CENTRAL AMERICA

Opposing Viewpoints™

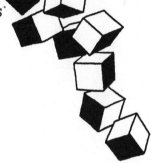

Other Books of Related Interest in the Opposing Viewpoints Series:

American Foreign Policy
China
Eastern Europe
Israel
Japan
Latin America and U.S. Foreign Policy
The Middle East
Problems of Africa
The Soviet Union
The Superpowers: A New Detente
The Third World

Additional Books in the Opposing Viewpoints Series:

Abortion
AIDS
American Government
American Values
America's Elections
America's Future
America's Prisons
Animal Rights
Biomedical Ethics
Censorship
Chemical Dependency
Civil Liberties
Constructing a Life Philosophy
Crime and Criminals
Criminal Justice
Death and Dying
The Death Penalty
Drug Abuse
Economics in America
The Elderly
The Environmental Crisis
Euthanasia
Genetic Engineering
The Health Crisis
The Homeless
Immigration
Male/Female Roles
The Mass Media
Nuclear War
The Political Spectrum
Poverty
Religion in America
Science & Religion
Sexual Values
Social Justice
Teenage Sexuality
Terrorism
The Vietnam War
Violence in America
War and Human Nature
War on Drugs

CENTRAL AMERICA

Opposing Viewpoints®

David L. Bender & Bruno Leone, *Series Editors*

Carol Wekesser, *Book Editor*
Janelle Rohr & Karin Swisher, *Assistant Editors*

OPPOSING VIEWPOINTS SERIES ®

Greenhaven Press, Inc.   PO Box 289009   San Diego, CA 92198-0009

Library of Congress Cataloging-in-Publication Data

Central America: opposing viewpoints / Carol Wekesser, book
    editor, Janelle Rohr & Karin Swisher, assistant editors.
        p.   cm. — (Opposing viewpoints series)
    Includes bibliographical references (p.   ) and index.
    Summary: Presents opposing viewpoints on Central
America, discussing such aspects as the political situation and
the involvement of the United States in conflicts there.
    ISBN 0-89908-484-2 (lib. bdg.). — ISBN 0-89908-459-1 (pbk.)
    1. Central America—Politics and government—1979-
2. Central America—Foreign relations—United States.   3.
United States—Foreign relations—Central America.   [1.
Central America—Politics and government.   2. Central
America—Foreign relations—United States.   3. United States
—Foreign relations—Central America.]   I. Wekesser, Carol,
1963-   .   II. Rohr, Janelle, 1963-   .   III. Swisher, Karin, 1966-
    IV. Series: Opposing viewpoints series (Unnumbered)
F1439.5.C456   1990   90-13922
327.730728—dc20   CIP

"Congress shall make no law . . . abridging the freedom of speech, or of the press."

First Amendment to the U.S. Constitution

The basic foundation of our democracy is the first amendment guarantee of freedom of expression. The Opposing Viewpoints Series is dedicated to the concept of this basic freedom and the idea that it is more important to practice it than to enshrine it.

Contents

Chapter 3: What Policies Would Strengthen Central American Economies?

Chapter 4: What Role Does Christianity Play in Central America?

Chapter 5: Is Peace in Central America Possible?

Why Consider Opposing Viewpoints?

"It is better to debate a question without settling it than to settle a question without debating it."

Joseph Joubert (1754-1824)

The Importance of Examining Opposing Viewpoints

The purpose of the Opposing Viewpoints Series, and this book in particular, is to present balanced, and often difficult to find, opposing points of view on complex and sensitive issues.

Probably the best way to become informed is to analyze the positions of those who are regarded as experts and well studied on issues. It is important to consider every variety of opinion in an attempt to determine the truth. Opinions from the mainstream of society should be examined. But also important are opinions that are considered radical, reactionary, or minority as well as those stigmatized by some other uncomplimentary label. An important lesson of history is the eventual acceptance of many unpopular and even despised opinions. The ideas of Socrates, Jesus, and Galileo are good examples of this.

Readers will approach this book with their own opinions on the issues debated within it. However, to have a good grasp of one's own viewpoint, it is necessary to understand the arguments of those with whom one disagrees. It can be said that those who do not completely understand their adversary's point of view do not fully understand their own.

A persuasive case for considering opposing viewpoints has been presented by John Stuart Mill in his work *On Liberty*. When examining controversial issues it may be helpful to reflect on this suggestion:

The only way in which a human being can make some approach to knowing the whole of a subject, is by hearing what can be said about it by persons of every variety of opinion, and studying all modes in which it can be looked at by every character of mind. No wise man ever acquired his wisdom in any mode but this.

Analyzing Sources of Information

The Opposing Viewpoints Series includes diverse materials taken from magazines, journals, books, and newspapers, as well as statements and position papers from a wide range of individuals, organizations, and governments. This broad spectrum of sources helps to develop patterns of thinking which are open to the consideration of a variety of opinions.

Pitfalls to Avoid

A pitfall to avoid in considering opposing points of view is that of regarding one's own opinion as being common sense and the most rational stance, and the point of view of others as being only opinion and naturally wrong. It may be that another's opinion is correct and one's own is in error.

Another pitfall to avoid is that of closing one's mind to the opinions of those with whom one disagrees. The best way to approach a dialogue is to make one's primary purpose that of understanding the mind and arguments of the other person and not that of enlightening him or her with one's own solutions. More can be learned by listening than speaking.

It is my hope that after reading this book the reader will have a deeper understanding of the issues debated and will appreciate the complexity of even seemingly simple issues on which good and honest people disagree. This awareness is particularly important in a democratic society such as ours where people enter into public debate to determine the common good. Those with whom one disagrees should not necessarily be regarded as enemies, but perhaps simply as people who suggest different paths to a common goal.

Developing Basic Reading and Thinking Skills

In this book, carefully edited opposing viewpoints are purposely placed back to back to create a running debate; each viewpoint is preceded by a short quotation that best expresses the author's main argument. This format instantly plunges the reader into the midst of a controversial issue and greatly aids that reader in mastering the basic skill of recognizing an author's point of view.

A number of basic skills for critical thinking are practiced in the activities that appear throughout the books in the series. Some of the skills are:

Evaluating Sources of Information. The ability to choose from among alternative sources the most reliable and accurate source in relation to a given subject.

Separating Fact from Opinion. The ability to make the basic distinction between factual statements (those that can be demonstrated or verified empirically) and statements of opinion (those that are beliefs or attitudes that cannot be proved).

Identifying Stereotypes. The ability to identify oversimplified, exaggerated descriptions (favorable or unfavorable) about people and insulting statements about racial, religious, or national groups, based upon misinformation or lack of information.

Recognizing Ethnocentrism. The ability to recognize attitudes or opinions that express the view that one's own race, culture, or group is inherently superior, or those attitudes that judge another culture or group in terms of one's own.

It is important to consider opposing viewpoints and equally important to be able to critically analyze those viewpoints. The activities in this book are designed to help the reader master these thinking skills. Statements are taken from the book's viewpoints and the reader is asked to analyze them. This technique aids the reader in developing skills that not only can be applied to the viewpoints in this book, but also to situations where opinionated spokespersons comment on controversial issues. Although the activities are helpful to the solitary reader, they are most useful when the reader can benefit from the interaction of group discussion.

Using this book and others in the series should help readers develop basic reading and thinking skills. These skills should improve the reader's ability to understand what is read. Readers should be better able to separate fact from opinion, substance from rhetoric, and become better consumers of information in our media-centered culture.

This volume of the Opposing Viewpoints Series does not advocate a particular point of view. Quite the contrary! The very nature of the book leaves it to the reader to formulate the opinions he or she finds most suitable. My purpose as publisher is to see that this is made possible by offering a wide range of viewpoints that are fairly presented.

David L. Bender
Publisher

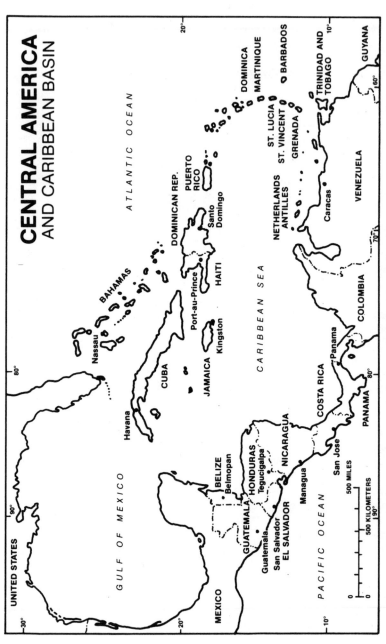

CENTRAL AMERICA
AND CARIBBEAN BASIN

Reprinted with permission of PACCA, Policy Alternatives for the Caribbean and Central America, 1901 Q Street NW, Washington DC 20009.

Introduction

"Out of these troubled times, a new world order can emerge."

George Bush

"Central America is America; it's at our doorstep. And it has become the stage for a bold attempt by the Soviet Union, Cuba, and Nicaragua to install communism by force throughout the hemisphere." In 1984, these words by U.S. president Ronald Reagan reflected the superpowers' view of Central America. To the U.S. and the Soviet Union, Central America was not a region of small, impoverished, but independent nations, but a battleground in the ideological war between capitalism and communism. By 1990, however, this ideological war had waned. The U.S. ceased military aid to the Nicaraguan contras, and the Soviet Union decreased its aid to Cuba, stating that future aid would be limited. These and other unexpected events created a new level of cooperation between the superpowers that softened the discord over Central America. Suddenly it seemed possible that the decades of superpower involvement in Central America were nearing an end. This possibility leads to questions about the future of a region long dominated by the world's powerful nations.

Since the U.S. defeat of the Spanish in the Spanish-American War of 1898, the U.S. has remained the dominant power in Central America, maintaining its political leadership through military and economic aid. This dominance was threatened when Fidel Castro established a Marxist state in Cuba in 1959 and allied with the communist Soviet Union in 1961. This move sparked a decades-long ideological battle between U.S. capitalism and Soviet communism in Central America.

Both superpowers claimed that their involvement in Central America was for the benefit of the people of the region. The Soviets supplied military aid to Cuba and the Nicaraguan Sandinistas to support the Marxist movements in these two countries. Reagan justified U.S. support of the Nicaraguan contras by calling the rebels "freedom fighters" and comparing them to the American revolutionaries of 1776. But as they watched their countries being torn apart, many Central Americans doubted the sincerity of superpower involvement. Because some of the contra leaders had supported dictator Anastasio Somoza, many Nicaraguans were suspicious of the U.S.-backed rebels. U.S. support of the contras, and of the oppressive governments of El Salvador,

13

Panama, Guatemala, and Honduras, increased Central America's political instability in the 1980s.

The 1980s brought civil wars to Nicaragua and El Salvador, wars fought with the help of U.S. and Soviet military aid. This decade of civil war led to a worsening of the poverty and instability of the region. Living standards fell by more than 15 percent from 1980 to 1987, causing more than two-thirds of Central Americans to live in poverty. The 1980s also saw the murders of thousands of civilians in El Salvador and Guatemala. Rather than improving the lives of Central Americans, superpower involvement had increased their suffering. It became clear to many Central Americans that the superpowers were involved merely for their own strategic interests. As Mexican author and diplomat Carlos Fuentes stated, "North Americans in responsible positions speak of not caring . . . whether the rights of others are respected, but whether its own strategic interests are defended."

Fuentes and others contend that major powers have so dominated Central America that the region has never had a chance to flourish—or fail—on its own. Instead of aiding Central America, superpower intervention "damages the fabric of a nation, the chance of resurrecting its history, the wholeness of its cultural identity," Fuentes states. Fuentes and others believe that if the superpowers end their involvement in the region, there is a chance that Central America's problems can be solved.

Many experts predict that Fuentes's wish will be granted and that superpower involvement in Central America will greatly decrease. The world is changing, these experts contend, and the superpowers no longer view Central America as a playground for their ideological tug-of-war. Other experts are not so optimistic. They argue that as long as nations such as the U.S. and the Soviet Union remain in power, weaker, poorer regions such as Central America will be the victims of superpower domination. In the words of Albert Einstein, "As long as there are sovereign nations possessing great power, war is inevitable."

The future of Central America remains uncertain. Can the region on its own overcome its legacy of poverty and political oppression? This and other issues concerning the region are explored in *Central America: Opposing Viewpoints,* which replaces Greenhaven Press's 1984 book of the same title. This volume contains all-new viewpoints and several new topics. The authors in this anthology debate the following questions: Why Is Central America a Conflict Area? Is U.S. Involvement in Central America Justified? What Policies Would Strengthen Central American Economies? What Role Does Christianity Play in Central America? and Is Peace in Central America Possible? The editors hope that these debates will provide the reader with insight into the issues surrounding the problems and possibilities for peace in Central America.

Why Is Central America a Conflict Area?

Chapter Preface

For four of five Central American nations, the 1980s were marked by brutality, poverty, and internal strife. Political violence and an impoverished citizenry are two factors that suggest conflict will continue to plague the region.

Political violence is perhaps the most obvious sign of the turmoil that engulfs Central American countries. El Salvador, for example, has experienced ten years of civil war. More than seventy thousand Salvadorans have died since the war began. The war has led to political killings: people being murdered because they support or oppose a particular side in the conflict. In 1989, sixty-four deaths were linked to political violence. This problem is also evident in Guatemala, which has one of the world's worst human rights records. In 1989 alone more than five hundred Guatemalans died and another two hundred disappeared as a result of internal political conflict.

Poverty also spurs conflict in the region. In Honduras, the poorest of the Central American nations, seven out of ten people are destitute. Many experts see a connection between Honduran poverty and the terror and repression Hondurans experience due to internal struggles for power. Many Nicaraguans also are impoverished. The country's economy was devastated by ten years of civil war. Observers contend that economic problems will make it difficult for democratic government to be established there. They predict that the government will be unable to improve the Nicaraguan economy quickly and will face protests from angry Nicaraguans who are poor and unemployed.

Conflict has thus undoubtedly been characteristic of Central America. The reasons behind these conflicts are further explored in the six viewpoints that follow.

"Growth without equity . . . had swollen the ranks of those who were calling for fundamental and far-reaching change in Central America."

Poverty Causes Conflict

Richard R. Fagen

Instability in Central America has its roots in the region's economic problems, Richard R. Fagen argues in the following viewpoint. He maintains that regional economic policies created an elite, wealthy minority and a vast, poor majority. In response, Fagen contends, Central Americans formed political factions that fought to control governments and reverse economic inequality. Fagen, the Gildred Professor of Latin American Studies at Stanford University in Palo Alto, California, is the co-chair of Policy Alternatives for the Caribbean and Central America, which works to promote democratic policy options in Central America. The following viewpoint is an excerpt from his book *Forging Peace: The Challenge of Central America.*

As you read, consider the following questions:

1. What is the author's definition of the agro-export model of development?
2. How did many Central Americans who once grew their own food become dependent on foreign imports, according to Fagen?
3. Why did many Central Americans form armed opposition groups, according to the author?

Richard R. Fagen, *Forging Peace: The Challenge of Central America.* New York: Basil Blackwell, 1987. Copyright © PACCA. Reprinted with permission of Basil Blackwell.

*The fundamental causes of dissatisfaction [in Central America] are
the existing social, political, and economic inequities.*

> General Wallace Nutting,
> retiring U.S. Army Chief of
> the Southern Command, 1983

The roots of the contemporary Central American crisis go far
back in time—much further than most citizens and policymakers in the United States are willing to look. The events of recent
years, however, can be very deceiving. For almost three
decades, from 1950 to 1978, Central America had one of the
highest growth rates in the world. Gross domestic product was
expanding at an average annual rate of at least 5 percent in all
five countries (Costa Rica, Nicaragua, Honduras, El Salvador,
Guatemala). Fueling this rapid economic growth for most of that
period were an expanding world economy, substantial foreign
aid and investment, and regional policies of agricultural diversification, trade expansion, and local industrialization. Per capita
income almost doubled during this period, new roads, dams,
and schools were built, and literacy increased. Yet, by the end
of the 1970s, Central America was in the grips of a profound
economic and political crisis. What went wrong?

Old Crops, New Problems

Central Americans have always lived from the land. From the
first incursions of the Spaniards in the 16th century, however,
indigenous subsistence agriculture began to be squeezed out by
export crops such as indigo. Communal and individual peasant
farmers were gradually—often violently—displaced by a relatively small number of landowning families who controlled
large estates. In the 20th century, this tiny agricultural elite,
along with, in some cases, foreign corporate owners, dominated
economic life by producing commodities—particularly coffee
and bananas—for foreign markets. This pattern of huge planta-
tions and crops for export is known as the agro-export model of
development.

A primary feature of an agro-export economy is its dependence
on a very few crops. In the 1920s, for example, coffee and bananas accounted for more than 70 percent of the export earnings
in all five republics—and more than 90 percent in Costa Rica, El
Salvador, and Guatemala. Even today, despite the addition of
sugar, cotton, and cattle during the export diversification drive
begun in the 1960s, the same two products account for more
than half of all exports in every country except Nicaragua. In
1980, these five agricultural commodities accounted for more
than 70 percent of Central America's total exports, and for more
than one-third of the region's total gross domestic product.

the products produced were not competitive outside the region. Thus, rather than improving the foreign exchange situation by generating new exports and cutting imports, the new industries often did just the reverse. In practice, then, the CACM failed to produce balanced and equitable development.

By the 1970s, successive oil shocks and the currency demands generated by imports of food, industrial inputs, and luxury goods placed foreign exchange reserves under significant pressure throughout the region. Export earnings from the agrarian sector simply could not keep up with the demand for dollars. Government efforts in several countries to increase the level of taxation were successfully resisted by elites. At a time when international banks were eager to lend, increased foreign borrowing seemed to offer a solution to the foreign exchange problem and a way to fund continuing growth. But this solution soon turned into yet another problem, as debt service joined the list of burdens that the local economies had to shoulder.

The Legacy of Poverty

For millions of Central Americans, poverty is a way of life. A tiny elite controls most of the region's land, wealth, and power. That leaves the vast majority of Central Americans with no land to live on or grow food on.

This staggering imbalance has bred a climate of revolution—one often ground in doctrines, such as Communism, that promise an equal distribution of wealth. The U.S. opposes Communism in this hemisphere. But repeated U.S. attempts to prop up individual countries through economic aid have done little to improve the situation.

Phil Sudo, *Scholastic Update*, February 9, 1990.

Thus, although growth continued well into the 1970s, the model had exhausted itself. Crises multiplied. Honduras withdrew from the CACM as a result of its five-day war with El Salvador in 1969, and the market was further weakened by the inability of debtor countries—particularly Honduras and Nicaragua—to pay their bills. As the economic and political situations became increasingly uncertain and unstable in the late 1970s, creditors and investors hesitated to increase their levels of exposure, and local capital fled to Europe and the United States. Growth slowed dramatically, unemployment soared, and millions of Central Americans found their already meager incomes even less adequate than they had been just a few years earlier.

If the growth generated through the late 1970s had been more equally distributed, the exhaustion of the agro-export model

21

might not have resulted in such profound crises. But rather than improving during this period, the distribution of income deteriorated. In almost every case the poorer groups in Central America—who were already living in poverty in 1960—were relatively worse off in 1980. What had been a substantial success from the point of view of overall economic growth was a disaster for most citizens of the region.

By 1980 the richest 20 percent of the population was receiving between one-half and two-thirds of total national income, depending on the country. At the other end of the spectrum, the poor were receiving almost nothing at all. In El Salvador, for example, the poorest 20 percent of the population received only 2 percent of national income, or the equivalent of $46 a year in constant 1970 dollars. In contrast, the 20 percent at the top of the pyramid received, on average, 33 times that amount—two-thirds of all national income.

Not surprisingly, efforts to broaden economic and political participation during this period were commonplace. New social forces not content with the status quo called for a wide variety of reforms. In rural areas, as the imposition of the agro-export model displaced tens of thousands of peasants from the land, new groups of politically conscious agricultural wage laborers were organized. Thousands of landless and jobless peasants migrated to the cities, swelling the shanty towns of the urban poor. New urban industries spawned an urban labor movement. Rapid population growth, the spread of schooling and the mass media, and the demonstration effect of both local and foreign wealth produced a younger, better-educated, and ultimately more frustrated population. Growth without equity, rising expectations, elite intransigence, and militarized repression had swollen the ranks of those who were calling for fundamental and far-reaching change in Central America. Universities, the Church, trade unions, and other grass-roots groups provided national leadership for these new social forces. Mass organizations, church-based communities, and political parties ranging from Christian Democrats to Social Democrats and Socialists were founded. . . .

Armed Opposition Increases

As political polarization increased, large numbers of Central Americans came to view nonviolent reform as impossible, and new impetus was given to armed opposition groups. Such movements were not new, but the extent of their support certainly was. Although not all voices advocated violence, many people had come to believe that the old order would not yield peacefully, and that more than tinkering would be needed to correct the structural problems that had come to characterize the economies and societies of the region.

"Political violence and . . . near chaos are the result of the increasingly desperate struggle of certain entrenched groups to retain land, prestige, and power at any price."

A History of Political Violence Causes Conflict

Thomas P. Anderson

In the following viewpoint, Thomas P. Anderson states that political unrest in Central America is the result of decades of violence perpetrated by the military and by the ruling classes in the region. The Spanish conquistadors established a tradition of oppression and military rule, Anderson maintains, a tradition that has continued in Central America throughout the twentieth century. Anderson, a history professor at Eastern Connecticut State University in Willimantic, wrote *Matanza: El Salvador's Communist Revolt of 1932* and *The War of the Dispossessed: Honduras and El Salvador, 1969.*

As you read, consider the following questions:

1. Why does the author believe Central American unity failed in the 1820s?
2. How do Central American constitutions usually differ from the U.S. Constitution, according to Anderson?
3. How does Anderson define Central American machismo?

To undertake an explanation of the politics of any one country is difficult enough. To attempt to explain the politics of four of them may seem presumptuous; yet there are certain reasons that make possible a comparative study of the four Central American countries of Guatemala, El Salvador, Nicaragua, and Honduras. This is not to say that their political traditions are identical. Any such statement would raise the hackles of a politically aware Central American, but there are similarities as well as divergences in the political life of these nations. On the other hand, Costa Rica—the fifth Central American state to be carved from the ruins of the Central American Federation—while having certain factors in common with the rest, has developed a unique political tradition in which violence has been largely eliminated and relative democracy is the rule. It has therefore been excluded from this study, though the reader who wants a contrast to the almost unrelieved pattern of violence in the other Central American republics might do well to undertake a study of Costa Rican institutions.

Volcanoes and Violence

Active peaks dot the area, such as Guatemala's Volcán del Fuego, which broods over the capital like a pagan god; the jet black Izalco of El Salvador, a tombstone marking one of the bloodiest massacres of Central American history; and the lovely Momotumbo, which can be seen from the windows of the formerly Somoza-owned Hotel Intercontinental, across Lake Managua. But the volcanoes also serve as an ominous symbol here, as they did for Malcolm Lowry when he wrote his violent and tragic masterpiece, *Under the Volcano*. This study will focus on the eruptive violence of the region, not simply as a phenomenon, but rather as a symptom of grave social and economic injustices that have so far made a peaceful and democratic life there impossible. Its primary thesis will be that this political violence and, at times, the near chaos are the result of the increasingly desperate struggle of certain entrenched groups to retain land, prestige, and power at any price. . . .

Some background on the region is necessary, along with a discussion of some of the region's most important political, social, and economic institutions.

The region invaded by the Spanish conquistadores was by no means entirely made up of volcanoes, although the backbone of the New World runs through the region, hugging the Pacific coast of it fairly closely in Guatemala, where it is at its highest, and then broadening out through El Salvador, a land of lush mountain valleys among a tangled welter of low peaks, and becoming confused and choppy, like a breaking sea, in Honduras. Nicaragua resembles El Salvador in its broad plains and rela-

24

tively low mountains. Lakes dot the mountain valleys, most impressively—Ilopango in El Salvador; Lake Managua, now an open sewer and a chemical bath, in Nicaragua; and, largest of all by far, Lake Nicaragua, the ever-tempting waterway for a possible isthmian canal.

© Kemchs/Rothco. Reprinted with permission.

When Alvarado and the other conquistadores stormed down from Mexico, they found civilization already flourishing, chiefly among Maya and related Toltec tribes, but also among the Aztec-linked Pipil of El Salvador. The newcomers subjugated, exploited, and, largely through their diseases, nearly killed off these people. But eventually a conglomerate race appeared, the mestizo, part Indian and part European. El Salvador, Nicaragua, and Honduras are predominantly mestizo nations, with a few Indians, while Guatemala remains some 40 percent Maya in speech and culture. This requires some qualification because, *indio* and mestizo literally move in shade from one to the other, the real distinction has come to be between indio, or *indígene,* and ladino, the latter being any person, of whatever ethnic origin, who takes on European-Hispanic ways. Thus, saying that Guatemala is 40 percent Maya means that 40 percent of its population is outside the dominant Spanish-European culture of the ladinos. . . .

Led by a *criollo* aristocracy (of European ancestry), Central America joined in the independence movement against Spain. At first claimed by Mexico, the region had asserted its independent existence by 1822 and established the Central American Confederation, comprising the five traditional states of Central America. But this unity did not last. Poor communications and the incessant struggle of liberals and conservatives had broken the confederation into its constituent parts by the 1840s, and separate governments were established.

The New Central American Governments

Each of these governments was republican in form, with a presidential system generally modeled on that of the United States. But while it was possible to import the forms of such a government, it proved impossible to impart much of the spirit. While the government of the United States grew organically out of colonial institutions, the newly established Central American governments represented a total break from the traditions of the colonial past. In colonial times, there had been virtually no local governments reflecting the will of the governed, but instead, a multitude of often overlapping authorities created by the crown-administered edicts written in Spain and imposed upon the New World. Further, instead of following the common-law system presumed in the United States as the basis of government, the Central Americans were saddled with a Roman law system which held that authority came from above and gave very little scope to judicial review.

The constitutions of Central America, both in the nineteenth century and in the twentieth, have reflected the confusions arising from the grafting of an alien governmental structure onto a Hispanic legal system. A good constitution, as Napoleon reminded us, should be "short and obscure," like that of the United States, which, with all its amendments, can be printed on half a dozen pages. Central American constitutions often run to several hundred pages. As there is little judicial discretion, even the most minute details of what we could term "positive law" find their way into the constitution itself, making the document inflexible and constricting. Most Central American constitutions are likewise difficult to amend.

This means that almost every major governmental upheaval, through coup or civil war, results in a new constitution being established. The constitutions become no more than party platforms and statements of aspirations for the current groups in power. They represent an ideology rather than a simple set of rules for governing.

Spanish Brought Terror

In Mexico, Guatemala, and elsewhere, Spaniards exploited Indians and forced them into varying degrees of servitude. Maya submission, the efforts of Las Casas and others notwithstanding, was simply non-negotiable. It was assumed, taken for granted, regarded as a privilege of victory, a natural fixture in the pursuit of empire. Under these terms, relations between Spaniards and Indians hardly fostered tolerance and respect. What it engendered was suspicion, distrust, hatred, and fear. Michael Taussig suggests how the Spanish maintained Indian subordination through widespread terror. . . . Terror and resistance, then, must be seen as omnipresent, as constructs that alter in form and rhythm but never disappear.

W. George Lovell, in *Central America: Democracy, Development, and Change*, 1988.

Whatever the constitution might say, the fact is that the president generally concentrates most of the authority of the republic in his own hands. This may be, as some authorities declare, because of the traditional Hispanic need for caudillos—strong, often military leaders exhibiting the traditional macho virtues and passing out rewards to their followers and punishments to their enemies. But, in any case, the very nature of the constitutional system has made this concentration of power practically inevitable. When constitutions are so constricting that nothing can be accomplished within their framework, the temptation of the executive branch will be to rule by decree, outside constitutional restraints. Presidents play a large part in the life of Central America. Sometimes they use their mandate to effect reform and then they step down, as did Juan José Arévalo in Guatemala. Sometimes they are more or less benevolent dictators, such as Tiburcio Carías Andino in Honduras. Often they are despots, such as Maximiliano Hernández Martínez in El Salvador or the various Somozas of Nicaragua. Occasionally they are demonic figures of legendary cruelty, such as Manuel Estrada Cabrera of Guatemala. There are even instances of ineffectual presidents, dominated behind the scenes by some minister of defense or a past president. But even in these cases the power remains in the institution of the presidency, no matter who might wield that power. . . .

One of the most important historical groups in Central America includes those who control the land. Even in colonial times, the crown and its agents left the great *hacendados* broad latitude to deal with the Indian laborers and to control the local administration of justice. With the coming of independence, this oligarchy broadened its scope to the national level of politics, making and unmaking presidents, frequently raising the standard of revolt, through the simple process of arming its own followers. In rural Honduras to this day, many of the great landholders bear the honorary title of colonel. . . .

The military, which has come to have such a dominant influence, has had a long period of evolution. In the nineteenth and the early twentieth centuries, the profession of arms was something that most members of the landed gentry indulged in as officers at some point in their career, either during internal strife or in one of the frequent Central American wars. The peacetime army tended to be a rather sorry affair of impressed peasants commanded by underpaid and demoralized officers. This began to change with the establishment of military academies, such as the *Politécnica* in Guatemala and the *Escuela Militar* in El Salvador. The emphasis from then on was on professionalism, with the students receiving a thorough grounding in mathematics, engineering, and science, along with more military subjects. The students of such schools tended to be recruited at a much younger age than are our own West Pointers. Generally a student would have ten years of education upon entry and be in his mid-teens. He graduated as a second lieutenant at around 19. Like novices in a seminary, the cadets, taken in at an impressionable age, learned to have no other loyalties but to their calling. The people they knew best were those in their own class, or *tanda*, and in these small groups (for the classes were never large), such a feeling of brotherhood grew that even being on opposing sides in a coup or revolution could not break the sense of kinship. This explains the frequent leniency toward the military instigators of an unsuccessful coup.

U.S. Training for the Military

As professionalism and esprit de corps increased, new opportunities to extend the education of the military were sought. The coming of World War II brought in Uncle Sam to fill that role. It appeared to the United States that one of the best ways to bind the Latin American nations to its cause was to train their military. The process has continued ever since, with large numbers of officers shipped off to train at Fort Bragg or at Fort Gulick in Panama. Some young officers, such as Anastasio Somoza Debayle, even received part of their military education at West Point. To the officer class, one of the most tragic aspects of the 1969 war between Honduras and El Salvador was that it was fought between officers who had gotten to know each other well in Panama and elsewhere as they learned the profession of arms. . . .

The politics of the area under discussion has long been bound up with violence. . . . Indeed, even without political turmoil, the society of these four countries might still be styled violence-prone. In El Salvador, murder and manslaughter together rank as the second highest cause of death in normal times, lagging behind only intestinal diseases and well ahead of respiratory ailments, the third highest killer in the country. In 1960, a normal year, that country had 1,313 arrests for murder while having only 243 traffic fatalities.

The reasons for the propensity to violence would require a highly complex sociopsychological study, one that is only hinted at in current writing on the subject; but it is possible to make certain suggestions concerning the deeper roots of this cultural malaise.

To begin with, like much of Hispanic America, this is a death-oriented society. Poverty and malnutrition combine to insure a very high infant-mortality rate (something on the order of 120 per 1,000 live births). Death becomes a constant and familiar companion. . . .

Life being brief, the emphasis shifts from prolonging one's life to living and dying in a heroic manner. As Octavio Paz so beautifully wrote: "Death defines life. . . . Death illuminates our lives. If our deaths lack meaning, our lives also lacked it. . . . Tell me how you die and I will tell you who you are." For most men, to die tamely, of some disgusting disease, is thus a disgrace, an unworthy death. The best death is that which gives one the chance to display one's manhood to the fullest. Here the concept of machismo is very important. It is a term against which most North Americans take offense, but it is a very real part of the regional culture of Central America and does not mean the kind of swaggering bravado that comes to our minds.

The Noble Defiance of Death

Rather, machismo is the noble defiance of death. It is the willingness to dare, to take physical risks, in the face of hopeless odds. Therefore, it has more to do with Don Quixote than with Don Juan. No one has put it as well as Julius Rivera has in his brilliant study, when he wrote:

A Macho gambles with Destiny, ready to win or lose. He

gambles with death, he gambles with God. A burning love affair is a victory over Destiny; a revolution, a victory over death; sin, a victory over god. When the three come together, man has accomplished his fulfillment.

Skill in arms and pride in their possession are traits in ladino society handed down from the time of the conquistadores. Every poor man has his machete; every man who can afford it, his firearms. You can be sure you have won the confidence of a Central American man when he shows you his collection of weapons, which, these days, can include an automatic rifle. These weapons are there to be used. While it might seem cowardly to assassinate or to shoot from ambush, to the people of the region, the very act of killing requires courage and machismo.

These tendencies can be exaggerated, but the acceptance of violence as the normal means of settling disputes, including political ones, is what sets the two cultures apart. The *golpe de estado* (or coup d'état) and the *cuartelazo* (or barracks uprising) are not regarded as aberrations, but rather as normal parts of the political process and sometimes the only, or best, way of effecting change.

"It is culture that principally explains . . . why some countries develop more rapidly and equitably than others."

Central American Culture Causes Conflict

Lawrence E. Harrison

The violence and instability characteristic of many Central American nations is a result of the region's culture, Lawrence E. Harrison contends in the following viewpoint. Harrison maintains the brutality and inequality of the Spanish conquistadors in the sixteenth century developed a culture that continues to breed violence in Central America. The author, who served in the Agency for International Development (AID) for twenty years, was a visiting scholar at Harvard University's Center for International Affairs from 1981 to 1983. He has contributed articles to many periodicals and newspapers, including *Foreign Policy* and *The New York Times*.

As you read, consider the following questions:

1. How do the early histories of Nicaragua and Costa Rica differ, according to Harrison?
2. Why does the author think it is inaccurate to blame Nicaragua's problems on outside forces, such as Britain and the United States?
3. How would Central America be different today if the region were populated by Costa Ricans, according to the author?

Excerpted from *Underdevelopment Is a State of Mind* by Lawrence E. Harrison. Lanham, MD: University Press of America, 1985. Reprinted with permission of the Harvard University Center for International Affairs and University Press of America.

Like many young people who worked for AID [Agency for International Development] in the early years of the Alliance for Progress (inaugurated on August 17, 1961, at Punta del Este, Uruguay), I was convinced that Latin America was in trouble principally because of U.S. neglect, and that a combination of money, Yankee ingenuity, and good intentions would transform the region to one of rapidly developing, vigorous democracies in a decade or two. After all, we in the U.S. shared the hope and the wealth of the New World with Latin America, we gained our independence at roughly the same time, and their constitutions and rhetoric sounded pretty much like ours. They hadn't done as well as we, but that could be remedied. The spectacular success of the Marshall Plan was much on our minds.

Cultural Differences

Less than seven years after Punta del Este, Teodoro Moscoso, the first U.S. coordinator of the Alliance for Progress and one of its most ardent and optimistic early promoters, had this to say:

> The Latin-American case is so complex, so difficult to solve, and so fraught with human and global danger and distress that the use of the word "anguish" is not an exaggeration.
>
> The longer I live, the more I believe that, just as no human being can save another who does not have the will to save himself, no country can save others no matter how good its intentions or how hard it tries.

A few years later, in an article in *Foreign Policy* in which I quoted Moscoso, I made the following observation:

> The differences between North America and Latin America are enormous, covering virtually all aspects of human life. The North American and the Latin American have differing concepts of the individual, society, and the relationship between the two; of justice and law; of life and death; of government; of the family; of relations between the sexes; of organization; of time; of enterprise; of religion; of morality. These differences have contributed to the evolution of societies which are more unlike one another than our past policymakers appear to have appreciated. In fact, it can be argued that there are some Asian societies (Japan is an obvious candidate) which have more in common with the societies of North America than do most of the societies of Latin America.

In the thirteen years since I wrote those words, I have been increasingly persuaded that, more than any other of the numerous factors that influence the development of countries, it is culture that principally explains, in most cases, why some countries develop more rapidly and equitably than others. By "culture" I mean the values and attitudes a society inculcates in its people through various socializing mechanisms, e.g., the home, the school, the church. . . .

Nicaragua and Costa Rica are neighbors. Both are well endowed with natural resources, but Nicaragua has an advantage in this regard. Yet Nicaragua's history is a tortured and chaotic one, while Costa Rica's is one of fairly steady progress and stability.

Values Impede Progress

After 25 years of working on Latin America's development problems, I am convinced that it is the way Latin Americans see the world—their values and attitudes—that are the principal obstacle to progress in Latin America. Those values and attitudes derive from traditional Hispanic culture, which nurtures authoritarianism, an excessive individualism, mistrust, corruption and a fatalistic world view, all of which work against political pluralism and economic and social progress. That culture also attaches a low value to work, particularly among the elite, and discourages entrepreneurship, thus further braking economic growth.

Lawrence E. Harrison, *The Washington Post National Weekly Edition,* April 14, 1986.

The early history of the two countries suggests a probable explanation: Nicaragua is in the mainstream of Hispanic-American culture, while Costa Rica's special circumstances as a Spanish colony, with a colonial experience in some ways reminiscent of the New England colonies, led to significant modifications of that culture.

One could argue that Nicaragua's underdevelopment relative to Costa Rica reflects the costs of Nicaragua's historical relationships with the outside world, first with the British, then with the Americans. While it is true that the British harassed the Costa Ricans in the seventeenth and eighteenth centuries, particularly in the cacao region of the Atlantic coast, the depredations they visited on the Nicaraguans were far more costly and sustained. Nicaragua's potential as a trans-isthmian canal site also attracted the special attention of the British and the Americans. And, of course, Nicaragua experienced the trauma of a prolonged U.S. military intervention, which further undermined the self-confidence and dignity of a people whose tragic history had left them with little of either.

Yet a reading of Nicaraguan history leaves considerable doubt that the country's evolution was determined by external forces. The continuous threads of authoritarianism, polarization of politics, and economic exploitation of the masses by the oligarchy, from 1522 until well into the twentieth century, appear to have been little influenced from the outside—except by Spain during the colonial period. No one will ever know what the course of recent Nicaraguan history would have been had the United States not intervened in 1912. But if past performance is any indicator, it might not have been very different from what actually has happened. . . .

A Different Kind of Colonist

Costa Rica's remoteness, its small Indian population, and its early poverty forced a colonial life style which was very different from that in the other colonies—and attracted a quite different kind of colonist. Because Costa Rica was poor, the Spaniards paid it relatively little attention, which protected it from many of the corrosive and suffocating effects of Spanish colonial administration. The *encomienda* and *hacienda* systems did not adapt well to Costa Rica's special circumstances, which saved Costa Rica from the morally corrupting effects of plantation agriculture. Colonists were by self-selection different from the conquistadors: they had to work the land themselves if they were to survive, and survival was a pressing issue for virtually everyone.

Poverty and isolation fertilized the soil from which Costa Rican democracy sprang. They also nurtured a kind of individualism—or perhaps more accurately, a modified traditional Spanish individualism—that cherished liberty and a sense of equality. . . .

The one factor that distinguishes Costa Ricans from Nicaraguans (and indeed from most other Hispanic Americans) is the Costa Rican's identification with other Costa Ricans. [In their book *Los Costarricenses*, Richard, Mavis Hiltunen, and Karen Zubris de Biesanz] put it this way: ". . . the *nation of brothers* of years gone by continues to be one big family in many respects. You still frequently hear people saying, 'everyone is a cousin of everyone.'"

The sense of family is doubtlessly reinforced by Costa Rica's relative racial homogeneity. Samuel Stone shows the following breakdown in a table on the ethnic composition of Central America.

The racial composition in Nicaragua has probably been more an obstacle to national unity than the table would imply, because the Nicaraguan elite has largely been white.

	Indians	*Whites*	*Blacks*	*Mixed Blood*
Costa Rica	1%	80%	2%	17%
Guatemala	60%	5%	—	35%
El Salvador	11%	11%	—	78%
Honduras	10%	2%	2%	86%
Nicaragua	5%	17%	9%	69%

In any event, there is ample evidence that Costa Ricans have felt a stronger bond to their countrymen than have Nicaraguans. That bond is reflected in Costa Rica's long-standing emphasis on public education and public health; in its more vigorous cooperative movement; in a judicial system notable by Latin American standards for its impartiality and adherence to fundamental concepts of due process; and above all in the resilience of its politics, its capacity to find peaceful solutions, its appreciation of the need for compromise.

Had Central America been peopled exclusively by Costa Ricans in 1824, the federation would have stood a much better chance of holding together. Similarly, the Central American economic integration movement, which looked so promising in the early and mid-1960s, might still be flourishing had Costa Rican values and attitudes prevailed in the region. . . .

Common Values

At the root of Costa Rica's economic lead over Nicaragua is the same set of values and attitudes that explains its greater social and political development. These are the values and attitudes that flow from a common leveling experience, one that has strengthened the identification of Costa Ricans with one another. High levels of literacy and public health are one manifestation. Political stability, with all that means for economic growth, is another.

That common leveling experience triggered a process of cultural change that is self-reinforcing. In an article comparing Costa Rica and Nicaragua, James L. Busey observes, "Previous stability lays the ground for understanding which makes possible future stability; previous chaos and resultant hatreds arouse deep bitterness which makes more difficult the task of establishing stable, constitutional government." And, we might add, the task of development.

35

"Contrary to the ethnocentric stereotype often held by North Americans, Central Americans are as hardworking as most other humans on this planet."

Central American Culture Does Not Cause Conflict

John A. Booth and Thomas W. Walker

In the following viewpoint, John A. Booth and Thomas W. Walker argue that turmoil in Central America is the result of hundreds of years of political and economic inequality combined with the disruptive influence of U.S. intervention. The people of Central America are industrious, the authors maintain, but have been hampered by a lack of natural resources and by the economic exploitation of wealthy landowners and foreign nations. Booth, who chairs the political science department at the University of North Texas in Denton, is the author of *The End and the Beginning: The Nicaraguan Revolution.* Walker, author of *Nicaragua: The Land of Sandino,* directs the Latin American Studies Program at Ohio University in Athens.

As you read, consider the following questions:

1. What regional traditions do the authors believe laid the groundwork for conflict in Central America?
2. Why did rebellion and turmoil erupt in Central America in the late 1970s, according to Booth and Walker?
3. What do the authors view as specific problems faced by the governments of Guatemala and El Salvador?

John A. Booth and Thomas W. Walker, *Understanding Central America.* Boulder, CO: Westview Press, 1989. Reprinted with permission.

We . . . seek to supply the reader with keys to understanding Central America by briefly and systematically describing the region and its major problems, its historical evolution, and the major social and political forces that have taken at least 200,000 Central American lives and displaced nearly 2 million refugees since 1978.

Much of what is wrong in Central America today stems from fairly simple, direct, and man-made causes. We believe that regional traditions of economic and political exploitation and the external reinforcement of those patterns of repression of the many by the few laid the groundwork for turmoil. Rapid but unbalanced economic growth, the product of deliberate public policy decisions by Central American elites, backed financially and militarily by the United States, created the conditions for popular rebellion and turmoil in the late 1970s.

The Five Nations of Central America

The "Central America" upon which we focus in this report consists of five countries: Guatemala, El Salvador, Honduras, Nicaragua, and Costa Rica. Belize and Panama will not receive individual attention. Though Belize is technically Central American, that English-speaking microstate has a history that is fairly distinct from that of the other states in the region. At present this tiny republic, which only became formally independent from Great Britain in 1981, does not figure significantly in the "Central American" problem. Panama, though often lumped with the other countries of the region, is not technically Central American. Its pre-Columbian indigenous cultures were South American, and from the beginning of the national period until 1903, Panama was an integral (though poor) part of the South American republic of Colombia. "The five," however, share a common political heritage from the colonial period—in which they were administered as a unit by Spain—to the early national period, when for fifteen years (1823-1838) they formed a single state called the United Provinces of Central America. In the late nineteenth century, several ill-fated attempts at reunification once again took place, and in the 1960s the five joined to form a common market. Out of this history comes a sense of Central American national identity and, among a surprisingly large segment of the region's educated elite, an almost utopian belief that someday the larger homeland will once again be united.

Central America, as defined above, is not a big region. Indeed, its combined land mass of 431,812 square kilometers is barely larger than that of the state of California (404,975 square kilometers). Moreover, its total 1988 population of around 25.9 million is just slightly more than California's (25 million). The country with the smallest surface area, El Salvador, is smaller even than the state of Maryland, whereas the largest, Nicaragua, is only slightly larger than Iowa. In population, the five vary between a low of 2.82 million in Costa Rica (Arkansas, in comparison, has 2.28 million) and a high of 8.61 million in Guatemala (New Jersey has 7.36 million).

The Wrong Kind of Development

It is an oversimplification to attribute today's crisis to the Spanish conquest, and one which misses the point that precisely the kind of "development" promoted in the 1960s and 1970s has produced the crisis.

Phillip Berryman, *The Religious Roots of Rebellion*, 1984.

Central America's natural resources are not particularly remarkable. However, under a different sort of political system than currently rules most of Central America, there would certainly be enough arable land to provide adequate sustenance for the present population, while at the same time producing some primary products for export. Yet the unregulated response to international market demands by the region's agrarian elite has led to land concentration, an overemphasis on export, and inadequate production of consumer food staples. Instead of growing beans, corn, rice, plantain, and cassava for local consumption, big landholders normally concentrate on lucrative exports such as coffee, cotton, sugar, and beef. Central America also has a variety of mineral resources, though apparently not in remarkable abundance. One possible exception is Guatemala, with its nickel and its newly discovered oil reserves. Historically, Central America, or more precisely, Nicaragua, was (for a while) viewed as the logical site for a future transisthmian waterway. However, the building of the Panama Canal and the development of modern air and surface communication have made it unlikely that this potential will ever be developed.

Hardworking People

Central America's main resource is clearly its people. Contrary to the ethnocentric stereotype often held by North Americans, Central Americans are as hardworking as most other humans on this planet. To verify that statement, one need only observe the hustle and bustle of most Central American cities at daybreak, or follow the activity of a typical Central American through the long hours of his or her daily routine. Central Americans are also remarkably resilient. The strength with which they have faced more than their share of hardship—including endemic repression, occasional civil war, foreign occupation, and frequent natural disasters, such as volcanic eruptions, earthquakes, hurricanes, and floods—is impressive to outside observers, especially those used to fairly safe natural and human environments.

This is not to say that there are not characteristics of the population of some Central American countries that pose problems. Guatemala, for instance, no matter which type of political system it adopts, will long have to struggle with the question of how to integrate the approximately half of the population that is Indian, and that, by and large, does not speak Spanish. Similarly, any government in El Salvador is going to face an enormous social headache posed by the country's high density of population. Moreover, all of the countries face severe problems of poverty that affect the vast majority of their people. But such poverty is not inevitable, and, overall, the human resources of the region are a very positive factor. The dignity, determination, and remarkable humor of the Central American people must be taken as a cause for hope.

In sum, Central America is small in size and population, poor in resources, and holds a wealth of problems and troubles—for its own people as well as for its neighbors and for the United States. Its small nation-states are riven by severe internal strains. They are pushed and pulled by international pressures, both economic and political, pressures that often intensify domestic strains rather than reduce them. The deepening U.S. involvement there and the efforts that numerous Latin American and European nations have made to promote negotiated settlements to the various open and latent conflicts in the region have made these strains and conflicts worthy of serious study.

"Cuban efforts . . . have included intensive and ongoing attacks against El Salvador and Guatemala with secondary subversion directed against Honduras and Costa Rica."

Cuban Intervention Causes Conflict

John Norton Moore

In the following viewpoint, John Norton Moore contends that increased Soviet and Cuban military involvement in the 1970s created civil strife in Central America. To spread Marxism throughout Central America, Cuba has supported revolutionary groups and attempted to militarize many of the nations in the region, Moore maintains. He suggests that by supporting Cuba financially and militarily, the Soviet Union has contributed to the region's instability. Moore is the director of the Center for Law and National Security at the University of Virginia in Charlottesville. He has written many articles and books on international law, including *Law and the Grenada Mission* and *The Secret War in Central America*, of which this viewpoint is an excerpt.

As you read, consider the following questions:

1. What three trends have shaped the conflict in Central America, according to Moore?
2. What does the author believe caused the militarization of Cuba and Nicaragua?
3. Why has Cuba supported Marxist-Leninist insurgencies in Central America, according to the author?

Excerpted from *The Secret War in Central America: Sandinista Assault on World Order* by John Norton Moore (Greenwood Press, an imprint of Greenwood Publishing Group, Inc., Westport, CT, 1987), pages 5-9, © 1987 by John Norton Moore. Reproduced with permission.

Conditions in Central America and the Caribbean have changed dramatically over the last quarter century. Three trends in the region have been particularly important in shaping the Central American conflict.

First, social modernization and a pronounced trend toward democracy have begun to transform the nations of the region. The former British colonies in the Caribbean have become independent and the old oligarchies that held power in many Central American countries have given way to a process of increasing social concern and democratization. The reformist coup in El Salvador in 1979, followed by the 1982, 1984 and 1985 elections, exemplifies this process. That Guatemala is moving toward democracy is suggested by its elections for a Constituent Assembly (held in July 1984) and for president, vice-president, members of congress, municipal mayors and members of city councils (held on November 3, 1985). Pursuant to these elections, President Vinicio Cerezo Arevalo was inaugurated on January 14, 1986. On January 27, 1986, Honduras inaugurated President Jose Azcona, marking "the first time in more than 50 years that one [Honduran] elected civilian succeeded another as chief executive." In Nicaragua the Somoza regime, a paradigmatic dynastic oligarchy, was overthrown in 1979 with initial broad-based support from labor, the business community, the church and other segments of Nicaraguan society. Even Haiti, long subject to dynastic rule, had a revolution and seems moving toward greater democracy. . . .

Rapid Economic Growth

Second, the region has experienced rapid economic growth through the decades of the 1960s and 1970s only to be whipsawed by a severe economic downturn following the 1979-80 second oil shock. Through the 1960s and 1970s economic growth in the region averaged 6 percent a year—more than double the population growth. This rapid economic expansion contributed to rapid modernization and social change. The rapidity of change has in turn brought an increasing awareness of the importance of human rights, but paradoxically has been accompanied by increased violence from the extreme left and the extreme right.

At the beginning of the 1980s, the global recession following the second oil shock produced the worst global economic downturn since the Great Depression, from which most Central American nations are just beginning to recover. Their economic troubles were compounded by a huge jump in the price of imported oil, dislocations due to rising levels of political violence, and an oil shock-induced rise in the cost of capital, reduction in trade, decrease in the prices of commodities such as coffee, ba-

41

nanas and cotton, an increase in inflation, foreign debt and debt
service payments, and an increase in unemployment. This severe economic recession intensified the rapidity of social dislo-
cation in many countries of the region.

Henry Payne. Reprinted by permission of UFS, Inc.

Third, during the decade of the 1970s there was a dramatic
United States decrease in military assistance to the region cou-
pled with an even more dramatic intensification of Soviet-bloc
military involvement in the region. In a post-Vietnam setting
and with an activist commitment to human rights, the United
States terminated military assistance to pre-revolutionary El
Salvador and Nicaragua in 1977 and to Guatemala in 1978.
Military assistance—including deliveries of ammunition—was
reinstituted to El Salvador in January 1981 only after the Carter
administration reacted to unmistakable evidence of an intense
Cuban-Nicaraguan effort to overthrow the post-revolutionary
government of El Salvador. Even today there are only about 55
United States military trainers in El Salvador. These 55 trainers
are not even advisors and do not participate in operational missions. The cutoff in military assistance to Guatemala has continued even after the election of civilian President Marco Vinicio
Cerezo, with the exception of a small grant in 1984 for military
officer training. In Latin America as a whole, the number of
United States military advisors plummeted from 516 at the beginning of the decade to 70 in 1981.

In sharp contrast, Soviet-bloc and radical regime military involvement in the region grew dramatically during the 1970s and

1980s. Soviet military deliveries to Cuba jumped from 13,300 metric tons in 1970 to 40,000 in 1978 and 68,300 in 1982. Following the Sandinista victory in Nicaragua, Soviet-bloc military deliveries to Nicaragua jumped from 850 metric tons in 1980 to 18,000 tons in 1984. . . . After the Sandinista victory, Cuban military advisors arrived in Nicaragua on July 19th, the day the Sandinistas took power. Within a week there were 100 Cuban advisors, and within three months there were several thousand. . . . The Soviet navy also participated in this buildup. In 1970 Soviet naval vessels spent 200 ship-days in the South Atlantic; in 1980 they spent approximately 2,600 ship-days, for a 13-fold increase. Before the October 1983 OECS [Organization of Eastern Caribbean States]-United States action in Grenada, this tiny island had some 800 Cubans, 49 Soviets, 17 Libyans, 15 North Koreans, 10 East Germans and 3 Bulgarians engaged in military and security-related activities.

The U.S. Disengages from the Region

The following comparisons put in perspective the combined effect of this United States disengagement and the Soviet-bloc and radical regime buildup in the region. By 1981 the Soviet Union had 50 times more military advisors in Latin America (largely in Cuba and Nicaragua) than did the United States. From 1962-82 the Soviets provided more than twice as much security assistance to Latin America (largely for Cuba and Nicaragua) as did the United States, or roughly $4 billion from the USSR compared to $1.5 billion from the United States. Even between 1981 and 1985, including four years of United States reaction to the Cuban-Nicaraguan secret war, the Soviet Union provided more military assistance to Cuba and Nicaragua than the United States provided to all of Latin America. (In 1984, the Soviet Union gave $4.9 billion in assistance to Cuba and Nicaragua, nearly 6 times the $837 million in United States assistance to all of Central America.) In 1984 the Soviet-bloc gave $250 million in military assistance to Nicaragua, nearly ten times the military assistance in one year alone that the United States gave to Nicaragua in the *sixteen-year period* from 1962-78 (a total of some $25.2 million). . . . A study by the U.S. Arms Control and Disarmament Agency indicates that in the period 1979 to 1983 the Soviet Union was the leading arms supplier to Latin America: its $3.6 billion in sales was more than five times the United States' $700 million. To put these comparisons in a global perspective, it should be remembered that Central America is not . . . contiguous to the Soviet Union, but is closer to Washington, D.C. than is California, historically an area of great importance to the United States and squarely within the OAS [Organization of American States] regional defense system.

The substantial Soviet-bloc military assistance to Cuba and Nicaragua following the 1959 seizure of power by Fidel Castro and the 1979 seizure of power by the Sandinistas has led to a militarization of society in those two countries. Cuba today has the second largest army in Latin America, exceeded only by Brazil which has 13 times the population of Cuba. On a per capita basis Cuba has a military 10-20 times greater than that of any other major nation in the hemisphere. In comparison, Mexico, with 7 times Cuba's population, has a defense establishment only half its size. Castro maintains an expeditionary army in Africa alone that is about five times the size of the total Cuban military under Cuba's former ruler, Fulgencio Batista. Cuba has an overt military presence in 20 countries around the world, ranging up to 19,000 troops in Angola alone. Cuba's military is equipped with high-quality modern weapons: it has more than 950 tanks and 200 jet fighters, including a substantial number of MiG-23's, a front line fighter of the Soviet air force. Moreover, its weapons are not purely defensive. For example, Cuba has developed an amphibious assault force capable of overwhelming its small island neighbors. . . .

A Struggle of Ideology

Two revolutionary movements seek today to replace the old dictatorships and old oligarchies of Central America. One is a democratic revolution whose goal is constitutional democracy, with its associated rights and freedoms. The other is a Marxist-Leninist revolution, which seeks to replace traditional dictators with new-style, Castroite dictators with the help of arms, advisers and doctrines from the Soviet Bloc. The struggle between the traditional Latin military regime and the two revolutions has dominated the politics of Central America during the last twenty years.

Jeane Kirkpatrick, in *Central America and the Reagan Doctrine*, 1987.

Even more troubling in terms of adherence to world order norms, Cuba has long had a doctrine of "revolutionary internationalism" in which it has sought to create and assist Marxist-Leninist insurgencies throughout the world and particularly in Latin America and the Caribbean. In fact, Cuba's Constitution openly asserts a right, contrary to the United Nations Charter, to assist "wars of national liberation." Since 1959 Castro has sought to foster insurgencies widely throughout the region. Indeed, Pamela Falk in her book *Cuban Foreign Policy* writes that "Cuba provided armed assistance to guerrilla insurgents in every nation of the Western Hemisphere except Mexico during the first two decades of revolutionary rule." And Ernst Halperin writes of prolonged Castroite guerrilla

campaigns in Guatemala, Venezuela, Colombia, and Peru, with lesser attempts in Mexico, the Dominican Republic, Nicaragua, Panama, Brazil, Argentina, and Paraguay. Then, after Che Guevara's disastrous failure in Bolivia, there came the campaigns of terrorism—"urban guerrilla warfare," as it is euphemistically called by its protagonists—in Brazil, Uruguay, and Argentina.

In 1959, an abortive effort to invade Nicaragua was investigated by the OAS, which linked the insurgents to the Castro government. This Nicaraguan invasion was only one of at least three invasions attempted by Castro in his first year in power. Che Guevara's own diary documents the failed effort in Bolivia during the 1960s. The OAS formally condemned Cuba for its attacks on Venezuela during the 1960s. On March 23, 1981, Colombia suspended relations with Cuba for its role in training several hundred M-19 guerrillas who then infiltrated Colombia with a mission of establishing a "people's army" to fight against the Colombian government. President Julio Cesar Turbay of Colombia commented in a *New York Times* interview: "When we found that Cuba, a country with which we had diplomatic relations, was using those relations to prepare a group of guerrillas to come and fight against the government, it was a kind of Pearl Harbor for us."

Subversive Efforts

Cuba's first efforts to foster subversion during the 1960s were generally amateurish and universally unsuccessful. In contrast, their more recent subversive efforts, beginning in the late 1970s, have been highly professional and are backed by a sophisticated military, indoctrinal, training, logistical, intelligence and propaganda effort. . . . Cuban efforts are broad-ranging and have included intensive and ongoing attacks against El Salvador and Guatemala with secondary subversion directed against Honduras and Costa Rica. To illustrate the magnitude of this problem for Latin America, Cuban military facilities have been used to train over 20,000 persons, including some from virtually every Latin American country. All four Central American nations just noted as targets of recent Cuban subversion have had substantial groups of insurgents trained at special guerrilla training camps in Cuba.

A trend that adds considerably to the danger of these attacks is an increasing cooperation in terrorism and subversion among radical regimes that share an antipathy toward liberal democracy and a willingness to use force to expand regime ideology.

"The North American imperialist strategists have put into effect a doctrine of low-intensity wars and conflicts in order to suppress the striving of . . . millions."

American Imperialism Causes Conflict

Jaime Barrios

The political and economic conflicts in Central America are caused by American efforts to end socialist revolutions in the region, states Jaime Barrios in the following viewpoint. Barrios, a member of the central committee of the Communist Party of El Salvador, believes the U.S. employs a policy of low-intensity warfare to disrupt Central American nations and socialist governments. Because the U.S. feels it must prove its global superiority, Barrios maintains, it continues to violate treaties and intervene in Central America even as other nations are resolving regional conflicts peacefully.

As you read, consider the following questions:

1. Why does Barrios believe the domino theory is an oversimplification of the situation in Central America?
2. How does the U.S. plan to fight socialist revolution in El Salvador, according to the author?
3. Why does Barrios think peace between the U.S. and the Soviet Union is not a guarantee of peace in Central America?

Jaime Barrios, "Low-Intensity Warfare: Reasons and Rationale," *World Marxist Review,* July 1989. Reprinted with permission.

The North American imperialist strategists have put into effect a doctrine of low-intensity wars and conflicts in order to suppress the striving of the dispossessed millions for revolutionary social and national liberation. Some of the progenitors of the concept, and commentators upon it, have made statements which give us a good idea of what it means in practice.

Events in Central America are often referred to in Washington as a "low-intensity conflict", which is unlike either a conventional or a nuclear war. Some experts even say in all seriousness that it is neither war nor peace but an elusive and complex blend of diverse phenomena, something like the Cheshire Cat, which used to disappear when looked at, leaving behind its broad grin.

An objective analysis of the conflicts in the region indicates that they are rooted in the internal contradictions of each particular country. These contradictions arise in the course of the class struggle, and as they become increasingly aggravated they help shape objective conditions for a radical turn in the nation's historical development, when revolution ceases to be a distant prospect and becomes something tangible and impending. If at this juncture the democratic forces can count on a reliable vanguard, the opportunity will not be missed. Again and again, one is prompted to repeat the well-known truth that revolutions have definite causes, develop in line with objectively operating laws and cannot be exported.

Social Conflicts

Acute social conflicts sometimes flare up almost simultaneously in several countries of the same geographical area, and this is what has happened in Central America. In such cases these conflicts assume a regional dimension, even though each particular conflict remains, in essence, purely internal. The "domino theory" invented by US strategists is an attempt at an extremely biased and oversimplified explanation of this coincidence—an explanation devised for the gullible.

When movements for national liberation and social emancipation gain ground, imperialism uses any pretext and a variety of techniques to intervene in the course of events. Then the forces at the head of the democratic process have to fight both against the local rulers and against the foreign power that is there to help them. If revolutionary action in a particular country has a broad social base and a reliable political leadership, the struggle inevitably becomes protracted. This is what the present US strategy is based on.

Many US theorists doctor facts in a bid to blame the guerrillas and the revolutionaries for low-intensity conflicts. In actual fact, these wars are a direct result of the counterrevolutionary strategy of counterinsurgency.

" . . . Well, like it was explained to me, we're movin' in only to protect those unarmed advisers we sent down here."

Ollie Harrington. *People's Daily World.* Reprinted with permission.

Former US Defense Secretary Caspar Weinberger is one of these "accusers". According to him, the term "war of national liberation" is ill-suited to low-intensity conflicts. A similar idea is propounded in the report entitled "A Strategy for Latin America in the 1990s", which political scientists have christened the "Santa Fe Document II". Specifically, it refers to the "growing danger" of "weak democratic regimes" being drawn into these conflicts, as is alleged to have happened to most of them in Latin America. A similar view is held by a commission for integrated long-term strategy which, in January 1988, submitted a report entitled "Discriminate Deterrence" to the US President. We hold that the term itself—low-intensity conflict or war—is merely a euphemism for *counterrevolutionary war against national liberation movements*. The Latin American researcher Gregorio Selser is quite right to note that the same phenomenon may well be described as "limited war", "cheap war" or "violent peace".

The fundamental postulates of the doctrine in question are still being tried and tested in the main proving ground of Central America. Washington is finding out whether the new strategy can help it control socioeconomic processes in Nicaragua, El Salvador and Guatemala and curb the rising popular struggle in Honduras and Costa Rica. Naturally, a related objective is to teach the revolutionaries in Latin America, and in the Third World as a whole, an object lesson and to prove the immutability of the United States' global might.

The Importance of Central America

As President Reagan said in his time, "If Central America were to fall, what would the consequences be for our position in Asia, Europe, and for alliances such as NATO [North Atlantic Treaty Organization]? If the United States cannot respond to a threat near our own borders, why should Europeans or Asians believe that we are seriously concerned about threats to them? If the Soviets can assume that nothing short of an actual attack on the United States will provoke an American response, which ally, which friend will trust us then?" Toward the end of his statement, the then US President exclaimed dramatically that the "national security of all the Americas is at stake in Central America. If we cannot defend ourselves there, we cannot expect to prevail elsewhere."

There are two key aspects to the imperialist doctrine of low-intensity wars: a tactic of counterinsurgency and a political pattern to be introduced into the countries comprising the theatre of operations. . . .

Washington has failed to present the Central American insurgents as "bandits". It has proved impossible to defeat them on the battlefield or to eliminate them by state terrorism. It was necessary to look for other ways of achieving the strategic objective of undermining the revolutionary policies of the forces the US found objectionable. *"Total" conflict means not only military operations but also vigorous political, diplomatic, economic, social and ideological action.* Hence the interpretation of these wars as primarily a clash of two opposite programmes, and only then as hostilities between armies. . . .

49

The counterrevolutionary political programme for low-intensity wars posits several models for different situations. In some cases, the objective is to *overthrow progressive regimes* (Nicaragua, Angola, Afghanistan, etc.) and in others, to counter the ongoing revolutionary struggle (specifically, in El Salvador and Guatemala) by an *alternative project* which has the broadest possible social base and is designed to *suppress the national liberation movement.*

Anger at U.S. Imperialism

The U.S. rulers are committing one murderous outrage after another against the people of Latin America. The U.S. death-squad government goes on murdering in El Salvador. . .in Panama U.S. stormtroopers occupy the country in full fascist operation and thousands of unnamed victims of the invasion lie buried in mass graves. . .the U.S. puppet-elect in Nicaragua prepares to take power, eleven years after the Nicaraguan people overthrew the hated Somoza regime. . .U.S. intervention and threats mount against the people of Haiti, Cuba, and elsewhere. . . .

It is time to seize the time and step forward with an outpouring of rage against the crimes of yanqui imperialism in Latin America.

Revolutionary Worker, March 19, 1990.

In El Salvador, a "nation-building" programme was adopted to create stable institutions capable of ensuring "national security" and to deny mass support to the revolutionaries. That was the goal of various civilian programmes, local development projects, indoctrination and the like. The ruling quarters tried to demonstrate the feasibility of a "new nation" and a "new state" that differed radically from the model advocated by the insurgent organisations. . . .

The "nation-building" drive called for *controlled elections,* civilian rule and a subsequent reshuffling of government agencies; even the enactment of a new constitution was not ruled out. This legitimation of a patently illegal regime with the help of an electoral process—a fetish that casts a spell on US public opinion—is an integral component of the whole political project of low-intensity wars. The "assertion of the people's will" takes place amid a reign of terror and is accompanied by scandalous cases of fraud. Against the background of protracted class struggle, the counterinsurgency programme is oriented on the centrist quarters, implying the isolation of both the Right and the Left.

A certain *modernisation of dependent capitalism* is also planned. An agrarian and banking reform was implemented and foreign

50

trade was nationalised in El Salvador under the Christian Democratic government. As a result, the oligarchy lost some of its economic power and some of its influence with the armed forces, which were managed by advisers from the Pentagon —even though, after the suppression of the popular uprising of 1932, the oligarchy had put the army in control of politics (the military had the decisive say in the selection of every president) and quietly lined its pockets under army protection.

In an effort to win back the ground lost in recent years, the oligarchy set up its own party—the Nationalist Republican Alliance (ARENA). This political group gradually came to dominate the legislative assembly and the Supreme Court and, in March 1989, won the presidential elections. The reforms that had been implemented turned out to be superficial and illusory. Besides, they were never really carried through so as not to aggravate the contradictions either within the ruling class or between it and US imperialism. Yet again, populism has demonstrated how little it is worth. . . .

The doctrine of low-intensity wars has been drawn up with due attention paid to US foreign policy and military failures in the Third World. The historic victory of the Vietnamese people forced the military strategists of imperialism to modify their old policy. The neoglobalist Reagan Doctrine is in fact an updated and adjusted version of the old strategy of intervention in the world's flash points. An attempt to *roll back* the social and political processes that allegedly threaten US "national security" and "national interests" is one of the major "innovations" introduced into a policy inherited from previous US presidents (which emphasised efforts to strengthen the allies and to preserve what was left of the United States' global dominance—which took a severe beating during the 1970s).

Easing of Tensions

Washington is aware of the intricate and complex nature of today's world, but it refuses to give up its old course even as international tensions are being eased.

As Fidel Castro noted, it is important to understand "how imperialism interprets peace and peaceful coexistence". There is justifiable concern that, as happened many times in the past, imperialism may be ready to accept "peace between the great powers, while reserving the right to intimidate, oppress, exploit and launch aggression against Third World countries".

The fact that various regional conflicts are being settled politically *does not mean that Washington has given up low-intensity warfare*. Every conflict of this kind has its own logic of settlement. There is no common yardstick here.

US imperialism is increasingly demonstrating its disdain of

the treaties it signed or was party to. Often, these agreements soon turn into scraps of paper. Witness the developments in Afghanistan, Nicaragua and Angola, where the United States is blatantly violating its obligations. Washington still aids and abets the opposition in Afghanistan, and the UNITA [National Union for the Total Independence of Angola] thugs. It frequently appears to regard negotiations as a way of playing for time and continuing with its old "containment of communism" strategy.

There is no reason to hope that imperialism will change its spots and become decent of its own accord. This view is borne out by the doctrine of low-intensity wars. Therefore, the enslaved nations will continue to fight for national independence and uphold their right to a better life by using the forms of struggle they themselves find necessary.

Distinguishing Between Fact and Opinion

This activity is designed to help develop the basic reading and thinking skill of distinguishing between fact and opinion. Consider the following statement: "Sixty-nine percent of Nicaraguans are racially mixed." This is a factual statement because it could be checked by looking at Nicaraguan population statistics in *The World Fact Book*. But the statement "The racial composition in Nicaragua has been an obstacle to national unity" is an opinion. Many people may not think Nicaragua has a problem with national unity. Others might argue that, even if Nicaragua lacks national unity, its racial composition is not the cause.

When investigating controversial issues it is important that one be able to distinguish between statements of fact and statements of opinion. It is also important to recognize that not all statements of fact are true. They may appear to be true, but some are based on inaccurate or false information. For this activity, however, we are concerned with understanding the difference between those statements which appear to be factual and those which appear to be based primarily on opinion.

Most of the following statements are taken from the viewpoints in this chapter. Consider each statement carefully. *Mark O for any statement you believe is an opinion or interpretation of facts. Mark F for any statement you believe is a fact. Mark I for any statement you believe is impossible to judge.*

If you are doing this activity as a member of a class or group, compare your answers with those of other class or group members. Be able to defend your answers. You may discover that others come to different conclusions than you do. Listening to the reasons others present for their answers may give you valuable insights into distinguishing between fact and opinion.

O = opinion
F = fact
I = impossible to judge

53

1. For almost three decades Central America had one of the highest growth rates in the world.

2. Central America accounts for only 13 percent of world coffee exports.

3. By 1980 the richest 20 percent of the Central American population was receiving between one-half and two-thirds of total national income.

4. Large numbers of Central Americans came to view nonviolent reform as impossible.

5. Political violence is the result of the desperate struggle of certain groups to retain land, prestige, and power at any price.

6. In El Salvador, murder and manslaughter together rank as the second highest cause of death.

7. Like much of Hispanic America, Central America is a death-oriented society.

8. The differences between North America and Latin America are enormous, covering virtually all aspects of human life.

9. Central America is a little larger than California.

10. Central America has a variety of mineral resources.

11. Central America's main resource is its people.

12. Central America is small in size and population, poor in resources, and holds a wealth of problems and troubles.

13. During the 1970s there was a dramatic decrease in U.S. military assistance to Central America.

14. By 1981 the Soviet Union had fifty times more military advisors in Latin America than did the United States.

15. Cuba has long sought to create and assist Marxist-Leninist insurgencies throughout the world.

16. Revolutions have definite causes and cannot be exported.

17. An agrarian and banking reform was implemented in El Salvador under the Christian Democratic government.

18. There is no reason to hope that imperialism will change its spots and become decent of its own accord.

19. Central Americans are as hardworking as most other humans on this planet.

20. The best death is that which gives one the chance to display one's manhood to the fullest.

Periodical Bibliography

The following articles have been selected to supplement the diverse views presented in this chapter.

Vidal Brown — "The Root Causes: Poverty and Politics," *World Press Review,* April 1988.

Business Week — "Cooling Off 'Hot Spots': A Promising Start," February 22, 1988.

Commonweal — "Enlarging the Cloth," September 8, 1989.

Commonweal — "Facing South," February 24, 1989.

James P. Dean — "U.S. Support Is Key to Democracy in Central America," *American Legion Magazine,* March 1987.

The Economist — "Changing the Script in Central America," December 16, 1989.

The Economist — "Hands Off the Isthmus," March 4, 1989.

Robert Kagan — "There to Stay: The U.S. and Latin America," *The National Interest,* Spring 1990.

Clifford Krauss — "Revolution in Central America?" *Foreign Affairs,* Winter 1987.

Charles Krauthammer — "Terror and Peace: The 'Root Cause' Fallacy," *Time,* September 22, 1986.

Saul Landau — "Remember Central America?" *Tikkun,* November/December 1989.

The Nation — "Termination Time," September 4, 1989.

The Nation — "The Thirty Years War," October 24, 1988.

Michael Novak — "Are You Sleeping Well, Fidel?" *Forbes,* February 5, 1990.

James Petras — "Roots of the FSLN's Defeat," *Against the Current,* May/June 1990. Available from the Center for Changes, 7012 Michigan Ave., Detroit, MI 48210.

Jonathan Rose — "The War-Torn Roots of Today's Turmoil," *Scholastic Update,* March 9, 1987.

Scholastic Update — "The Struggle for Peace and Democracy," special issue, February 9, 1990.

Kenneth N. Skoug Jr. — "Our Last Adversary," *Department of State Bulletin,* September 1988.

Tad Szulc — "Castro: Dilemmas of the Last Idealist," *New Perspectives Quarterly,* Winter 1988.

Robert E. White — "Blaming the Villains, Not the Victims," *Commonweal,* October 21, 1988.

George F. Will — "Without Reagan, There Would Be No Contras," *Conservative Chronicle,* March 14, 1990. Available from *Conservative Chronicle,* PO Box 11297, Des Moines, IA 50340-1297.

Is U.S. Involvement in Central America Justified?

Chapter Preface

Nicaragua holds elections and the U.S.-supported Violeta Barrios de Chamorro defeats the Marxist Sandinistas. Thousands of Panamanians celebrate as U.S. troops invade their country, overthrow Manuel Noriega, and install as president Guillermo Endara, the winner of the Panamanian elections. Many Americans point to these events as evidence that U.S. involvement in Central America has brought democracy and political stability to the region. It is America's responsibility to promote democracy in the world, these Americans believe. Former U.S. president Ronald Reagan, for example, stated, "We can and must help Central America. It's in our national interest to do so; and, morally, it's the only right thing to do." Reagan and others maintain that U.S. involvement has brought fair, democratic elections not only to Nicaragua and Panama, but also to El Salvador, Honduras, and Guatemala.

Other Americans, however, think that U.S. involvement has done anything but stabilize the region. As evidence they point out that nearly 45,000 Nicaraguans were killed in that nation's civil war, a war in which the U.S. supplied the rebels with more than $265 million in aid. U.S. involvement promotes oppression in Central America, many experts contend, because the U.S. has a pattern of supporting dictators like Anastasio Somoza and Manuel Noriega who, although loyal to U.S. interests, are often inhumane to their own people. These dictators sometimes become disloyal or embarrass the U.S. when their brutality to their own people is revealed to the world. At this point, these experts contend, the U.S. often abandons such dictators and helps overthrow them, thus promoting more violence and instability in the region. As Mexican author Carlos Fuentes states, "The other fundamental reason, along with colonialism, of turmoil, instability, terrorism, hunger, and weakness in the area [is] United States interventionism."

Whether U.S. involvement in Central America benefits or harms the region and its people is a subject of much disagreement. The authors in the following chapter debate how American involvement affects Central America and whether such involvement is justified.

57

*"The Monroe Doctrine still is the lamp by which
our policy should be guided."*

The Monroe Doctrine Justifies U.S. Involvement

Phyllis Schlafly

In 1823, President James Monroe proclaimed the entire western
hemisphere off limits to further European colonization. Many
presidents since Monroe have used this proclamation, known as
the Monroe Doctrine, as a primary reason for U.S. involvement
in Central America. The Monroe Doctrine benefits the U.S. by
protecting American interests in Central America, Phyllis
Schlafly contends in the following viewpoint. Communism in the
region threatens the security of the U.S., she argues, and the
U.S. has the right to protect itself by helping to establish democratic governments in Central America. Schlafly is a conservative
commentator, the author of many books and articles, and the
publisher of *The Phyllis Schlafly Report*, a monthly newsletter.

As you read, consider the following questions:

1. Why does Schlafly think the Monroe Doctrine can be used
   to justify American action against communism in Central
   America?
2. What examples does the author give of Castro's mistreatment
   of political prisoners?
3. What will happen if the U.S. does nothing to stop communism
   in Central America, according to the author?

Phyllis Schlafly, "Reaffirming the Monroe Doctrine," *The Phyllis Schlafly Report,* May 1987.
Reprinted with permission.

The Monroe Doctrine was proclaimed in President Monroe's message to Congress on December 2, 1823. It was a response to an attempt by Imperial Russia under Czar Alexander to colonize our Pacific coast, from Alaska to San Francisco. History teaches that sometimes, the more things change, the more they remain the same.

The essential part of the Monroe Doctrine is contained in these words: "The political system of the allied powers is essentially different from that of America. We should consider any attempt on their part to extend their system to any portion of this hemisphere as dangerous to our peace and safety." The "allied powers" were defined as Russia and other European governments.

Enthusiastic Support

President Monroe's courageous statement was made at a time when America had no standing army and only five sailing ships in our navy. But we had a proud sense of national identity. His statement was enthusiastically supported by Congress and the American people. His Secretary of State, John Quincy Adams, advised: "There can, perhaps, be no better time for saying, frankly and explicitly, to the Russian government that the future peace of the world cannot be promoted by Russian settlements on any part of the American continent."

The Marquis de Lafayette immediately called the Monroe Doctrine "the best little bit of paper that God ever permitted any man to give to the world." Daniel Webster later called it a bright page in our history.

The Monroe Doctrine was never limited to preventing territorial aggression. The key word is "system"—it prohibits extending the "system" of Russia or other European powers to the Western Hemisphere. Furthermore, Monroe said, we can't believe that our friends to the south would ever voluntarily adopt the Old World system. The Monroe Doctrine thus declared the fundamental difference between our republic and Old World empires or dictatorships.

The Monroe Doctrine does not define our relationship with Latin America, but states our policy toward aggressive governments of the Old World. It originated as a policy of U.S. national security, and this rationale of self-defense has been reaffirmed many times in the 20th century.

Throughout the 19th century, the Monroe Doctrine was successful as a deterrent. Even though we were a small nation of only ten million people, European nations didn't want to tangle with us.

Before Soviet boss Nikita Khrushchev moved his offensive nuclear missiles into Cuba in 1962, he taunted us: "Now the remains of this Monroe Doctrine should best be buried, as every

dead body is, so that it does not poison the air by its decay."
News of its death was premature, as Mark Twain would have
said.

National Honor

The support the American people gave to President John F.
Kennedy in removing those missiles is evidence that the Monroe
Doctrine is not only part of our national heritage, it is part of
our national honor. That's the same reason why the American
people supported President Ronald Reagan's dramatic rescue of
Grenada so overwhelmingly.

The Symms Amendment, passed by big majorities in Congress
in 1982 and again in 1984, reaffirms our commitment to the
Monroe Doctrine. President Reagan recognized this in his 1987
State of the Union Message when he reminded us that his commitment to stop Communism in the Western Hemisphere did
not start by spontaneous generation on the day he took office.
"It began," he said, "with the Monroe Doctrine in 1823 and continues today as our historic bipartisan American policy."

Dusting Off the Doctrine

Marxism/communism has failed, and is no longer welcome anywhere. Even the republics of the Soviet Union and the masses in
Red China are weary of the communist system, and are willing to
shed their blood to change it.

That's precisely why the Monroe Doctrine should be dusted off
and reinstated for the Western Hemisphere. . . . That Doctrine is
as valid—and more important to our own security—than it was in
1823.

The United States has no territorial ambitions. But it is the only
nation in the West having the military and diplomatic clout to
prevent Soviet interference in the affairs of American countries,
as in El Salvador, which is currently under siege.

Latin Americans may be jealous of their Big Brother to the North,
but they should thank their lucky stars that the U.S.A. is not an
aggressive or predator nation, but one that only wishes them
well—and stands ready to prove it.

Henry Mohr, *Conservative Chronicle*, January 17, 1990.

James Monroe established a cornerstone of American foreign
policy, and he planted it so firmly in our national consciousness
that it still evokes an enthusiastic response from modern audiences. . . .

President Monroe once said that "national honor is national
property of the highest value." He bequeathed to us a property

60

that is part of our national honor. The Monroe Doctrine is a doctrine for all seasons. May it live forever.

Historians will probably look back on Ronald Reagan's rescue of Grenada in October 1983 as a turning point in official American policy toward Communism. Using a minimum of force, the United States prevented the establishment of another Communist state in the Western Hemisphere.

Two years later, the U.S. State Department published a selection from the 35,000 pounds of documents captured when our Marines landed in Grenada. They provide important insight into Soviet actions and plans in the Caribbean. It's clear from these documents that the Soviet Union was arming Grenada to function as a Soviet base supplied by weapons going through Cuba. . . .

The captured documents prove that (to paraphrase Gertrude Stein) a Communist is a Communist is a Communist. The Grenada Documents, which include thousands of internal memoranda of a Communist regime in power, detail a police state just like Cuba, Afghanistan, Angola, Vietnam, and every other satellite country. The documents describe how to repress political opponents, the press, the clergy, and the private sector.

The captured documents confirm that the Communists have not changed their ways; they are still a major threat to the Free World, and that what is at stake in this confrontation is freedom itself. . . .

The Grenada invasion broke the mystique of the Brezhnev Doctrine that, once a country goes Communist, it must always remain Communist. Grenada exposed this for what it really is: just the impudent boast of a bloody dictator. The Grenada invasion not only proved that Communism is reversible, but it legitimized the use of force to liberate the captive peoples. Grenada demolished the notion that it isn't appropriate for a Western democracy to use any but "political" or "negotiated" means to resolve conflicts.

A Voice from Castro's Prisons

Armando Valladares is a very brave man. He survived 22 years in Castro's prisons. When he tells the world what it was like, it sounds very similar to Alexander Solzhenitsyn's descriptions of the Soviet Gulag. Only Cuba is a lot closer to America.

A one-time supporter of Castro, Valladares was imprisoned in 1960 because he criticized the dictator's growing dependence on the Soviet Union. He was released in 1982 as a result of French and Spanish intervention in his behalf.

Some of the most interesting of Valladares' revelations are his descriptions of the "new class" in Castro's Cuba which lives "a way of life completely unknown to the Cuban people." The "new class" is a favored group of government and police officials and Communist Party dignitaries.

The "new class" has access to "special" stores and products, exclusive homes which were confiscated from the middle class in pre-Castro Cuba, travel privileges, and a favored brand of justice. For example, a professional boxer, Jose Gomez, got away with committing murder without any punishment, but the possession of a Bible can land an average citizen in jail. In Communist Cuba, he says, "equal justice does not exist."

Two Goals for Central America

The United States has two interests in Central America. One is to keep it from becoming a place where Russian advisers stroll across the waistline of the Americas. The other is to make it a democratic place, whose free people can spend their time getting richer instead of being herded into armies and bureaucracies.

The Economist, March 26, 1988.

"In the first days of the Revolution," Valladares said, "Castro promised that the beaches would become the property of the people and that he would abolish private beaches. However, he has done nothing about this." Valladares says that the Club Biltmore, where the well-to-do gathered in prerevolutionary Cuba, is today exclusively reserved for colonels of the political police and other officials of the Ministry of the Interior. Other beaches are similarly barred to the Cuban people, notably Jibacoa, where access is limited only to Soviet personnel and other foreigners.

Valladares says that there are 24,000 to 30,000 Soviet personnel in Cuba. He says that Soviet officials control the Cuban economy and industry (including the sugar industry), as well as the military. He says that "the Soviets have total control of the Cuban equipment, weapons, and transportation systems. The Cuban military does not even have access to its own bases."

Political "Rehabilitation"

Essentially, all important decisions and operations are controlled by Soviet officials. Soviet "specialists" run the prisons with an iron hand. When political prisoners chanted "Soviets, go home!" in an incident known as "Black September," they were given "the harshest of floggings."

Castro has 140,000 political and criminal prisoners in 68 Cuban penitentiaries. Havana province alone has 48,000 prisoners out of two million residents. For a quarter of a century, Castro has used the penitentiary system to carry out a ruthless system which he calls political and social "rehabilitation." It is quite different from anything in American prisons.

Valladares and his fellow prisoners were encouraged to "reform" by such inducements as systematic beatings, mutilation, starvation (in his case, for 46 days), and hard labor. Those who refused to cooperate with this rehabilitation program were gagged and murdered.

The strictest penal institution is located on the Isla de Pinos, an island south of Cuba made famous as *Treasure Island* by Robert Louis Stevenson. Valladares says that the conditions there are "identical to those of the Soviet concentration camps under Stalin." Castro and the Communists have converted *Treasure Island* into what Valladares calls the "Siberia of the American continent."

For the "free" citizens of Cuba, the Castro regime has restructured the work week. "Occupational work" is required on Mondays through Saturdays, while "voluntary work" is expected from all on Sundays. Those who choose not to "volunteer," or who attend church services, are subject to public humiliation and investigation as revolutionaries.

The Castro regime enforces its work demands on all starting at an early age. Some young students are taught manual labor at youth "camps" before entering the factories, and uncooperative youths are sent to specially designed adolescent concentration camps.

Cuban officials apparently thought that, if they released Valladares, he would drift into obscurity among other Cuban refugees. Although he must know how vindictive the Communists are against defectors who tell the truth about Communism, he has chosen to give the world his authentic, first-hand information.

"After almost a quarter of a century of Communism in Cuba," he says, "no one can continue to excuse its crimes by talking of the immaturity of the political process. No philosophy, no symbol, can justify the impunity with which Castroism kills its enemies."

Mistakes in Nicaragua

After the Sandinistas overthrew Anastasio Somoza in 1979 and captured Nicaragua, I asked a friend living in that country, "Are they Communists?" She replied, "only 100%."

But somehow the liberal intellectuals and politicians were fooled. In 1979 the Sandinistas wrote a letter to the Organization of American States promising free elections, freedom of religion, free trade unions, a free press, civil rights, human rights, and a just judicial system. The liberals believed, or pretended to believe, that the Sandinistas were merely agrarian reformers or democratic do-gooders.

So the OAS expelled the government of Somoza. The Carter Administration withdrew U.S. aid from Somoza, and gave economic aid to the Sandinistas while the Soviet bloc armed them with weapons.

During the first year and a half after the Sandinistas took over, the Carter Administration sent them $118 million in U.S. aid. In addition, the Carter Administration actively supported loans to the Sandinistas from international lending institutions, helping them to get $262 million from the InterAmerican Development Bank. The Sandinistas received three times the economic assistance that Somoza got in the previous 40 years.

Spirit of Monroe Doctrine Still Alive

In his December 2, 1823, message to Congress, President James Monroe declared that, "the American continents, by the free and independent condition they have assumed and maintain, are henceforth not to be considered subjects for future colonization by European powers." The spirit of this doctrine remains vitally important for U.S. regional strategic interests. . . .

The letter of the Monroe Doctrine remains a foundation upon which U.S. hemispheric policy rests. A key U.S. policy objective should be to deny any Soviet-bloc power the ability to exert its political and economic influence within the Americas.

Mark B. Liedl, *Issues '88: A Platform for America*, 1988.

So the Communist Sandinistas grabbed the power, the police, the military, the radio station, the information ministry, and the foreign ministry. They filled all positions of power with Communists and squeezed out the non-Communists. The Sandinistas persecuted the church, wiped out the Jewish religion, attacked the Indian tribes on the northeastern coast and relocated them, closed down the trade unions, suppressed the newspapers, and carried out a methodical murder campaign. . . .

President Reagan has asked the fundamental question: "Must we sit by while Central Americans are driven from their homes like the more than a million who have sought refuge out of Afghanistan, or the 1-1/2 million who have fled Indochina, or the more than a million Cubans who have fled Castro's Cuban utopia?"

If we do nothing, . . . we had better get prepared for at least five million refugees to flood into Texas, Arizona, New Mexico, California, Louisiana, and Florida. They won't have to come on boats like the Vietnamese; they can just walk north.

When individual Americans, who enjoy our freedom, security and comforts, voluntarily risk their lives and fortunes to help valiant Freedom Fighters in a foreign country to win their freedom, those Americans should be honored for their sacrificial efforts.

The United States won its freedom in our seven-year Revolutionary War in significant part because valiant men from other countries (notably Lafayette) were noble and generous enough to travel across the Atlantic and risk their lives fighting with the colonial Freedom Fighters.

When the Communists were trying to capture Spain in the 1930s, some U.S. citizens voluntarily joined what they called the "Abraham Lincoln Brigade" in order to fight and die for Communism in Spain. Most of us would judge their goals as wrong, but their motives were sincere and they certainly placed their lives on the line to prove it.

We don't hear any more about American citizens joining Communist military operations abroad. The evidence of Communist inhumanity to man, from the U.S.S.R. to Poland to Afghanistan to Cambodia, is too massive.

But there are valiant Americans who, from our abundance of freedom and plenty, voluntarily undertake dangerous missions to try to light the lamp of freedom in other lands. Americans have helped in Nicaragua, Afghanistan, Cambodia, Mozambique and Ethiopia. That role is too risky and too costly for most of us, but we can salute the few who show such courage. . . .

President Reagan said, "Make no mistake—the Soviets are challenging the United States to a test of wills over the future of this hemisphere.". . .

The Monroe Doctrine still is the lamp by which our policy should be guided.

"The Monroe Doctrine is the most illustrious cadaver in all the Americas."

The Monroe Doctrine Does Not Justify U.S. Involvement

Carlos Fuentes

President James Monroe established the Monroe Doctrine in 1823 in an attempt to prevent further European involvement in the western hemisphere. Even then, the doctrine was hypocritical, Carlos Fuentes states in the following viewpoint, for only with the help of France could the U.S. have gained its independence. Fuentes believes the Monroe Doctrine is used to further U.S. imperialism in Central America, not to protect the region from Europeans. The U.S. will lose its prestige if it continues to employ the Monroe Doctrine as a foreign policy while the Soviets promote peace, Fuentes maintains. Fuentes, a former Mexican ambassador to France, is an acclaimed Mexican novelist and poet whose works include *Christopher Unborn, The Good Conscience,* and *Constancia and Other Stories for Virgins.*

As you read, consider the following questions:

1. Why does Fuentes believe the Brezhnev Doctrine is dead?
2. Against whom does the U.S. use the Monroe Doctrine, according to the author?
3. What does Fuentes think will happen if the U.S. and Cuba take down the Miami and Havana walls?

In December 1968—more than twenty-one years ago—Gabriel García Márquez, Julio Cortázar and I traveled to Prague. Our purpose was to show our solidarity with the Czechoslovak reform movement, which has come to be called the Prague Spring. That August, the troops of the Warsaw Pact had invaded Czechoslovakia to terminate Alexander Dubcek's experiment in democratic socialism. . . .

What Dubcek and his advisers—Foreign Minister Jiri Hajek, President Ludvik Svoboda, the economist Ota Sik and the journalist Jiri Pelikan—were seeking was, in light of the changes now taking place in Central Europe, remarkably modest. "Socialism with a human face," simply put, consisted in carrying out Marx's dictum about the withering away of the state and its gradual replacement by the energies of civil society. Czechoslovakia, which had a tradition of political democracy and a well-developed industrial base, not only could take that step but actually did take it. . . .

That is, *glasnost* and *perestroika* were born twenty-two years ago in Czechoslovakia. It is only natural that they now return to their native land and replace the doctrine used to justify the aggression of 1968. The Brezhnev Doctrine announced that the Soviet Union had the right to intervene militarily to insure that any nation already within the Soviet sphere of influence (or even one that might someday be within it) did not drift away. In so doing, Brezhnev supplied powerful arguments to U.S. hardliners: Those who fall into the hands of the Soviet Union never escape.

Monroe and Brezhnev

When García Márquez, Cortázar and I reached Prague in the cold winter of 1968, the operative fiction—Kafka-cum-Schweik —was that the Russians were not there at all, that the "spring" could continue right into winter. While we couldn't refer directly to the Brezhnev Doctrine, we could talk about the Monroe Doctrine, so that when we mentioned U.S. intervention in Latin America, everyone understood that we were talking about Soviet intervention in Eastern Europe.

Today the Brezhnev Doctrine is dead, and the Soviet government's witty Foreign Ministry spokesman, Gennadi Gerasimov, whose sense of humor derives from Gogol and Bulgakov, says that now it's the Sinatra Doctrine that's operative in Eastern Europe: "I'll do it my way" is the order of the day. Or as we say in Mexico, *Cada chango a su mecate*—"Every monkey up his own tree." But the demise of the Brezhnev Doctrine in Europe, from the Elbe to the Vistula and from the Danube to the Baltic, is not being echoed by the demise of the Monroe Doctrine in the other theater of the cold war, the U.S. sphere of influence in Central America and the Caribbean.

© Kirk/Rothco. Reprinted with permission.

The Monroe Doctrine is the most illustrious cadaver in all the Americas. It was born with more holes than a Swiss cheese. How could President Monroe, in 1823, proscribe any European presence in the New World without weakening the legitimacy of the United States, whose independence would never have been achieved without the military intervention of Bourbon France? It was not only the active participation of freelancers like Lafayette but also de Grasse's fleet and Rochambeau's troops that clinched the English surrender at Yorktown.

The Falklands War

The application of the Monroe Doctrine as a weapon of intervention by the United States in Latin America reached the highest pitch of fantasy during the Falklands/Malvinas war. United Nations ambassador Jeane Kirkpatrick urged the Argentine military to embark on its disastrous adventure. In exchange for that support, the Argentines would train the Nicaraguan *contras*. But both the Argentine government and President Ronald Reagan had to realize that, when the chips were down, Washington would naturally support its old NATO [North Atlantic Treaty Organization] ally, Britain, and not its remote South Atlantic lackey, President Leopoldo Galtieri.

Once again it was clear that the United States did not intend to use the Monroe Doctrine against Europe but against Latin America. It was simply a weapon to be deployed against any

Latin American government that might be in conflict with Washington, any government that Washington might claim was working for "extra-continental" interests. It was the same argument the United States used against Mexico and the Germany of the Kaiser, against Argentina and the Axis powers, against Guatemala, Cuba, Brazil, Chile and Nicaragua with regard to "international communism." It is, therefore, hardly surprising that Latin American nations have from time to time preferred to align themselves with the distant empire, Moscow, rather than the all-too-nearby one, Washington. If only Latin Americans had been allowed to follow, unobstructed, their own national destinies without pressures from either side, how much confusion, how many perversions, how many reversals and, of course, how many human tragedies might have been avoided.

Increased Nationalism

It is one of the paradoxes of this *fin de siècle* that in the era of economic interdependence and instant communication political nationalism should be enjoying such a powerful resurgence. From Armenia and Turkestan to the Ukraine and Lithuania, from Northern Ireland to Brittany and the Basque country, regional nationalism is sending tremors through the seemingly solid foundations of European unity. The "single European home" is going to require an original and flexible federalism if it is going to respond successfully to these challenges.

In Latin America, nationalism is not limited to more or less isolated regions but is an important factor in the identity of extant nations. Mexican, Nicaraguan or Venezuelan nationalism is not spilling over frontiers and endangering neighboring countries and is certainly not destabilizing states. These nations define themselves by means of nationalism. We must, therefore, recognize nationalism as a dynamic factor essential for the solution of internal problems, which should remain free of outside meddling. We Latin Americans will be able to face the challenges of our times only if we first overcome this problem of external intervention.

Mexico and Brazil have the advantage of having consolidated their national sovereignty. Now they can test that sovereignty against the problems of political and economic modernization. Countries like Nicaragua, on the other hand, must defend their nascent national institutions against constant external aggression. In fact, the Sandinista government has defeated that foreign-supported aggression—just as Benito Juárez defeated the Mexican *contras*—and now demands that its last vestiges be expunged. The end of the *contras* should also be the end of the long history of U.S. intervention in Nicaragua. . . .

There is no way to compare what is happening in Nicaragua

with the situation in El Salvador. The Farabundo Martí National Liberation Front was not invented abroad; it arose in El Salvador and will either survive or die there. The *contras* never won a battle in Nicaragua; the F.M.L.N. controls much of El Salvador and is capable of launching an offensive in the capital itself to prove to President Alfredo Cristiani that he should negotiate seriously or face the prospect of an interminable bloodletting in a no-win situation. To accuse Nicaragua of sending arms to the F.M.L.N. is to apply yet another doctrine, one invented by the Mexican conservative ideologue Lucas Alamán: blaming internal problems on foreign governments.

Self-Interest Overrides Democracy

US leaders have favored democracy only when it produced governments that supported US policies. Otherwise, they have sought to subvert democracy. Washington's pro-democratic rhetoric has masked policies of self-interest and *realpolitik* that overrode support for democracy when the two aims collided.

Stephen Van Evera, *Defense & Disarmament Alternatives*, March 1990.

The Bush Administration is being criticized for its lack of initiatives with regard to the changes in Eastern Europe. I think it is more to be criticized for its abysmal behavior—threats or inaction—in Central America and the Caribbean. To go on arming the Salvadoran government while demanding that the Soviet Union stop arming the Nicaraguan government is not only a refusal to recognize that Moscow has in fact suspended all arms shipments to Central America but also a refusal to negotiate the compromise that Soviet President Gorbachev and Latin American diplomats have so often suggested, namely, that *no one* ship arms to Central America. . . .

Bush cannot limit his response to Gorbachev in Central America to a denunciation of Soviet arms—which, of course, are his justification for sending U.S. arms. He must support the principle that neither great power send arms and thereby proclaim the Sinatra Doctrine for all of Central America. Every country should go its own way, with no outside intervention whatsoever. Then we would see just how quickly negotiations would take place in El Salvador and with what vigor national institutions would develop in Nicaragua.

Bush's hypocrisy in Central America is an insult. He takes a paternalistic attitude that does not recognize the ability of Salvadorans or Nicaraguans to resolve their own conflicts or determine their own destinies. Is there anyone who really believes that the victory of the F.M.L.N. in El Salvador or of Daniel

Ortega in Nicaragua would endanger the Untied States or constitute a Soviet beachhead in Central America? In the Gorbachev era, with Solidarity governing Poland, with the Czechoslovak Politburo in total collapse, with a multiparty Hungary requesting admission to the Council of Europe, with the removal of the Berlin wall, how can anyone think that Gorbachev has either the intention or the ability to set up Stalinist dictatorships whose advantage to the Soviet Union would be doubtful, and logistically impossible, in countries so geographically remote? No one would want to be a spoke in the wheel of such a troika—assuming troikas had wheels.

The Problem of Cuba

The real problem, of course, is Cuba. Fidel Castro is increasingly isolated from his old allies in the Communist world. A stormy session of the Cuban Cabinet in 1968 debated the question of whether Cuba should denounce the invasion of Czechoslovakia. The Brezhnev Doctrine reinforced the perpetuation of the Monroe Doctrine in the Americas. The Cubans hoped the Czechoslovaks would resist, but there was no Sierra Maestra anywhere near the Danube. Castro, once again, was obliged to follow the policy he could enact instead of the policy he wanted to enact.

Is it possible for Fidel Castro to lead today the revolution he always wanted: Latin American and far-reaching, but a revolution that would not sacrifice democratic freedoms or social transformation? Will age, the tentacles of the system or perhaps a love of the personal exercise of power keep him from it?

The human drama in this dilemma cannot be overlooked. Castro can claim that for Cuba the cold war is not over. And everything suggests that George Bush, like his predecessors, does not want a reformed Cuba but a defeated Cuba. Given such a reality, there can be no movement on either side, just paralysis. If only Bush and Castro would simultaneously and dramatically declare an end to the cold war in the Caribbean, the mutual opening of frontiers and the demolition of their two walls. That's right, the Havana wall, so that Cubans could have free access to information and so that political prisons could be emptied. But the Miami wall must also come down: The blockade must be lifted and U.S. citizens allowed to travel to Cuba, trade with Cuba and recognize Cuba. And let's hear no more of Radio Martí's stridency.

But if in the New World we either cannot or choose not to act with the clearsighted dramatism of the Europeans, it is certainly necessary that the first steps be taken for the eventual removal of the Miami and Havana walls. This must be done delicately, over a reasonable period of time and with good faith on both

71

sides. Relations between Cuba and the United States, as lop-sided as they are, and as insolent and aggressive as the White House has been and continues to be toward its former protec-torate under the Platt Amendment, reveal a mutual insecurity. Castro is afraid that any relaxation of tension will be used against him by the gringos. Bush is afraid that, deprived of an enemy in Europe, the United States will have nowhere to show off its Manichean machismo. Where else can he demonstrate, with quasi-religious piety, that the Good Empire is facing up to the Evil Empire but in Cuba and Central America? The rest of the world, however, sees in Bush's regime the profound insecu-rity of an empire in decline, and its belief in and respect for the United States continue to diminish.

Restoring Prestige

An initiative by George Bush that would bring the agenda of the United States in the Caribbean and Cuba up to date would restore his country's diplomatic prestige, which Mikhail Gorbachev and his brilliant policies have stolen.

Are we going to be witnesses to the paradox that it will be the Soviet Union that dispenses with its useless ideological baggage while the United States persists in dealing with the world only in ideological terms? If the Soviet Union can give up the Brezhnev Doctrine for the Sinatra Doctrine, the United States can give up the James Monroe Doctrine for the Marilyn Monroe Doctrine: Let's all go to bed wearing the perfume we like best.

"We have a broad vista—stretching from Guatemala to Panama—of new possibilities for democratization. . . .With our help and the help of other democracies, it can and will be done."

U.S. Involvement Promotes Democracy

James A. Baker III

The United States is the most democratic nation in the world, and therefore has a duty to lead the nations of Central America to democracy, James A. Baker III maintains in the following viewpoint. Baker, who is the secretary of state for the Bush administration, contends that U.S. actions in Central America brought about free, democratic elections in Panama, El Salvador, and Nicaragua. By promoting democracy and providing economic assistance, he argues, the U.S. helps to improve the lives of Central Americans.

As you read, consider the following questions:

1. What does Baker believe is the new mission of the United States?
2. How did American emphasis on democracy bring about free elections in Central America, according to the author?
3. How will American economic aid promote democracy in Central America, according to Baker?

James A. Baker III, "Democracy and American Diplomacy," a speech delivered to the World Affairs Council, Dallas, Texas, March 30, 1990.

73

When the President took office, he talked about a new breeze blowing for freedom. That breeze has become a gale-force wind. Around the world, the old dictatorships of left and right have been swept away, and the people have been heard. Their wants are basic: freedom to think, freedom to speak, freedom to worship, freedom to work. And all of their freedoms are bound up in the call for democracy—the freedom to choose one's own government.

We all have been surprised at how quickly the long-cherished democratic ideal has been translated into the reality of free and fair elections. Ever since World War II, democratic values have been shadowed by the threat of totalitarian aggression. Now, as the threat is reduced and the shadow recedes, those values are bright and shining and out in the open.

Already a great, new debate—actually a great, old debate—has broken out, an argument as old as our republic. Now that the adversaries of democracy are weaker, some say we should retire, mission accomplished, to tend to our problems at home. I am not among them. In the new world struggling to be born, like the old world now rapidly passing away, there is no substitute for American leadership.

Let me put it this way: Beyond containment lies democracy. The time of sweeping away the old dictators is passing fast; the time of building up the new democracies has arrived. That is why President Bush has defined our new mission to be the promotion and consolidation of democracy. It is a task that fulfills both American ideals and American interests. . . .

The Meaning of Democracy

Democracy means individual rights and individual responsibilities. With all the talk about changing systems, architectures, processes, and structures, it would be easy to overlook the individual. But the essence of democracy is to treat the individual's rights and responsibilities as two sides of the same coin of freedom. Just as the individual human being has ideal aspirations, he or she also has limits and imperfections. So the process of democracy, as President Vaclav Havel of Czechoslovakia pointed out, is an endless journey in pursuit of our ideals—a journey spurred on by the reality that life is not always as just as we might want it to be. . . .

Democracy does not stand alone. Geometry teaches us that the triangle is the most solid configuration. The political geometry of successful democracy should teach us that a free society must be upheld by economic progress and basic security. War and poverty are the great opponents of democratic rules, democratic tolerance, and individual rights.

Many of the recent democratic revolutions in Europe began

when people understood at last that economic progress depended on freedom in the workplace and freedom to own property—and that such freedoms in turn depended upon a government responsive to the people. Dogmas, attempting to eliminate the entrepreneurial spirit while commanding the production of wealth, produced neither bread nor freedom.

U.S. Should Encourage Democracy

To accomplish its objectives in Latin America, the U.S. must encourage democratic pluralism. The U.S. must open its markets to Latin America while insisting that these nations adopt free market and private sector oriented economic policies allowing private foreign investment and imports from the U.S. The U.S. must enforce the Monroe Doctrine.

Mark B. Liedl, *Issues '88: A Platform for America,* 1988.

We must, therefore, build up the economic and security aspects of the new democracies even as the political base is put into place. A people with hope for a better life, at peace with themselves and their neighbors, is a people for whom democracy will be not just a temporary experiment but a permanent course. A strategy of simply applauding elections and then hoping for the best ignores the painful lessons of the past. Only a strategy that buttresses democracy with economic reforms and greater international security can give us the strength for the tough transitions that will transform the revolutions of 1989 into the democracies of the 1990s.

Foreign Policy and Democratic Values

American foreign policy abroad must reflect democratic values. This may seem all too obvious. Yet, there are those who would have America, in the name of its ideals, isolate itself from a world too often hostile to democracy. And there are others who argue for a realpolitik that has a place only for economic or military or political interests and leaves our values at home.

We can recognize in this dualism a little bit of ourselves. How often do we strive for the ideal only to fall short? How frequently do we conclude after some self-serving action that maybe it was not entirely the right thing to do?

As individuals, we succeed when we use each side of our nature to help the other, when we do things in this world not for selfish reasons or because we are satisfied with the status quo but in order to change it, guided by our ideals.

In my view, we must adopt the same approach to our foreign policy. America's ideals are the conscience of our actions. Our power is the instrument to turn those ideals into reality. Our foreign policy, our understanding of other nations, is the blueprint for the job.

As we enter a new era of democracy, the old arguments of idealism vs. realism must be replaced by idealism plus realism. If we do not understand this, then we shall risk the loss of enduring public support for our policies. I think history illustrates amply that the American people will not support for long a policy that violates their sense of humane values, no matter how it is justified as being in the national interest. I am equally convinced that Americans will reject a policy based primarily on moral exhortation which ignores our power to act. As we applaud the new trends toward democracy, we feel good. But those trends are opportunities and challenges, not permanent facts. We have to do more than feel good; we must do good.

Democracy in Diplomacy

Democracy is a "force multiplier": a potent instrument for rallying international action. A policy that draws upon our domestic values and enjoys the support of the American people automatically makes our influence more effective. But a policy centered on democracy is also a "force multiplier" in that we can use it to engage our friends and allies behind a mutual purpose. It can give hope to those peoples still suffering under dictatorship.

It would seem to be common sense for the United States to lead alliances of free market democracies in Asia, Europe, and the Americas in support of democracy and economic liberty. We can use our common values to pool our strength, advancing everyone's interests in a free and peaceful world. . . . In Central America, we have urged our friends and allies to calibrate their actions along a democratic standard, not just their immediate geopolitical interests narrowly understood. We have done so because we believe that democracy and the national interests of the democracies reinforce each other. . . .

These observations about democracy and our foreign policy are not speculative. They are rather guide-posts for practice, and they have played a major part both in our thinking and in some of our recent foreign policy achievements.

I would cite as [an] example events in Central America. When the President took office, U.S. policy toward that important region—our own neighborhood—was in trouble. It was the most divisive issue we faced. Congress and the executive branch had failed to reach any lasting agreement on how to approach the problem, or for that matter, even how to define it. The American people were divided, too—an almost certain recipe for failure.

The only way out of this tangle was to return to American principles. The President decided to define democracy as the regional objective and elections as the means to achieve that result. In each case, this turned the focus where it belonged. In Nicaragua, the Sandinistas' conduct of their society—an outpost of oppression in a region of democracies—became the central issue, not the Nicaraguan Resistance. In Panama, Gen. [Manuel] Noriega's brutal rejection of a free election verdict stripped him of his claim to legitimate rule and began the difficult trek toward Panamanian democracy. Another free election in El Salvador, conducted despite violence, gave President [Alfredo] Cristiani the popular mandate to pursue a negotiated settlement to the war and a chance to demonstrate a serious approach to human rights.

A New Partnership

My Administration will work to build a new partnership for the Americas—a partnership built on mutual respect and mutual responsibilities. And we seek a partnership rooted in a common commitment to democratic rule.

The battle for democracy is far from over. The institutions of free government are still fragile and in need of support. Our battlefield is the broad middle ground of democracy and popular government—our fight against the enemies of freedom on the extreme right and on the extreme left.

George Bush, Speech to the Council of the Americas, May 2, 1989.

An emphasis on democracy enabled us to cut the Gordian knot that prevented bipartisanship. On March 24, 1989, a bipartisan accord was signed at the White House, enabling Republicans and Democrats to join around a common purpose. Outside of Washington, the American people could be rallied in support. The United States was heard at last to be speaking with one voice. Directly as a result, the Congress voted humanitarian aid for the Resistance through February 28, 1990.

We then took the bipartisan emphasis on democracy and approached the Central American countries. The Esquipulas agreement expressed their wish for peace, democracy, and the end of support for bloody revolutions in other countries. What was lacking was an effective mechanism to turn the wish into reality. Then, at Tesoro Beach, the Central American presidents agreed on a joint plan to be developed within 90 days to demobilize the Resistance, and it was widely interpreted as a defeat for the United States at the time. But the other side of the joint plan was a requirement that the Sandinista government hold internationally supervised elections a year earlier than scheduled—February 25, 1990.

This provision helped us to convince our European allies that they should condition their economic aid to Nicaragua on the holding of free and fair elections. They did. In April 1989, a donors' conference for Nicaragua was sponsored by Sweden. President Daniel Ortega later admitted that he received only a small fraction of what he had hoped to get before elections.

Agreement from Moscow

Finally, we were able to use all of these developments together to take a more effective approach to the Soviet Union. We had the "force multiplier" of democracy to present the Soviets with a growing international consensus on elections. We could and did argue that if Moscow's aid were seen to be sabotaging legitimate governments—whether a freely elected democracy in El Salvador or the elections process in Nicaragua—there would be strong repercussions on overall U.S.-Soviet relations. And we were able to contrast the Soviet feeding of conflict with their evident desire for a more cooperative relationship in dealing with regional problems. As a result, even before the elections, Moscow publicly agreed to respect both the electoral process and its outcome.

We were prepared to make sure that the elections were as clean—as free and fair—as possible. Congress supported the President's request for money to support election activities, which enabled us to flood Nicaragua with international observers. The National Endowment for Democracy also contributed funds shared by the Nicaraguan parties. We considered that essential because it enabled the democratic opposition, UNO [Unified Nicaraguan Opposition], to compete on at least the minimal level against a Sandinista party utilizing the resources of the entire state. Finally, we protested vigorously and pointed out clearly every instance of unfair and arbitrary procedure. Democracy, we felt, was a fast-growing plant if only the sunshine of publicity could expose those who would kill it at the root. The pressure was on the Sandinistas to play it straight.

I recite all of these facts because I believe they set a context, a climate that was most conducive to democracy in Nicaragua through the voting itself. The individual Nicaraguan—the individual upon whom democratic hopes depended—knew that he or she was not alone. Voting in a free and fair election was not a desperate, lonely act but a step toward a better future.

Now that a democratic government has been elected in Nicaragua, we know that Nicaragua's recovery from years of civil war and the blight of Marxist economics will be costly and painful. There and in Panama, we must help to turn the new hopes into the reality of progress. That is why the President has proposed a new $800 million fund for democracy—our part of a multilateral effort to put our neighbors back on their feet. This is not charity. It is an investment in the democratic values we share with our neighbors. For we have a broad vista—stretching from Guatemala to Panama—of new possibilities for democratization, demilitarization, and development which offers a bright future for all the peoples of the region. With our help and the help of other democracies, it can and will be done. . . .

A Fear of Democracy

When I studied classics in college, I found to my surprise that most of the ancient philosophers feared democracy. Those who study the 18th century arguments over our Constitution also will encounter this fear. It was a lingering suspicion that the individual would be corrupted, that the ordinary man or woman simply was not up to the task of self-government.

Our Founding Fathers overcame that fear and left to us a legacy of confidence in the citizen that constitutes our greatest political and moral strength. Our foreign policy has been at its best when it drew from that strength and made of our country a great force for good in the world. Now, after hard years of defending democratic values, our original confidence has been renewed.

Ordinary people are truly the heroes of our time. Ordinary people broke through the [Berlin] Wall. Ordinary people turned out the dictators. Ordinary people voted for democracy in Central America.

As once our Founding Fathers drew upon confidence in the citizens to build a new democratic society, so now our foreign policy must build upon that same confidence to build a newly democratic international society. That is our opportunity and our challenge. With the help of every American, I am sure we will meet it.

"In the Americas, the U.S. and George Bush are associated with indiscriminate bombings of civilians; the organization, training and financing of death squads; and programs of mass murder."

U.S. Involvement Does Not Promote Democracy

Noam Chomsky

Noam Chomsky is a well-known author and political activist who protests U.S. involvement in Central America. A linguistics professor at the Massachusetts Institute of Technology in Cambridge, Chomsky has written many articles and books, including *Necessary Illusions: Thought Control in Democratic Societies.* In the following viewpoint, Chomsky maintains that the U.S. uses its influence to protect U.S. business interests in Central America and to keep in power dictatorships that promote U.S. policies. The U.S. does not foster democracy in Central America, he suggests, but instead promotes the continuation of poverty and inequality.

As you read, consider the following questions:

1. Why does the author believe that Eastern Europeans are luckier than Central Americans?
2. What does Chomsky see as the two major sources of power in Central America?
3. What are the major goals of the U.S. in Nicaragua, according to the author?

Noam Chomsky, "U.S. Still at War Against the World." This article was originally published in *Resist,* #226 (May 1990), One Summer St., Somerville, MA 02143. Reprinted with permission.

Twenty years ago, if you wanted to have a serious discussion about the prospects for Eastern Europe, you would have focused attention on the reigning superpower, the Soviet Union. Today, for precisely the same reasons, if you want to have a serious discussion about what lies ahead for Central America, you will focus on the reigning superpower, the United States.

Space for Truth and Hope

A Guatemalan journalist, and former Harvard Neiman Fellow, Julio Godoy, returned to Guatemala for a brief visit. He had fled after his newspaper, *La Epoca*, had been blown up by terrorists from the state security forces. That event aroused no interest here whatsoever. It was not reported, though it was well-known. At the time, the media here were very much exercised over freedom of the press; the U.S.-funded journal in Nicaragua, *La Prensa*, had been forced to miss a couple of issues due to a shortage of newsprint, and that led to an absolute torrent of outrage and abuse in *The Washington Post*, and elsewhere, about Sandinista totalitarianism, so naturally they could not be expected to notice that U.S.-funded security forces had silenced the one, tiny independent voice that had tried a few weeks earlier to open up in Guatemala.

That is just an illustration of the total, complete contempt for freedom of the press in the U.S. media, unless a display of libertarian passion can serve some function, like job enhancement, or simply serving the state. Now Godoy, when he returned to the U.S., contrasted the situation in Central America with the situation in Eastern Europe (and that's a natural comparison—it takes real intellectual discipline for the educated classes to miss the point), and he makes some pertinent observations.

One observation he makes is that East Europeans are "luckier than Central Americans," because "while the Moscow-imposed government in Prague would degrade and humiliate reformers, the Washington-made government in Guatemala would kill them. It still does, in a virtual genocide that has taken more than 150,000 victims, [in what Amnesty International calls] 'a government program of political murder.' "That, he says, "is the main explanation for the fearless character of the students' recent uprisings in Prague: the Czechoslovak army doesn't shoot to kill. . . . In Guatemala, not to mention El Salvador, random terror is used to keep unions and peasant and student associations from seeking their own way." The press conforms or disappears, as in the case of *La Epoca*.

There is an important difference, Godoy says, "in the nature of the armies and of their foreign tutors." Eastern European armies are "apolitical and obedient to their national government." In the U.S. domains, the "army is the power," and their

81

foreign tutors have been training them to use it for many years. One is tempted to believe, he says, "that some people in the White House worship Aztec gods—with the offering of Central American blood." And he quotes a Western European diplomat: "As long as the Americans don't change their attitude toward the region, there's no space here for the truth or for hope." That's the crucial point. If we remember that, we know exactly what we should understand and what we should do.

PUNCH

"There's a scare that peace may break out in Central America."

Another journalist, John Saxe-Fernandez, writing in the mainstream journal *Excelsior* in Mexico, describes the deterioration of U.S. relations with Latin America during the 1980s. He writes that what is most striking "is the contrast between Soviet foreign policy in socialist Europe, and U.S. policy in the Western hemisphere. . . . In Europe, the USSR and Mikhail Gorbachev are associated with the struggle for freedom of travel, political rights, and respect for public opinion. In the Americas, the U.S. and George Bush are associated with indiscriminate bombings of civilians; the organization, training and financing of death squads; and programs of mass murder such as that carried out against six Jesuit intellectuals. . . . It is unfortunate that the U.S. Congress has approved the equivalent of 4.5 million dollars a day to prop up a government like Alfredo Cristiani's. But Washington's policy towards El Salvador is consistent with its practice, under various rationalizations and pretexts, in the rest of the region."

In fact, it's been U.S. policy, open and public policy dating back to the 1950s, to take control of the security forces in Latin American countries and use them to enforce the preferred U.S. model for those regions. And it's no secret what that model is. The model is agro-export under control of U.S. corporations, cheap labor for assembly plants, and so on, in a climate conducive to private investment, and in the case of foreign investment, a climate that will ensure adequate repatriation on returns of invested capital. No nationalist regimes (the term used to describe the main threat to American foreign-policy, in top-level documents) that are responsive to pressures from the population for improvement in low living standards, or for production to meet domestic needs, can be tolerated, as is made explicit, over and over again, in these terms.

As for the Latin American military, the documentary record is completely frank about its role. U.S. AID [Agency for International Development], which trained the security and police forces in several Latin American countries, described these forces as "one of the major means by which the government assures itself of acceptance by the majority," and is able to abort dissident activities before "major surgery" is needed. But, when major surgery *is* needed, you turn to the military. Since the early 1950s, U.S. policy documents describe efforts to take control of the Latin American military, which has been termed "the least anti-American of any political group" in Latin America. It must be imbued with "the understanding of, and orientation toward, U.S. objectives." Once they've gotten that into their heads, they can play their assigned role in overthrowing civilian governments, if "in the judgment of the military," these governments are not pursuing "the welfare of the nation."

We'll Call It Democracy

One obvious consequence of all of this is a complete rejection of the right to exist of any popular organizations that might threaten the two legitimate sources of power in Latin America— the United States and the local oligarchies and business communities that are subordinate to U.S. power. As long as *they're* in charge, the playing field is level, and if they're willing to run elections now and then, we'll call it democracy. If anyone else has a chance to participate, like the great mass of the population, we've got to call out the death squads or one of the other techniques to level the playing field.

Democracy as an Alibi

The U.S. government invokes democracy with respect to Panama, Nicaragua or Cuba in the way the East European governments invoked socialism—as an alibi. Latin America has been invaded by the United States more than a hundred times in this century. Always in the name of democracy and always to impose military dictatorships or puppet governments which safeguarded the money that was in danger. The imperial power system does not want democracies; it wants humbled countries.

Eduardo Galeano, *The Guardian,* May 2, 1990.

This basic conception of "democracy" underlies U.S. policy worldwide (and that includes here at home, a long and interesting topic in itself). In Latin America, you don't need any subtle means to achieve these ends. You can use torture and mutilation and mass slaughter when you need to; or, if the local military can't do the job, direct invasion, as in the Dominican Republic in 1965. These are the basic factors that determine what happens in Central America, and there isn't the slightest reason to think that many of them are changing. . . .

In Central America, the number of people murdered outright, by U.S.-backed security forces, is about 200,000 in the last decade. It's interesting to watch the reaction to all this in the U.S. press, where it's called an inspiration for the triumph of democracy and freedom throughout the world. It's led to absolute euphoria among educated circles here. So, for example, in the *Boston Globe,* you can read Tom Wolfe tell us that the 1980s were "one of the great golden moments that humanity has ever experienced." We're "dizzy with success," as Stalin used to say.

In fact, there are two conflicting currents of American opinion. They are vastly different in power, but they are both there. One of them is elite circles, which are dizzy with success, and they want to proceed as they have always done. To the extent they succeed, the prospects for Central America are quite obvious—first, misery and death; second, rule by U.S. proxies, that is, the business classes, the oligarchy and the military; and third, destruction of what remains of the natural environment. That's one current. The other current is that of the dissident sectors, the solidarity movements. Whatever prospects there are for a decent future lie in their hands, in whatever changes they can bring about in the way the U.S. deals with its subject populations. It looks like a pretty unequal struggle, but it is, in fact, the only hope—and not only for Central America.

The conventional framework that has been constructed to prevent us from seeing any of these things is this: There's been a Cold War since World War II, and now, thankfully, it has ended with a complete U.S. victory—the United States being the inspiration for peace and democracy. According to the conventional understanding, the Cold War has been a conflict between two superpowers, and there are several versions to this. The orthodox, and dominant, version says that the cause of the Cold War is Soviet aggressiveness, and therefore, the major themes of the postwar world are containment and deterrence. We've tried to contain and deter the Soviet Union and protect the world from its aggressiveness.

A Simplistic Dichotomy

The most vulgar form of this version is that there are two forces in the world —on the one side "a nightmare," and on the other, "the defender of freedom." That's the version preferred by the John Birch society, or fundamentalist preachers, or American liberal intellectuals, who reacted with absolute joy and rapture when these sentiments were expressed, in the very words I quoted, by Czech President Vaclav Havel before Congress, which also just collapsed in amazement and wonder at these novel and astonishing sentiments.

There's a critique of this that says that the Soviet threat was exaggerated, misunderstood, an error, and that has tainted our noble intentions. The Cold War was really an "imaginary war"— that's the position of parts of the European Left. There's also a sharper critique that says that the superpower confrontation was the result of the interaction of the two superpowers, with the U.S. playing a role. The contrast is not simply that of the "nightmare" versus the "defender of freedom," but it's a little more mixed, and, contrary to the cherished beliefs of Pat Robertson, the American Legion and educated American left liberal opinion, the United States is not just the "defender of freedom" in say, El Salvador, Guatemala and a couple of other places one can think of. Well, without giving a history of the Cold War, I think that all of these perspectives are misleadingly formulated, and one cannot understand the past and evaluate what is coming unless some correction is introduced.

For years I've been trying to make what seems to me to be a very simple point—if you want to understand what the Cold War has been, you should look at the events of the Cold War. . . .

If you look at the Cold War in terms of the events that constituted it, then the Cold War hasn't ended at all. One side of it has called the game off, at least temporarily, but the other side is proceeding as before—with some of the constraints removed, though there are others that act in the opposite direction, such as the relative decline of U.S. power. That means that the U.S. half of the Cold War, the war against the Third World, is going to continue. There's no reason to expect it to be called off.

Enemies in the Third World

Now there are going to be some problems with this. One problem is that the technique of controlling the domestic population is going to have to shift. We've already seen that in Panama—a new technique of population control was required for post-Cold War intervention. Domestically, the drug war is one of the major devices of population control. It has little to do with drugs, but a lot to do with frightening people, increasing repression in the domestic Third World, and terrorizing the rest of the population so they will support intervention, and the police, and so on. This is not going to work very long. The Third World is going to have to be recognized as the actual enemy, as it always has been, as the pretexts for fighting the war against it gradually erode. . . .

Supporting Repression

The central goal of U.S. policy in [Central America] never was the holding of elections, much less democracy. In Honduras, Guatemala and El Salvador, the United States put its considerable weight behind elections that would ensure continuance of regimes dominated by rich elites and ruled by military repression. The aim was to persuade reluctant moderates in Congress to fund counterinsurgency strategies.

Kenneth E. Sharpe, *Los Angeles Times*, February 21, 1990.

There's another method that is very much favored by the Democratic doves, and that is diplomatic fakery. The Nicaraguan elections are a case in point. Let me go this time to the Costa Rican journal *Mesoamerica* for a reaction, from Tony Avirgan: "The Sandinistas fell for a scam perpetrated by Costa Rican president Oscar Arias and the other Central American Presidents—it cost them the 25 February 1990 elections." Referring to the peace plan of August, 1987, he says, "for Nicaragua, it was a good deal—move national elections forward by a few months, and allow international observation in exchange for having the Contras demobilized and the war brought to an end. . . . The Nicaraguan government did what it was required to do under the peace plan," but no one else did a thing. That was the scam.

In fact, Arias, the White House, Congress and the Central

86

American Presidents never had the slightest intention of implementing any aspect of the plan. The U.S. immediately virtually tripled CIA [Central Intelligence Agency] supply flights to the Contras. Pressure was placed on the Central American Presidents to limit the plan solely to Nicaragua so that they didn't have to observe any of its conditions, which of course, the U.S. never would. Within a couple of months the peace plan was totally dead. So, going on with Avirgan's description, "the deal had been broken. . . . Violeta Chamorro promised to end the war. Her relationship with the contras and the U.S. made that feasible. . . . War weary Nicaraguans voted for peace.". . .

The fact of the matter, of course, is that it was obvious in advance that the U.S. was never going to tolerate a free and fair election. It was very clear that the embargo and the Contra War were going to continue unless people voted for the enforcer. This was made official when the White House announced that the embargo would stay on, meaning death, unless you vote for our candidate. You have to be some kind of Nazi or unreconstructed Stalinist to regard anything like that as a free and fair election. If these things were ever done by our enemies. . . I leave it to your imagination. . . .

What Lies Ahead

As far as Nicaragua is concerned, the U.S. has a couple of major goals. The first goal is to gain control of the army and police—that's always been the standard doctrine, otherwise the population can get out of hand. The second goal is to destroy any independent press and any popular organizations. Let me stress that when liberals call for restoring the "Central American mode" and imposing "regional standards," that's what they are talking about; these are the regional standards under U.S. rule. A third, and more general, policy is to ensure the rule of the legitimate forces, the U.S. and local business and oligarchy.

The rest of Central America is already in the "Central American mode," so we don't have to restore it. The idea is to just to keep the stranglehold there, put them on the back-burner for a while, while we turn to Eastern Europe and try to impel it toward the Latin American model. Central America is to be kept within the U.S. system, available for cheap labor, resource extraction, and pollution export, until such time as it becomes totally unviable and unlivable. At that point we can "defend freedom" somewhere else.

"As demonstrated by everyone from Cuban and Central American exiles to Chinese students in Beijing. . .people all over the world look to America for leadership in the struggle for democracy."

U.S. Involvement Is Welcome

Emilio Bernal Labrada

In the following viewpoint, Emilio Bernal Labrada, a Cuban refugee, maintains that Central Americans welcome U.S. involvement in Central America. The people of the region want democracy, and look to America for help in creating democratic governments, he argues. Labrada believes that, while some Central American leaders may outwardly protest American involvement, they secretly wish the U.S. would use its influence to bring democracy to the region. Labrada is an author and a frequent contributor to the *Washington Inquirer,* a weekly newspaper published by the Council for the Defense of Freedom, an organization that works to fight the spread of communism.

As you read, consider the following questions:

1. Why do Americans blame themselves for the world's problems, according to Labrada?
2. Why does the author believe U.S. intervention is better than non-intervention?
3. What events does Labrada cite as examples of U.S. unreliability?

Emilio Bernal Labrada, "The Myth of the Ugly American," *Washington Inquirer,* October 27, 1989. Reprinted with permission.

Slowly, but surely, the myth of the "Ugly American" is becoming just that—a myth. At least as it is perceived by the rest of the world, particularly U.S. neighbors to the south. As one of those "neighbors" who has lived in the U.S. and has traveled to nearly every country in this hemisphere over the last 30 years, I believe it's about time someone spoke out about how Latin Americans really feel—as opposed to how our self-styled spokesmen *say* we feel.

Americans have convinced themselves—thanks to what must be called their enemy within: the liberal press—that they are to blame for most of the world's ills, as unprincipled exploiters and worshipers of the almighty dollar. The notion is strongly supported by the entertainment industry's propaganda which trashes America's efforts to prevent the Cuba-Nicaragua axis from chewing up Central America. No wonder so many Americans think of themselves as the big bullies on the block! In general, the press points an accusing finger at U.S. administrations for preferring rightist regimes to leftist revolutions.

The Lesser Evil

The irony is that most Latin Americans support this position. Except for demagogues and diehard revolutionaries, this U.S. tilt toward right-of-center is considered by far the lesser evil. Latin Americans are well aware that a leftist revolution does much more terrible and permanent damage to a country than any rightist regime. Furthermore, in recent years, Latin America's military have shown a constant tendency to step away from power and hand it back to civilians.

Central Americans in particular are privately disappointed over the scuttling of the Nicaraguan freedom fighters, who had a chance to free their country and to decisively defeat communist tyranny on the mainland of the hemisphere. . . .

Although Latin America's leaders prefer to posture, talk about negotiations with Marxist guerrillas and oppose U.S. "interference," the truth is that they are all the while secretly hoping for it. Down deep, their professed devotion to democracy and freedom is at odds with the principle of non-intervention. When those ideals are threatened by totalitarianism in today's interdependent world community, they can sometimes be protected or restored only through some sort of intervention—whether unilateral or multilateral.

Make no mistake about it. As it did in the Dominican Republic in the '60s—this writer was there with the OAS [Organization of American States] at the time—and in Grenada in the '80s, U.S. intervention can solve some very serious immediate and sequential problems: like the cost of defending the whole Caribbean—plus Central America—from communist takeovers, for example. Non-intervention, on the other hand, merely guarantees the survival of ruthless despots and gives totalitarianism a free hand. Furthermore, while intervention may risk lives, doing nothing certainly means casualties—in the skies over Scotland and in kidnapings in the Middle East, no less than in the drug wars in our cities.

No government, however, will publicly admit the desirability of U.S. intervention, since doing so would be politically risky and invite, atop a barrage of rhetoric, retaliatory violence from the left. Could Guatemala, for example, afford to antagonize a heavily armed, expansionist Nicaragua—particularly when viewing the U.S. record of backing off from its friends?

The U.S., unfortunately, has built up a reputation as an unreliable friend in need, starting with the 1961 Bay of Pigs disaster in Cuba, proceeding with Viet Nam in the '70s and continuing in the '80s with the Contra sellout. The liberation of Grenada was a minor, isolated exception. . . .

And lest someone shout *"glasnost!"* and *"perestroika!"*, such notions have clearly not percolated to this Hemisphere. Castro, for one, rejected them right in Gorbachev's face. Recent events confirm this attitude with a vengeance: Castro has not only come out in support of the bloodbath in Beijing, but has done some bloodletting of his own to wipe out any domestic threat to his power—while appearing to "clean house."

Distasteful as they are, rightist-military dictatorships have at least proven capable of evolving into democracies in recent times. Since 1959, in Venezuela, through 1984 in Argentina—not to mention much-maligned Chile, where the military regime has accepted electoral defeat—at least ten Latin American countries have discarded military rule and restored democracy.

But what has happened in communist dictatorships like Cuba? The record speaks for itself. It is no coincidence that El Salvador's guerrilla war has greatly intensified since the rug was pulled out from under the Resistance.

Others Look to America

Americans need hardly worry about being unpopular for their actions, but for their inaction. As for their principles, as demonstrated by everyone from Cuban and Central American exiles to Chinese students in Beijing holding up the Statue of Liberty, people all over the world look to America for leadership in the struggle for democracy.

To summarize, the real problem is the lack of U.S. intervention. It merely ensures a free hand for continued Soviet/Cuban intervention. It's the absurd attitude of the man whose neighbor's house is on fire, but decides to let it burn down lest he be accused of meddling. The trouble is that one day the arsonist may burn down the rest of the block.

As long as Americans abstain from giving prompt, effective assistance to put out the fires lit by the enemies of democracy in neighboring countries, Castro will continue to hold sway. Meanwhile, the freedom-loving peoples of the Hemisphere are finding refuge—where else?—in America itself, the one remaining place that seems safe . . . for the time being.

"The Central American conflict has deepened because of US attempts to suppress the struggle for revolutionary anti-imperialist and democratic transformations."

U.S. Involvement Is Not Welcome

Roberto Regalado Alvarez

The U.S. has used assassination and torture to spread imperialism and to protect America's interests in Central America, Roberto Regalado Alvarez states in the following viewpoint. He contends that Central Americans want socialist revolution, not the capitalism forced upon them by the U.S. military. Regalado Alvarez believes that although the U.S. attempts to isolate Cuba, Central Americans look to Cuba as evidence that U.S. imperialism can be successfully fought. Regalado Alvarez is a sector head for the Communist Party of Cuba.

As you read, consider the following questions:

1. What does the author believe was the real reason for America's campaign against Central American drug trafficking?
2. Why does Regalado Alvarez think bourgeois democracies are preferable to repressive tyrannies?
3. Why is socialist revolution in Central America difficult, according to the author?

Roberto Regalado Alvarez, "Latin America: Changes in the Offing," *World Marxist Review*, July 1989. Reprinted with permission.

The situation in Latin America and the Caribbean is marked by a sharpening of the economic crisis, the insupportable burden of the external debt, and dangerous social and political instability. There is a widening gap between the transnational bourgeoisie, with its vast profits, on the one hand, and the popular masses and middle strata, which have to pay the price for the consequences of the fashionable neoliberal policy, on the other.

During Ronald Reagan's presidency, the United States stepped up its interference in the region in an effort to strengthen its imperialist diktat, taking a tough stand on economic issues, notably the external debt, from which it strove to extract political dividends and to prevent the formation of a united front of debtor countries by negotiating separately with each of them.

Reagan made use of a hypocritical campaign against drugs trafficking as a means of political pressure, seeking to discredit the Latin American revolutionary movement and to destabilise Panama in order to create the conditions for revising some of the terms of the treaties under which the Canal is to be returned to Panama.

Adapting Imperialism

The Bush Administration began its term by trying to adapt the old imperialist policy to the realities of a changing world, but in formulating its policy with respect to Latin America it is bound to be confronted with the contradiction between the narrowly pragmatic and inflexible strategy in the Western Hemisphere and its direct effects: the deepening crisis and the growing instability in the region, which pose a threat even to undivided US domination.

The Central American conflict has deepened because of US attempts to suppress the struggle for revolutionary anti-imperialist and democratic transformations, and to prevent the consolidation of the Sandinista Revolution, the expansion of the military and political activity of the Farabundo Marti National Liberation Front in El Salvador, and of the Guatemalan National Revolutionary Unity. The Reagan Administration's policy in Central America was based on the "doctrine of low-intensity conflicts", including the imposition of a war of attrition on Nicaragua, and the establishment of counterinsurgency states in El Salvador and Guatemala. However, these US efforts were frustrated by mass action and the resolve of the revolutionaries in these countries, as evidenced by the rout of the Somoza bands in Nicaragua, and the crisis of the regimes in El Salvador and Guatemala. . . .

The countries of Latin America and the Caribbean are now faced with a crisis of the "governability of the democracies", which is reflected in the rapid decline of the prestige of their authorities within months, or even weeks, of their takeover. Since these are, in many cases, right-wing conservative, liberal or Christian democratic parties, they are the ones primarily affected by this process. . . .

Matt Wuerker. Reprinted with permission.

US intervention in the internal affairs of Latin American countries is another factor in the crisis of the "governability of the democracies". *US ruling circles regard as democratic only those political systems which guarantee the preservation of the capitalist system and subordination to US geopolitical interests.* US imperialism holds any methods to be valid when it comes to maintaining its definition of democracy, preferably a liberal bourgeois democracy, although it relies on military dictatorships in times of crisis. . . .

Bourgeois democracies are, of course, preferable to repressive tyrannies, if only because they offer some opportunities for strengthening the progressive social forces, but US intervention and the constant threat of military coups hang like the sword of Damocles over the constitutional governments, especially those faced with the contradiction of following the dictates of an unfair international political and economic order, and heeding the demands of their peoples for urgent transformations.

The Cuban people's victory on January 1, 1959, the first so-cialist revolution on the American continent, gave a powerful impetus to the revolutionary forces by demonstrating that power could be won a mere 90 miles away from mighty US im-perialism.

Our revolution was a historical lesson for the ruling circles of the United States as well. Their policy was to isolate Cuba by launching a campaign of antisocialist vilification. At the same time they began to hone their counterinsurgency instruments: the Inter-American Defence Council was resuscitated, the Alliance for Progress set up, and military aid programmes ex-tended. US specialists began to work out methods of assassina-tion and torture, among whose victims were many popular lead-ers, revolutionary activists and innocent people.

The Latin American revolutionary movement has gained valu-able experience, which is already yielding fruit in Central America. The revolutions in Grenada and Nicaragua in 1979 dispelled the myth that Cuba was simply an exceptional phe-nomenon.

No other revolution has succeeded in our hemisphere in the past ten years. Apart from the potential of developments in El Salvador, the left-wing forces of the continent are not yet capa-ble of using the effects of the current crisis to take power, and to start deep transformations in countries where the objective conditions have matured.

This can be explained by the increased US intervention, and by US emphasis on counterrevolutionary, counterinsurgency wars on a global scale. In this way the *United States has raised the price that has to be paid for taking and retaining state power.* There is also the strengthening of some sections of the classes and social strata supporting capitalism, and the inadequate po-litical involvement of the impoverished masses.

Political Alliances

In view of the situation in the world and in their own coun-tries, the left-wing forces of our continent are combining vari-ous forms of struggle, giving preference in some cases to mili-tary-political elements, and in others, to the consolidation of po-litical alliances: the Farabundo Marti National Liberation Front frustrated the US counterinsurgency project, and plunged the state power structure in El Salvador into crisis; and the incorpo-ration of the Guatemalan Party of Labour in the Guatemalan National Revolutionary Unity opens up fresh prospects for the liberation movement. . . .

In Cuba, a process is now under way to rectify mistakes and negative trends. The construction of socialism requires a policy that accords with our situation as a poor, underdeveloped country virtually without natural resources, next door to US imperialism and thousands of kilometres from the socialist community. The Cubans are a dedicated, hard-working people brought up on the principles of internationalism. The present economic situation makes it possible to assure our people of a fitting living standard, even if it still falls short of European standards. . . .

Those who spread the simplistic notion of Cuba's international isolation ignore the development of its relations with countries on every continent, the recent deepening of our relations with governments and peoples in Latin America and the Caribbean, and the efforts for continental unity.

Our country's activity in the international arena testifies to its resolute support of the principle of settling conflicts through negotiation on the basis of respect for the interests of all the parties involved, above all of those who express the people's true aspirations. . . .

Is Revolution Possible?

There is the question of *whether a socialist revolution is possible now in Latin America*. Theoretically, it is, but US domination, the economic dependence and vulnerability of the countries of our continent and the improvement of the mechanisms of aggression and military pressure make it very difficult.

However, what is possible in Latin America today is the *victory of a popular, democratic and anti-imperialist revolution* for the assertion of independence and national sovereignty as the prerequisite for political, social and economic transformations paving the way to socialism.

VIEWPOINT

"The war and the horrors of an unrestrained soldiery are sustained by the wealth of the United States."

U.S. Involvement Promotes Violence in El Salvador

Richard N. Goodwin

U.S. military aid to the Salvadoran government only increases the violence and instability in Central America and does not serve U.S. interests, Richard N. Goodwin states in the following viewpoint. He contends the Salvadoran government is a brutal right-wing regime whose death squads have murdered thousands of innocent peasants. Contrary to the hopes of U.S. leaders, continued U.S. aid will not help El Salvador establish a peaceful democracy, but will probably result in an anti-American Marxist government taking power, Goodwin maintains. Goodwin, a writer and commentator, was an assistant to former presidents John F. Kennedy and Lyndon Johnson.

As you read, consider the following questions:

1. What role has Roberto D'Aubuisson played in the violence in El Salvador, according to Goodwin?
2. Why does the author feel that democracy in El Salvador is a charade?
3. What examples does Goodwin give to show that U.S. support of repressive governments often backfires?

Richard N. Goodwin, "Aid to El Salvador Is Aid to Murder," *Los Angeles Times*, June 6, 1989. Reprinted with permission.

El Salvador is no longer a country, it is a battlefield. It has been engaged in civil war for [an] entire decade. In that time more than 70,000 Salvadorans have been killed; at least one out of every 10 people has been forced from home and village; an even larger number have sought sanctuary outside its borders.

The protagonists in this conflict have been a loose band of guerrillas who claim allegiance to some vaguely defined form of Marxism, opposed by the authoritarian Salvadoran military allied with some wealthy businessmen and landowners. Yet the war is basically an American war. We send more than $1 million a day to support the power of the army and the rich. These resources alone sustain this long and bloody conflict.

Although successful in keeping the war going, we have failed to halt the worst abuses of power or to construct a government willing to bring some measure of freedom and social justice to that ravaged land.

Murders by the Right Wing

In the early '80s, right-wing forces, led by Roberto D'Aubuisson, organized a number of "death squads" to murder suspected guerrilla sympathizers and innocent peasants alike. Individuals, even entire families, were slaughtered in their homes or simply disappeared. When the courageous archbishop of El Salvador, dared to protest these outrages, D'Aubuisson had him shot at the altar of his church.

Although most Americans are barely aware of El Salvador's existence, and almost none could locate it on a map, these outrages were so blatant that an ordinarily indifferent public was stirred. An annoyed but compliant State Department felt compelled to assist a "moderate" Christian democrat, Jose Napoleon Duarte, into the presidency; our chosen leader of a client state.

Unfortunately Duarte proved to be ineffectual. Necessary reforms were not made and the Salvadoran military simply ignored his wishes and commands. In deference to American sensibilities—and at the command of American authorities—death squads were abandoned and the notorious D'Aubuisson disappeared, temporarily, into the shadows.

To replace him, the extreme right, organized as the ARENA Party, selected a nominal leader more congenial to American sensibilities—Alfredo Cristiani, a millionaire businessman, educated at Georgetown and well-versed in the phrases that would please the continuing stream of American visitors to his country.

U.S. Supports ARENA Party

I met with Cristiani while he pleasantly discoursed of the need for human rights, democracy, improved education and health care for the masses. Following this conversation, I talked with the American ambassador. There was no doubt that the United States had decided that the ARENA Party, under the freshly polished leadership of Cristiani, would take over the country at the close of Duarte's term.

YOUR TAX DOLLARS AT WORK IN EL SALVADOR.

Clay Bennett, *St. Petersburg Times,* reprinted with permission.

And so it was. Cristiani was sworn into office in what our government termed El Salvador's "first peaceful transition of power from one elected civilian to another." But the crowd attending the ceremony more realistically reserved its loudest cheers for the entrance of Roberto D'Aubuisson who, lacking any official position, is clearly the leader—the *don*—of El Salvador. His henchmen occupy key security positions and the leaders of the military are his loyal subordinates.

There is little doubt that "democracy" in El Salvador is a charade; the new government is simply the old gang with a new front man. The vice president, hand-picked by D'Aubuisson, has already indicated his intention to reconstitute the death squads. The country will be run by the radical right, its use of brutality unrestrained by law; the wealth of the nation—including the immense flow of U.S. aid—will be allocated to the military and the wealthy few. Meanwhile, massacres of the past, and the murder of the archbishop, will go unpunished; after all, the perpetrators now control the instruments of legal power.

All this is happening with the full approval of the United States, which is pledged to pour millions of dollars into continuing the interminable conflict.

For the people of El Salvador, it is the continuation of tragedy. The majority of peasants and urban workers care little for either the guerrillas or the government. They want only peace—the chance to live and work free from the omnipresent shadow of terror, to reap the rewards of their own labor, to avoid the confiscations of the wealthy and the guns of the soldiers. So little to ask. But they are unlikely to get it; not as long as the war and the horrors of an unrestrained soldiery are sustained by the wealth of the United States.

We should know by now that we can supply guns and money to Central America, but we cannot control their use. We can call for democracy and human rights, but we cannot make them happen. In Nicaragua we supported Anastasio Somoza and got the Sandinistas. In Panama, we supported Manuel A. Noriega, and we got . . . Noriega. Now we are about to support the criminal D'Aubuisson and his gang. The consequence will probably be the eventual rule of an anti-American Marxist government. But a lot of people will be slaughtered along the way, and a lot of our money will be stolen.

A Vote for Murder and Torture

To vote for continued aid to El Salvador is to vote for murder and torture, to vote for increasing the possessions of the wealthy at the expense of the impoverished peasants. And it is, in all probability, to vote for the installation of still another hostile government in a part of the continent where America, if not loved, was respected, its leadership acknowledged. . . .

From the peaceful sterility of Washington chambers, we will send forth the means to unleash the most savage impulses of men. There will be no blood on the Capitol steps. But the blood of thousands will stain the soil of El Salvador. No U.S. interest will have been served. But the innocence that protects our freedom, the principles that restrain our own buried lawlessness —will be further eroded.

"An attack on El Salvador's elected government by violent persons of any persuasion is no excuse for withdrawing American aid."

U.S. Involvement Does Not Promote Violence in El Salvador

Jeane Kirkpatrick

Jeane Kirkpatrick, the U.S. representative to the United Nations from 1981 to 1985, is a senior fellow at the American Enterprise Institute, a conservative think tank in Washington, D.C. In the following viewpoint, Kirkpatrick argues that the U.S. must continue to aid the government of El Salvador to prevent Marxist guerrillas from taking power. While both right and left-wing groups are responsible for atrocities, democratic elections have shown that the people still support the Salvadoran government, Kirkpatrick states. Only by continuing to support this government, she writes, can the U.S. ensure that the guerrillas will be defeated, that the violence will end, and that a peaceful, democratic El Salvador will develop.

As you read, consider the following questions:

1. What has the FMLN done to increase the repressive acts of the Salvadoran government, according to Kirkpatrick?
2. Why does the author feel the Soviet Union is responsible for increasing violence in El Salvador?
3. What three errors have the guerrillas made, according to the author?

Jeane Kirkpatrick, "Violence Is No Excuse for Withdrawing Aid," *Conservative Chronicle*, June 6, 1989. Copyright, 1989, Los Angeles Times Syndicate. Reprinted with permission.

Pity the people of El Salvador who must live, work and try to govern themselves under the violent assault of Marxist guerrillas ready to die. In more than a decade of guerra prolongada (prolonged war), FMLN [National Liberation Front] commanders have honed the techniques of modern guerrilla warfare. They know how to fight and how to talk, how to choose targets and win international attention. They know how to terrorize and demoralize internal opponents, how to confuse and mobilize international audiences.

"To beat an army, it is not necessary to annihilate all its men nor capture its arms, only to cause the collapse of its morale. In the previous campaign, we wanted to prove that we could win the war. Now we want to push the army to the point where its morale will collapse," guerrilla commander Joaquin Villalobos explained in 1982 after the FMLN's first Final Offensive (in January, 1981) had failed and tactics had been revised.

Guerrilla Tactics

The FMLN learned how to secure a steady supply of arms and assistance from outside El Salvador, how to conduct an urban guerrilla war, and how to use that war to undermine the reputation of and international support for successive governments.

They have made it work exactly as Brazilian Communist Carlos Marigella said it would work. Marigella explained in his "The Mini-Manual of the Urban Guerrilla" that even a small band of violent men can create a situation in which a government has no alternative but to intensify repression.

"The police roundups, house searches, arrests of innocent people and of suspects, closing off streets, make life in the city unbearable." In the wake of these repressive measures, Marigella continues, "The general sentiment is that the government is unjust, incapable of solving problems, and resorts purely and simply to the physical liquidation of its opponents." Eventually as repression grows, "The political situation in the country is transformed into a military situation in which the militarists appear more and more to be the ones responsible for errors and violence, while the problems in the lives of the people become truly catastrophic."

When the FMLN unleashed its campaign of violence in San Salvador, the government responded with repression. More than 1,000 Salvadorans were killed in the first days of fighting, among them six priests at the University of Central America shot at point-blank range.

These events set in motion the familiar scenario. The U.S. government demanded, and Salvador's President Alfredo Cristiani promised, prompt investigation of the murders and punishment of their perpetrators. FMLN supporters everywhere jumped to the conclusion that right-wing death squads were responsible, and that the government was somehow to blame—if not for murder, then at least for being unable to control the violence. With convoluted logic, they argued that the FMLN's violence proved it should be given power, and that the government's violence proved it should be deprived of power.

Cullum/Copley News Service. Reprinted with permission.

Congressmen who had always opposed aid to El Salvador (and to the Nicaraguan resistance, for that matter) saw new reason to terminate aid. Once again, their demand was echoed by American clerics who proclaimed their "preferential option for the poor" without noticing that those poor had, in election after election, proclaimed their preference for democracy.

Secretary of State James Baker noted that the new violence in El Salvador was fed by a flow of arms from Cuba and Nicaragua, and that the Soviet Union had special responsibility because its arms and money funded the violence. Soviet policy in Cuba and Central America, therefore, remains the principal obstacle to an across-the-board improvement in the U.S.-Soviet relationship, Baker observed.

It all sounded like a replay of debates earlier in the 1980s, but there is an important difference.

By participating in election after election—in spite of guerrilla threats and international skepticism—the people have proven they were ready and able to govern themselves. And by opposing election after election, the FMLN has proven that it is interested in power, and not at all in democratic process.

The existence of democracy eliminates any excuse for violence from private armies and death squads of any political persuasion.

Historical Errors

As El Salvador's former President and founding father Napoleon Duarte argued in 1984, violent guerrillas fell victim to three historical errors: They despaired of the possibilities of peaceful democratic change in their country; they believed that structural changes were possible only if institutions were smashed, not reformed; they failed to understand that under conditions of democracy, a war against the government is a war against the people.

It is tragic for El Salvador that violent persons outside the law destroy the resources and services desperately needed by these poor people.

"Force," Duarte argued, "can only be acceptable when there are no institutional processes available to open the political system, and then should be used only for the purpose of opening the system."

An attack on El Salvador's elected government by violent persons of any persuasion is no excuse for withdrawing American aid. It is rather a reason to be steadfast in support of these free institutions.

Ranking American Foreign Policy Concerns

This activity will give you an opportunity to discuss with classmates the values you and your classmates consider important in foreign policy.

Michael Keefe for the Denver Post, reprinted with permission.

This cartoon examines U.S. foreign policy concerns. The authors of this chapter all debate U.S. foreign policy priorities within the context of U.S. involvement in Central America. Many believe American political values are becoming twisted, and that the U.S. has no right to intervene in other countries' affairs. Others, however, believe our involvement is essential.

105

Part I

On your own, rank the foreign policy concerns listed below. Decide what you believe to be the most important priorities for American foreign policy in Central America, and be ready to defend your answers. Use number 1 to designate the most important concern, number 2 for the second most important concern, and so on.

_____ protecting national security
_____ protecting human rights
_____ promoting democracy in other countries
_____ defeating communism
_____ promoting self-reliance in other countries
_____ promoting friendship between countries
_____ promoting free elections
_____ ending dictatorships
_____ supporting governments friendly to the U.S.
_____ providing economic aid to poor countries
_____ providing military aid to stem revolutions

Part II

Step 1.   After each student has completed his or her individual ranking, the class should break into groups of four to six students. Students should compare their rankings with others in the group, giving reasons for their choices. Then the group should make a new list that reflects the concerns of the entire group.

Step 2.   In a discussion with the entire class, compare your answers. Then discuss the following questions:

1. Did your individual rankings change after comparing your answers with the answers of others in the group?
2. Why did your reasons differ from those of others in the group?
3. Consider and explain how your opinions might change if you were:
   a. the president of a Central American country.
   b. the president of the United States.
   c. the president of a country that opposes U.S. involvement in Central America.

Periodical Bibliography

The following articles have been selected to supplement the diverse views presented in this chapter.

Elliott Abrams	"Hear No Evil, See No Evil," *National Review,* February 19, 1990.
Elliott Abrams	"Throw the Rascals Out," *National Review,* April 1, 1990.
Alexander Cockburn	"The Invasion of Nicaragua," *The Nation,* May 7, 1990.
Rowland Evans and Robert Novak	"El Salvador Prepares to Fight On Alone," *Conservative Chronicle,* May 16, 1990. Available from the *Conservative Chronicle,* PO Box 11297, Des Moines, IA 50340-1297.
Douglas Farah	"Can Benign Neglect Solve El Salvador's Problems?" *U.S. News & World Report,* November 6, 1989.
Seymour M. Hersh	"The Iran-Contra Committees: Did They Protect Reagan?" *The New York Times Magazine,* April 29, 1990.
David Isenberg	"The Pitfalls of Covert Operations," *USA Today,* November 1989.
Saul Landau	"General Middleman," *Mother Jones,* February/March 1990.
Abraham Lowenthal	"Latin America and the Caribbean," *Vital Speeches of the Day,* May 1, 1990.
Michael Massing	"New Trouble in Panama," *The New York Review of Books,* May 17, 1990.
Bill Moyers	"Scrapping the Constitution," *The Progressive,* January 1990.
The New Republic	"Who Won Nicaragua?" March 19, 1990.
Douglas W. Payne	"How the Sandinistas Lost," *Freedom at Issue,* Supplementary issue, June 4, 1990. Available from Freedom House, 48 E. 21st St., New York, NY 10010.
The Progressive	"Scandal in El Salvador," January 1990.
Steven V. Roberts and Linda Robinson	"Can Enemies Become Mortal Friends?" *U.S. News & World Report,* May 21, 1990.
Frank Smyth	"Salvadoran Abyss," *The Nation,* January 8-15, 1990.
Phil Sudo	"A History of Intervention," *Scholastic Update,* February 9, 1990.
Caspar Weinberger	"How They Deceived the President," *National Review,* May 14, 1990.

3 CHAPTER

What Policies Would Strengthen Central American Economies?

Chapter Preface

Central America is a poor region. Seventy percent of Central Americans cannot provide for their most basic human needs: food and shelter. Many experts believe that stronger economies would ease the poverty and decrease some of the region's political turmoil.

Experts have proposed a variety of ways to strengthen Central America's economies. Many favor establishing a strong market system promoting private enterprise. As U.S. president George Bush has said, "The future of Latin America lies with free government and free markets." Bush and others believe that the free market system rewards the industrious members of society because those who work the hardest make the most money. These people then reinvest their money, which helps create new businesses and new jobs and spurs economic growth. In this way a free market economy would benefit all Central Americans, some experts maintain, for it would make the region as a whole wealthier and more prosperous. Once private enterprise is thriving, Bush and others contend, the rest of the economy will follow suit. As evidence, they point to Costa Rica, which is the most economically stable Central American nation and also a nation with a strong market system.

Other experts disagree that a market economy alone will help ease Central America's poverty. They contend that most Central Americans are too poor to buy land or start a private business because of the inequity of income and land distribution in the region. About 20 percent of the people collect more than 50 percent of the region's income, and in Honduras 2 percent of the farmers own nearly half of the farmland. Because only the wealthy could afford to invest in a market economy, these experts maintain, such an economy would only further enrich the wealthy, impoverish the poor, and bring greater instability to the region. As author and Stanford University professor Richard A. Fagen states, "Growth without equity. . .will only set the stage for yet another cycle of conflict." Fagen and others favor redistributing income and land to increase the region's economic equality. Only when economic equality exists can all Central Americans benefit from increased growth, employment, and income, these experts contend.

The economies of Central America need help. What form this help should take and what methods will strengthen the economies of the region are questions that spur much disagreement. The authors in the following chapter debate these issues.

"The crucial development challenge is . . . to combine economic growth with more equitable distribution of land, opportunities, and welfare."

Redistributing Wealth Would Strengthen Central American Economies

Richard R. Fagen

Central America's economic and political problems were caused by poverty and inequality, and will not improve until wealth is equally distributed among the Central American people, states Richard R. Fagen in the following viewpoint. He contends that economic growth and development will occur only when wealth is redistributed, taxes are increased and made more progressive, and Central American nations are relieved of their foreign debt. Fagen is the Gildred Professor of Latin American Studies at Stanford University in Palo Alto, California. The following viewpoint is an excerpt from his book *Forging Peace: The Challenge of Central America.*

As you read, consider the following questions:

1. What does Fagen believe is the result of growth without equity?
2. How can the wealthy help meet the basic needs of the majority of Central Americans during times of scarcity, according to the author?
3. What responsibilities does the U.S. bear in assisting the Central American economies, according to Fagen?

Richard R. Fagen, *Forging Peace: The Challenge of Central America.* New York: Basil Blackwell, 1987. Copyright © PACCA. Reprinted with permission of Basil Blackwell.

If a Contadora formula for demilitarization can be implemented in Central America, what are the prospects for development? Almost everyone agrees that the region's economies have significant potential for growth. Central America has good land, underutilized supplies of labor, and a history of very rapid economic growth from 1950 to 1978. But development means more than economic growth. Whereas growth can be measured by increases in gross national product, development can only be measured by improvements in the human condition. Development means enhancing the economic and social well-being of the majority of citizens.

The crucial development challenge is thus to combine economic growth with more equitable distribution of land, opportunities, and welfare. Equitable distribution was missing from the flawed history of the 1960s and 1970s, and those mistakes must not be repeated if the violence and the destruction of the 1980s are not also to be repeated. Growth without equity—without a fundamental redistribution of assets, benefits, and power—will only set the stage for yet another cycle of conflict. In short, peace is a necessary condition for development, but neither demilitarization nor growth, alone or together, will guarantee the kind of stability-enhancing development essential to the *maintenance* of peace.

Formidable Dilemmas

The architects of postwar development in Central America will face a formidable set of dilemmas. The 1980s have been a period of global economic crisis, as manifested in the virtual stagnation of growth in world trade and a plunge in the prices of primary commodities. These trends have been devastating for Central America, as well as for other developing countries that depend heavily on commodity exports. Debt has accumulated, capacity to repay has shrunk, unemployment and malnutrition have increased, and forced austerity is almost everywhere the rule.

Moreover, Central America has been tragically scarred by the human and material devastation of almost a decade of conflict. War-related physical damage in El Salvador totals at least $1 billion; in Nicaragua the toll approaches $500 million. Fairly conservative estimates of the cost of repatriating and resettling refugees and displaced persons in the five republics come to another $1.5 billion. The Central American republics cannot absorb these costs unaided. Yet unless these immediate needs are met, development will be even more problematic. A strong case can thus be made that the region will need from $2 to $3 billion in immediate foreign assistance simply to finance essential postwar reconstruction and resettlement.

Beyond reconstruction and resettlement loom fundamental issues of political and economic change. Agrarian reform, programs to meet basic needs, and mechanisms to encourage democratic participation are among the key problems that must be faced if new patterns of development are going to be sustained. Even this short list suggests how potentially divisive the development process inevitably will be—particularly in El Salvador and Guatemala, where military and oligarchical power have traditionally blocked just such reforms. Precisely these demands—for land reform, basic human needs, and democratic participation—forcefully articulated by peasants, workers, the Church, and sectors of the middle class, have been ruthlessly repressed over the past decades. In other words, *real development implies a new and different social pact in which the majority of Central Americans are given voice and eventually opportunities and benefits that they have not traditionally enjoyed.* This new social pact will not be forged with the stroke of a pen. A long, difficult, and conflict-ridden road lies ahead. . . .

A Few Reap All the Riches

In almost every country in Central America, the top 20 percent of the people collect more than half the nation's income. Meanwhile, the poorest 20 percent receive almost nothing. In some nations, such as El Salvador, as few as 14 families control virtually all the wealth. The pattern has persisted through times of economic prosperity and hardship alike.

Though these figures are based on 1980 data, experts say the gulf between rich and poor remains as wide as ever. If anything, they say, it has gotten worse.

Scholastic Update, February 9, 1990.

Land means both livelihood and power in Central America. Only Nicaragua has instituted an agrarian reform radical enough to break the link between the landed elite and political power—and only after a widely supported popular insurrection put a revolutionary government in power. But revisions in the structure of land ownership are not enough. Questions of credit, productivity, crop diversity, and markets must also be addressed. In El Salvador (admittedly the most difficult case), even if all the arable land were divided into the smallest possible viable individual plots, more than one-third of all peasant families would still have no land. New ways of organizing production to include the landless must be found.

Significant changes in the ownership and use of land raise other crucial questions. Since the economies of Central America

112

will continue to depend heavily on the production, consumption, and export of agricultural products, decisions about who works the land, producing which crops and with what technology, become central in determining everything from foreign exchange earnings to levels of employment and food consumption. It makes a great deal of difference, for example, if the production of staple foods for domestic consumption is given priority over the production of beef cattle for export. In the first case, employment and food self-sufficiency are enhanced; in the second, export earnings are given priority. Rational choices between these options require effective agrarian planning bolstered by realistic price, credit, and tax policies—a pattern rare in the past.

Effective agrarian reform would favor multicrop agriculture aimed at satisfying basic food needs over monocrop export. This pattern of land use offers a much better framework for reducing the excessive use of pesticides and the wanton destruction of the rain forest. For example, intensive use of pesticides on cotton fields in Central America in the 1960s and 1970s led to high levels of pesticide poisoning, as toxins such as DDT accumulated in humans, livestock, and the entire food chain. Also, the expansion of logging and cattle ranching, and the resulting displacement of peasants, are causing some 4,000 square kilometers of Central American rain forest to be destroyed annually. These trends must be reversed.

Industrial Reform

Traditionally, Central American industries have been highly protected by tariffs and oriented to limited sectors of the domestic market. A new development program for the area would expand the industrial sector by concentrating on some mix of agroindustrial production (the processing and refining of agricultural products), export-oriented light industry, and the manufacture of basic consumer goods for expanding domestic and regional markets.

Although in the medium-term industry cannot possibly become as important in overall development as agriculture, there is significant room for growth. Equitable development would put increased purchasing power in the hands of people who previously spent little on manufactured goods. A rational development program would attempt to ensure, through an appropriate mix of exchange rates, prices, and taxes, that the majority of this new purchasing power would be spent on goods produced in the region, thus further stimulating local production. Furthermore, since relatively low wages and the proximity to North American markets give a marginal advantage to exports from Central America, growth in manufactured exports is also

113

possible. Some foreign investment will undoubtedly be necessary for exports to expand, but the prospects for an increased inflow of private capital seem reasonably good, provided the region is at peace.

Fiscal Reform

With the partial exception of Costa Rica, Central American countries have very weak fiscal institutions. Tax rates are extremely low and frequently regressive, and evasion and corruption abound. Everywhere budgets run huge deficits, covered (if at all) by the printing of money (as in Nicaragua) or by massive infusions of politically motivated aid from the United States (as in Costa Rica and El Salvador).

Land Reform Acts as a Safety Valve

The land distribution pattern in Honduras is highly inequitable: the richest 2 percent of farmers own 44 percent of all farmland while the poorest 64 percent of farmers own 9 percent. There have been attempts over the years to mitigate this inequality through land reform. Although the land reform has not been well enforced, it has acted as a safety valve for pressure from Honduras' landless and landpoor.

Kevin Danaher, Phillip Berryman, and Medea Benjamin, *Help or Hindrance? United States Economic Aid in Central America,* September 1987.

At first glance, fiscal reform might appear to be one of the easier aspects of a new development program to implement. With military expenditures declining and the tax base expanding through renewed growth, national balance sheets should improve. Unfortunately, the situation is not so simple. Like agrarian reform, fiscal reform strikes directly at the heart of class-based privilege and traditional political power. To ask the wealthy to pay—whether directly or indirectly—a higher percentage of their income (and wealth) to help finance equity-enhancing development is to ask them to renounce both privilege and power. As the stubborn resistance to the tax reforms proposed by the Duarte government in El Salvador demonstrates, these privileges are rarely given up voluntarily. To date, fiscal reform has been accomplished with some success only in Costa Rica and Nicaragua, the two countries that have undergone significant structural reforms in other areas.

Basic Needs

A development program that neglects basic needs in food, health, housing, employment, and education is doomed to failure. What was possible in the 1950s and 1960s will not be possible in the 1990s. As has been seen since the early 1970s, growth alone cannot lead to social stability unless the living and working conditions of the majority of Central Americans can be improved substantially. Furthermore, few analysts seriously believe that the benefits of growth will "trickle down" to the bottom 60 or 70 percent of the population rapidly enough to meet even their minimal needs and expectations. Thus, for any development program to stand a chance of success in the 1990s, it must incorporate appropriate mechanisms for the delivery of basic goods and services to the majority of the population.

Austerity, however, adds another dimension to this issue. Hard times will be the common lot of most Central Americans in the years immediately ahead, even if programs of economic recovery are quite successful. In times of scarcity, the delivery of minimal levels of goods and services to the majority of the population requires that the well-off also bear a fair share of the burden, through equitable tax policies and other measures. The even-handed distribution of austerity is just as important as the distribution of benefits. . . .

Democratic Participation

Democracy means more than elections. Throughout this century, El Salvador, Guatemala, Honduras, and Nicaragua under the Somozas have held show elections characterized by limited participation and massive fraud. Even elections conducted more honestly, however, do not exhaust the full meaning and substance of democracy.

Democracy means opportunities for ordinary people to choose, organize, and participate, free of fears for their lives and livelihoods. Thus, elimination of repression, encouragement of grassroots participation, freedom of speech and organization, independence of the judiciary, and civilian control of the military are fundamental to democratic politics. In El Salvador, Guatemala, and Honduras, where the armed forces have long blocked needed reforms, there is little hope of constructing real democracy in the midst of war and continued military domination of politics—no matter how many elections are held.

Furthermore, democracy in its fullest sense is essential to the reform process. Without multiple opportunities for popular participation, changes will neither come fast enough nor go deep enough to ensure that economic benefits flow to the majority and not, as before, to a small minority. Precisely for this reason, democratic participation has always been seen as extremely dangerous—literally subversive—by entrenched elites. The existing structure of privilege cannot survive the full democratization of political life—any more than disproportionate wealth can survive agrarian and fiscal reform.

115

The five small republics of Central America can only prosper in the context of vigorous regional trade and cooperation. Despite its shortcomings, the CACM [Central American Common Market] was a stimulus to regional trade in the 1960s and 1970s. With peace, reduced tariffs, and expanding markets, the CACM could be reinvigorated.

The Roots of the Crisis

The roots of today's crisis can be traced, not to a lack of development, but to a particular model of agro-export development that impoverishes the many while rewarding the few. It is this tendency to concentrate wealth and power in a few hands—not exports *per se*—that is the central flaw of this economic model.

The agro-export model not only fails the test of equity, it also violates simple rules of supply and demand: by concentrating wealth in too few hands the agro-export model fails to create the consumer buying power needed to sustain a market economy, and by sowing seeds of conflict it scares away investment capital. . . .

There is no reason to believe that the revival of an export strategy—even the current emphasis on "nontraditional" exports such as flowers, spices, fruits and vegetables—will have any different impact from that of earlier decades. The export-oriented model has proven that it will not get money into the hands of the majority to create the demand needed to support a local market. *As long as the majority is impoverished, a market economy cannot flourish.*

Kevin Danaher, Phillip Berryman, and Medea Benjamin, *Help or Hindrance? United States Economic Aid in Central America,* September 1987.

More innovative and long-term regional projects are also required. Central America lacks an integrated system of railroads and a rational structure of ports and skipping facilities. El Salvador, for example, has no access to the Atlantic Coast, and other nations' facilities are duplicative and frequently too small to achieve economies of scale. Building a genuine economic community in the region would require the development of such shared infrastructure. In the beginning, the construction of regional transportation and shipping would be as important in its political symbolism as in its economic potential. . . .

Fundamental Changes Needed

This sketch of the changes that will have to be made—first to begin and then to sustain an equitable process of development—is daunting. That should not be surprising. The crisis that gave rise to the current conflict was and continues to be profound, and its reversal will require fundamental changes in the economies

116

and societies of the region. It does not follow, however, that the changes or the outcomes will be identical in each country. On the contrary, just as diversity characterizes Central America today, so it will continue to be a fundamental characteristic of the region in the future. A mix of development strategies is needed, desirable, and inevitable.

Similarly, the power to make the necessary changes does not reside in any one place—not in Washington or in Managua, not in San Salvador, Guatemala City, San Jose, or Tegucigalpa—although each government and each nation must do its part. If there is cause for optimism, in fact, it is precisely because millions of Central Americans in all five countries have increasingly become convinced that the past has not served them well. The United States thus has a double responsibility: first, to step aside and allow Central Americans to determine their own histories and their own futures; and second, as a respectful neighbor, to encourage and support needed changes where possible.

"A strong free-market economy is the only secure base upon which a prosperous and just society can be built."

Privatization Would Strengthen Central American Economies

Robert W. Kasten Jr.

Robert W. Kasten Jr., a Republican U.S. senator from Wisconsin, is on the Senate Appropriations Committee and the Budget Committee. In the following viewpoint, Kasten argues that Central American economies can be improved only with increased private ownership and decreased taxes. The U.S. can assist Central America by opening American markets to the region and by assisting in the development of a free-market system, he states. Private ownership, not wealth redistribution, is the key to prosperity, Kasten believes, and Central America will flourish only when it begins to guarantee the right of private ownership.

As you read, consider the following questions:

1. What does Kasten believe caused Central America's economic problems?
2. What seven reforms does the author believe would strengthen the Central American economies?
3. How would a Marshall Plan hurt Central America, according to Kasten?

Robert W. Kasten Jr., "Capitalism from the Ashes," *Policy Review*, Spring 1989. Reprinted with permission of The Heritage Foundation, 214 Massachusetts Ave. NE, Washington, DC 20002.

Political turmoil in Central America has been aggravated by the worst economic crisis in the region since the global depression of the 1930s. From 1980 to 1983, the region's per capita income dropped 12 percent; in El Salvador, it dropped 20 percent—following an already sharp decline over the preceding two years. Central America's external debt rose $10 billion, and $1.5 billion of foreign capital fled the area.

These indicators do not even begin to tell the story of the devastating human cost of the crisis. According to the Economic Commission for Latin America, almost 70 percent of the 20 million people in the region are unable to provide for their most basic human needs—food, shelter, and medical care. The percentage of malnourished children under age five is unacceptably high—17.9 percent in El Salvador, 28.5 percent in Guatemala and 43.6 percent in Honduras. The infant mortality rate for the region is 56.9 per thousand births, compared with 10.4 per thousand in the United States.

The United States can help relieve this distress—and improve the prospects for political stability—by forging a new political and economic contract with the democracies of Central America. Under this contract, the U.S. would offer aid, trade, and security assurances in return for Central American economic reforms and liberalization. . . .

Rich in Resources

The present depression in Central America did not result from regional backwardness. Central America is endowed with a rich variety of natural resources, ranging from fertile soil and petroleum to abundant water available for irrigation and power. Central America is ideally located for international trade, and its people are ingenious and hard-working. Indeed, during the 1960s and 1970s these factors combined to produce growth rates of about 5 percent per year.

The economies of Central America traditionally depended on the export of basic commodities such as cotton, sugar, beef, coffee, and bananas. The Central American Common Market (CACM), formed in the early 1960s, initially led to high growth in manufacturing as well, as member countries raised tariffs while eliminating trade barriers among themselves to create a larger market. Foreign capital came in at satisfactory rates and capital flight was small. Inflation was almost nonexistent.

Reasons for Collapse

What went wrong? The external economic shocks (worldwide inflation, oil price shocks, and recession) of the 1970s and early 1980s contributed to the economic collapse in Central America. So did the region's devastating wars over the last decade. The

Nicaraguan economy has been paralyzed by the Sandinista suppression of almost all private economic activity by *campesinos* and urban market women. Communist guerrillas have systematically blown up electric pylons, bridges, and buses in El Salvador.

Joining the Global Economy

The old days of massive U.S. aid pushing statist "development programs" clearly are over. And no one should mourn their passing. Internal development spurred on by deregulation and openings to the global economy is the key to Latin America's future.

Haroldo J. Montealegre, *The Wall Street Journal,* June 29, 1990.

Throughout the region, growing government interference in the private economy in the 1970s and 1980s aggravated a cultural resistance to entrepreneurship, risk-taking, and the amassing of wealth. An inflationary surge in the 1970s caused the region's governments to begin an unhealthy expansion of their public sector. Their response to double-digit inflation was to increase public spending for salaries and subsidies to private firms. Higher income and payroll taxes only added to the problem of unemployment. Rising joblessness led to the expansion of public sector jobs programs and other social welfare programs.

As a consequence, public spending in the region rose significantly—from 14 percent of GDP [gross domestic product] in the early 1970s to 24 percent in the early 1980s. The result was huge budget deficits. To service the rising tide of public debt, the governments printed more money—which led to even more inflation and exchange rate instability.

The multilateral development banks exacerbated the growing economic crisis by forcing governments to impose high-tax austerity on their peoples as a condition for further extensions of credit. Too often, agencies like the International Monetary Fund have focused on the fiscal balance sheet at the expense of essential economic growth.

Fortress Central America

Another factor contributing to the economic decline was CACM protectionism. The region's "fortress Central America" approach to trade seriously weakened export industries. The protected industries found it difficult to compete successfully in third markets, and this limited their sources of much-needed foreign exchange. Moreover, protectionism slowed the development of non-traditional agricultural exports and industrial exports. Lacking alternative exports with which they might generate foreign exchange, the region's economies were especially vulnerable to the plunge in basic commodity prices that took place during the early 1980s.

The eventual collapse of the CACM in 1979 led to the adoption of unilateral trade policies between each pair of countries, and the consequent elimination of intra-regional free trade.

Central America also has suffered from a ponderous and all-pervading superstructure of bureaucratic practices, economic regulations, and mandated business procedures that have proved a costly and counterproductive brake on wealth creation.

Guatemala provides a typical example. Guatemala's cartelized banking system strangles credit to small and medium sized businesses by demanding up to 200 percent collateral for expansion loans. Guatemala's economy is also hampered by the government's bureaucratic inertia—a dogged resistance to even the most necessary changes, such as the computerization of basic functions (for example, customs, immigration, and licensing).

In Honduras, a small businessman seeking approval of a new venture faces a maze of official procedures as well as a mountain of paperwork. In the cultivated shrimp industry, an investor must take 120 separate steps to obtain a business license; some of these steps can be done simultaneously, but others must be done in sequence. This process takes an average of *one and a half years.*

Investment controls, wage and price controls, sweetheart deals for government-owned enterprises, forced sales to government at below-market prices, and barriers protecting cartel profits—all of these have been as common as they have been devastating to the Central American economies.

Seven Reforms for Central America

The new contract between Central America and the United States would be designed to restore economic growth to the region: the United States would free its markets for goods from the region, provide security guaranties, and continue effective development assistance, in return for these seven economic reforms by the Central American democracies:

1) *Lower marginal tax rates.* With the possible exception of Costa Rica, all of the region's governments impose high and progressive tax rates on individual effort and enterprise. In El Salvador, a marginal tax rate of 43 percent is imposed on incomes above $25,000, and a rate of 60 percent above $50,000. The Honduran tax code features a rising scale of eight tax brackets, with a top tax rate of 40 percent. Guatemala has an even steeper scale of rates, including a 48 percent top bracket.

Lower and less progressive tax rates would increase economic activity in these countries and reinvigorate their anemic revenue bases.

121

2) *Monetary stabilization.* A four-country region with four small currencies is not an ideal recipe for investment, price stability, and economic competitiveness, especially when exchange rates among the currencies are controlled not by the market but by central bank fiat. Bureaucratic setting of exchange rates among countries too small to be sizable markets in themselves is an unaffordable luxury.

Ultimately, the Central American countries will have to either adopt the U.S. dollar as the unit of account and exchange, or revitalize the *peso centroamericano*, a unit of exchange similar to the European Economic Community's ECU money-basket currency. The *peso centroamericano* has not been used effectively in the past because of the disarray of the CACM, but it remains clear that whichever currency is finally settled on must be backed by more than the promises of four or five central banks.

Promoting Market Principles

Political and economic liberties go hand in hand. Fragile democracies are reinforced by strong economies. And open societies give scope to the creativity and entrepreneurship essential to economic success. Strategies of deregulation, privatization, and market-based structural adjustment work. Free and open markets are the key to broad-based and sustainable economic growth.

James A. Baker III, Statement before the Senate Foreign Relations Committee, February 1, 1990.

3) *Privatization of government-owned enterprises.* Costa Rica has joined the worldwide movement toward privatization by reducing the cost of state-run enterprises from $66 million in 1983 to less than $5 million today. President Oscar Arias is justly proud of his success in converting a large government-owned sugar corporation into a 200,000-member cooperative.

Private contracting for traditionally government-run services is starting to appear in Central America. Contracting-out and privatization both offer great opportunities for turning workers into owners, thus broadening the hitherto narrow ownership base of private enterprise.

4) *Encouragement of foreign private investment.* Central America desperately needs the technological expertise as well as the physical capital of foreign investors. To attract investment, though, there must be a stable business climate in which investors face no risks beyond those of the competitive marketplace and acts of God.

Investors need binding assurances against arbitrary expropriation. Investment disputes should be subject to impartial third-party arbitration, and investors should have strong guarantees by the government of their right to repatriate earnings and otherwise move their capital across borders.

5) *Rule of law.* Economic reform requires the creation of independent judicial systems, administering established rules of law in economic transactions. The judicial system of a country must enforce contract law and resolve tort claims impartially before that country can expect increased foreign investment.

6) *Debt-equity swaps.* Central America has a burdensome foreign debt. There is no panacea for this problem, but debt-equity swaps are a useful beginning. In these swaps, a country's foreign debt is purchased in the U.S. at a large discount, converted by the debtor country's central bank into local currency, and then invested in local enterprises.

Reducing foreign debt through debt-equity swaps has the added advantage of forcing countries to make investment in their countries attractive to prospective swappers. Chile has gone the furthest in establishing regular procedures for these swaps; nearly $3 billion has now been repatriated in this fashion.

7) *Economic empowerment.* Property rights and the security of ownership—hallmarks of any true capitalist system—are the keys to prosperity. . . .

The goal of Central American economic reform ought to be the conversion of workers into owners, of propertyless peasants into genuine citizens with a full share in their national destiny. Swaps of debt for employee stock ownership would help to promote a worker stake in the economy. In Costa Rica and Guatemala, the expanded ownership is being promoted by Solidarity Associations—private employer-employee alliances that seek to surmount the old divisions between labor and management.

Fallback Reform: Incubator Zones

If economy-wide reforms should prove politically unrealistic, the governments should establish enterprise zones to incubate capitalism in certain areas of each country. These zones would feature the reduction or elimination of taxes, regulations, and other government-imposed restrictions on private enterprise. As wealth creation, living standards, and general prosperity begin to flourish in these zones, the task of convincing the rest of the people about the benefits of capitalism will become much easier.

The Central Americans have themselves pointed the way by creating "free zones" to promote exports. Free zones feature reduced tax and tariff burdens for export industries. All five of the Central American countries have authorized the creation of free zones at one time or another, and several are in operation today, notably in Costa Rica. The bustling activity at the free zone in Iquique, Chile, should serve as an example.

123

The Central American democracies are seeking greater market access by applying for membership in the General Agreement on Tariffs and Trade (GATT), which will give them a powerful boost into the world marketplace. Reviving the Central American Common Market would help integrate these countries into the global economy.

The U.S. can aid this process by revitalizing the moribund Secretariat for Economic Integration in Central America (SIECA) and by underwriting the formation of a new "Central American Democratic Community" (CADC) to supersede the Organization of Central American States created by the 1962 Charter of San Salvador. Such an effort might include greater status for the appointive and advisory Central American Parliament, an idea enthusiastically promoted by President Cerezo of Guatemala.

Principles of Economic Freedom

A commitment to democracy is only one element in the new partnership that I envision for the nations of the Americas. This new partnership must also aim at ensuring that the market economies survive and prosper and prevail. The principles of economic freedom have not been applied as fully as the principle of democracy. While the poverty of statism and protectionism is more evident than ever, statist economies remain in place, stifling growth in many Latin nations.

George Bush, Speech before the Council of the Americas, May 2, 1989.

The United States ought to appoint a prominent ambassador to the new Community, exercising direct supervision over the existing Regional Office for Central America and Panama (ROCAP) of the U.S. Agency for International Development (AID). One radical proposal goes even further, calling for the consolidation under the CADC ambassador of the AID mission to all of Central America. While this proposal may be too extreme, the idea behind it—that is, treating the four democratic nations as an economic and increasingly as a political unit—deserves to be kept in mind as the nations evolve in that direction.

Opening the U.S. Market

As part of the contract, if the Central American governments embark on the reforms proposed here, the U.S. can help strengthen the region by negotiating a Free Trade Agreement —modeled on those we have concluded with Israel and Canada—with the newly revived CACM. Because the U.S. is Central America's biggest customer, and transportation costs to the U.S. are much lower than to any other market, we are in a unique position to strengthen Central America through expanding trade.

Exports—particularly agricultural products—are the lifeblood of the Central American economy. But all too often, nontariff barriers imposed by the U.S. have posed extremely costly obstacles to Central America's traditional exports (for example, sugar and textiles). U.S. quotas on sugar products alone have cost the region almost as much in foreign exchange as the U.S. has contributed in economic aid.

Another part of our contract would be continuation of the kinds of development aid that have proven effective in the past. These include aid programs for education and vocational training, health and nutrition, and infrastructure (this last category includes housing, water, sewage systems, roads, bridges, irrigation, and energy).

The health, housing, and education needs of the Central American poor can best be met by a strong market economy with a tax base capable of providing a safety net for the weakest citizens. U.S. development assistance should focus on meeting those human needs until the reinvigorated Central American economies can take up the slack. This commitment to a social safety net will help improve the political climate for capitalist reforms in Central America.

However, government-to-government assistance must not be considered the centerpiece of our pro-growth reform package. Aid programs do nothing to solve the underlying problems of economic stagnation and slow private-sector job creation. They don't encourage the supply-side economy, which is the only reliable source of prosperity. . . .

A Window for Consensus

Many in Central America are coming to accept the wisdom of a policy along the lines proposed here. The intra-regional entrepreneurial group FEDEPRICAP [Federation of Private Business in Central America and Panama], based in Costa Rica and with affiliates in other countries, supports these initiatives. A new generation of Central American leaders, many of them U.S.-trained, are now rising to ministerial posts. They bring with them a commitment to broad-based prosperity—instead of continued protection of vested interests. . . .

A strong free-market economy is the only secure base upon which a prosperous and just society can be built. Now more than ever before, we have an opportunity to help Central America move in this direction.

"The Sandinista defeat, like the defeat of the Marxist Left generally, is the defeat of fantasy. The communist remedy to social injustice proved worse than the malady."

Renouncing Marxism Would Strengthen Central American Economies

Octavio Paz

The defeat of the Sandinistas in Nicaragua signaled the defeat of Marxist-Leninist economies in Central America, according to Octavio Paz, the author of the following viewpoint. To develop and prosper, Paz believes Central Americans should embrace a free-market economy that is integrated with other nations. He contends that such an economy, modeled after the European Common Market, would promote equality and economic justice in Central America. Paz, a well-known Latin American author and intellectual, wrote the acclaimed *The Labyrinth of Solitude*, a philosophical analysis of Mexico.

As you read, consider the following questions:

1. What does Paz believe is the main reason for the fall of the Sandinistas?
2. What will happen to the Central American nations if they do not unite, according to the author?
3. How does Paz think nations can prevent nationalism from destroying economic integration?

The 1990 Nicaraguan election has dealt the all but final blow to the Marxist-Leninist alternative in this hemisphere; it initiates the closing episode of the tumultuous era that began in 1959 with the Cuban Revolution and will conclude with the presumed fall of Fidel Castro.

Thankfully, this part of the world, like Eastern Europe, has finally given up Marx for Montesquieu. Even the Sandinistas, by showing mature acceptance of their defeat, have apparently learned to value the checks and balances on power that are the fundamental guarantee of Western civilization.

A Doomed Attempt at Marxism

Even if the Sandinistas had won the election, it was already clear to them that their primitive attempt to establish a Marxist-Leninist government in Nicaragua was doomed. Although the US-backed Contras contributed to the pressure on the Sandinistas to accept free elections, they were not the decisive factor. The transformation of the Sandinistas was primarily a consequence of the momentous changes in the Soviet Union and Eastern Europe: It had become clear to the Sandinistas that the kind of help they needed to carry out their revolution would not be forthcoming from Mikhail Gorbachev or their rapidly collapsing communist allies in Eastern Europe. Without Soviet backing, the Sandinistas knew quite well, Cuba's support was useless. Because it is so isolated, Cuba carries little political or military weight on its own. . . .

The effect of the Nicaraguan elections on Cuba is unclear. History is not only a matter of impersonal social forces, but of human beings; of chance and accidents. Fidel Castro is an historical accident. Persons are unpredictable, and Cuba is a personalized regime.

However, the Nicaraguan election makes Castro's choice strikingly clear: either he can take the path of Daniel Ortega in Nicaragua, who has followed the lead of Poland, East Germany and Czechoslovakia; or he can follow the path of Ceausescu in Romania. With each passing day, Castro seems less disposed to take the path of the Sandinistas. . . .

The End of Anti-Americanism

Significantly, the Sandinista defeat can also be read as a falling out of the "anti-gringo" sentiment that has plagued Latin America long past its historical reality. After all, the Nicaraguan people elected the candidate openly endorsed by the president of the US, who has been a key supporter of arming the Contras. And, contrary to predictions, the US invasion of Panama did not unleash the nationalist backlash that would have cemented the Sandinista hold on power.

The abandonment of anti-gringo sentiment, which can be seen throughout Latin America, will be a key factor in confronting the problems of a Central America at peace.

The End of Marxism

The upset win of Violeta Barrios de Chamorro in Nicaragua spells the end of a failed Marxist economic experiment.

For the first time in history, the Central American countries including Panama have freely elected leaders who advocate market economics. And prospects for regional peace seem to be improving by the week.

Bruce Babbitt, *World Monitor*, May 1990.

The new peace will present Violeta Barrios de Chamorro with two pressing tasks: reconciliation—among forces that have bitterly, and bloodily, fought for years—and economic reconstruction.

The first task can only be resolved by the Nicaraguans themselves. The second task, economic reconstruction, can be successfully resolved only through broad integration not only with the rest of Central America, the Caribbean and Mexico—but with the heretofore vilified United States as well.

Following Europe's Example

The precedent of European integration is very important not only for the future of Central America, but for the surrounding region as well. If the Europeans, after 2,000 years of killing each other, have found a way to understand one another, then so can Central Americans, Mexicans and North Americans. If the French and Germans can get together, why can't we?

The division of Central America into various countries is an artificial remnant of extreme decolonization. Since these countries lack economic as well as political viability on their own, the only solution for them is to unite into a regional common market and political association like the European Community. These would be linked in turn with a larger integration in a North American community. If these tiny countries remain alone in the 21st century, they will remain the poor and impotent pawns of outside powers—a situation which has already led to so much bloodshed in this century.

Now that ideological rift has diminished in Central America, the main threat to the promise of integration, as in Eastern Europe, will be resurgent nationalism.

Here too, democratization is the best guarantee against nationalist reaction. In Mexico, for example, the anti-American sentiment has resided mainly in intellectuals and the upper class. In the last century, the anti-Americans were the aristocrats who inherited European tradition. The Conservative Party of Mexico, for example, asked the help of Napoleon to defend against the "gringo menace."

In the 20th century, the custodians of anti-Americanism have been on the Left, not the Right. Today, anachronistic intellectuals, primarily of the Left, are the last to change.

The Practical Appeal of Integration

The kind of democratic developments we witnessed in Nicaragua, however, will facilitate Central American integration with one another and with the US. When the same people who would migrate to the North can freely elect their leaders, outdated nationalist sentiment will readily yield to the practical appeal of economic integration.

Integration alone will not close the gap between rich and poor or reconcile freedom and equality. It is only the precondition for such a possibility. As in the US and Europe, the likely order will be a mixed economy: a free market with state intervention as a means to alleviate gross inequality.

The Sandinista defeat, like the defeat of the Marxist Left generally, is the defeat of fantasy. The communist remedy to social injustice proved worse than the malady. Now, our challenge is to find the political imagination to address those injustices that have outlived their untenable solution.

"The responsibility for starvation and misery in Central America belongs . . . to the U.S. and its 'free market system.'"

Renouncing Capitalism Would Strengthen Central American Economies

Revolutionary Worker

In the following viewpoint, a writer from *Revolutionary Worker* contends that the free-market economic system promoted by the U.S. has brought poverty and economic instability to Central America. The U.S. has encouraged Central American nations to grow export crops rather than food staples, leaving thousands of people hungry, the writer argues. In addition, *Revolutionary Worker* maintains that the free-market system caters to a few wealthy Central American families, leaving the majority in poverty. *Revolutionary Worker* is the weekly newspaper of the Revolutionary Communist Party, USA.

As you read, consider the following questions:

1. How did the U.S. ruin the Nicaraguan economy, according to *Revolutionary Worker*?
2. How does the author believe export-oriented agriculture has affected Central America?
3. What was the real reason for the failure of the Nicaraguan Sandinistas, according to *Revolutionary Worker*?

"American-made Poverty," *Revolutionary Worker*, March 5, 1990. Reprinted by permission of the *Revolutionary Worker*, the weekly newspaper of the Revolutionary Communist Party, USA. Title and some subheadings have been changed by Greenhaven editors.

One of the things the U.S. rulers are saying about the 1990 Nicaraguan elections is that a major reason the people did not vote for the Sandinistas is Nicaragua's messed-up economy. They claim that the Sandinista policy is the cause for the crisis and that the economy can only get better now that a pro-U.S. government will take over. On every level, this is outrageous hypocrisy on the part of the U.S.

Number One: The bloody handprints of the U.S. are all over the economic crisis in Nicaragua. The U.S. put extreme economic pressure on the Sandinista government. In 1985, for example, the Reagan administration declared a trade embargo against Nicaragua. In order to justify the embargo, Reagan issued a presidential decree which said that Nicaragua posed "an unusual and extraordinary threat to the national security and foreign policy of the United States" and declared a "national emergency." The vicious and unjust war by the U.S. against Nicaragua through the 1980s put huge strains on the economy. The Contras caused terrible suffering and damage in the Nicaraguan countryside.

Number Two: All over the world, Third World countries already under full U.S. domination and carrying out the U.S. program for a "free market economy" are in crisis. The country of Ivory Coast in west Africa has been praised in the West as a "model of free market economy." The Ivory Coast now grows more cocoa for export than ever, but the fall in world cocoa prices has hit the economy hard and people are starving. The government in the Philippines, desperate for new loans from the International Monetary Fund, is cutting food subsidies and taking other steps against the people in order to comply with IMF demands. Poverty and starvation are the order of the day for oppressed people in the U.S. empire.

Examples of Misery

But there's no need to go across the oceans to see "free market" disasters. Central America, which the U.S. imperialists arrogantly call their "backyard," is full of U.S.-dominated countries with wrecked economies. Here are a few examples of the misery that Uncle Sam has brought to these countries and their people (much of this information is from *The Central America Fact Book* by Tom Barry and Deb Preusch):

• Two-thirds of the people in all of Central America live in poverty. The situation is worst in the rural areas. In the Guatemalan countryside, four out of five people cannot afford the minimum basic necessities like food, shelter and clothing.

• There was some economic growth in the region up until the mid-1970s. But by the early 1980s per capita income in Central America was back to the levels of the 1960s. The UN [United

Nations] declared in 1984 that the region is in "an economic breakdown unlike any seen in Central America since the 1930s."

• About 85 percent of the goods exported by the Central American countries are agricultural products, and most of their imports are commodities like machinery, chemical fertilizers, and steel from the U.S. and other developed countries. The export-oriented agriculture has forced these countries deeper into the web of debt and crisis. In 1960 a ton of coffee bought about 40 tons of fertilizer. By 1982 a ton of coffee could buy less than two tons of fertilizer.

A Nightmare Come True

For us, capitalism is not a dream to be made reality, but a nightmare come true. Our challenge lies not in privatizing the state but in deprivatizing it. Our states have been bought at bargain prices by the owners of the land, the banks and everything else. And for us, the market is nothing more than a pirate ship—the greater its freedom, the worse its behavior. The world market robs us with both arms. The commercial arm keeps charging us more and more for what it sells us and paying less and less for what it buys from us. The financial arm that lends us our own money keeps paying us less and charging us more.

We live in a region where European prices and African wages prevail, where capitalism acts like the kind man who said, "I'm so fond of poor people that it seems to me there are never enough of them." In Brazil alone, for example, the system kills 1,000 children a day by disease or starvation.

With or without elections capitalism in Latin America is anti-democratic—most of the people are the prisoners of need, doomed to isolation and violence. Hunger lies, violence lies: They claim that they are part of nature, they feign belonging to the natural order of things. When that "natural order" grows disorderly, the military comes on the scene, hooded or barefaced. As they say in Colombia: "The more the cost of living goes up the less life is worth."

Eduardo Galeano, *The Guardian*, May 2, 1990.

• Between 1960 and 1984 the amount of debt owed by the Central American countries to foreign countries and banks increased over 40 times. The total debt comes to about $800 for every person in this region. Costa Rica is said to be in better shape economically than the other Central American countries, but the value of all the exports from this country in 1984 was only one-fourth of its external debt. Austerity programs demanded by the IMF in return for loans have hit the people hard. In El Salvador the cost of living jumped almost 250 percent between 1975 and 1984, and there were big cuts in food subsidies and social services.

• A small U.S.-backed elite rules in each country and owns most of the land and big businesses. In El Salvador fourteen powerful families (known as *los Catorce*) control the wealth, but six out of ten peasants do not own any land. In Honduras, two-thirds of the fertile land is in the hands of big landowners who make up only 5 percent of the farmowners. In Costa Rica only 300 landowners control 25 percent of the agricultural land.

• Three out of four children in Honduras, Guatemala and El Salvador are malnourished. In 1984, 40 percent of all the people in Guatemala could not afford a minimum diet.

• There is one head of cattle for every two people in Central America. In Honduras 65 percent of the farmland is used for cattle grazing. But most of the beef is not for the people to eat but for export. In Honduras per capita beef consumption dropped 10 percent between 1965 and 1975; in the same period the country's meat exports to the U.S. tripled.

• In the Salvadoran countryside there is only one hospital bed for every 100,000 people and one doctor for every 8,000 people. Four out of five people do not have latrines and three out of four have no safe drinking water. Over 200,000 Salvadoran children are in danger of going blind from severe vitamin A deficiencies.

Imperialism to Blame

The responsibility for starvation and misery in Central America belongs to the imperialist system, in particular to the U.S. and its "free market system." The U.S. rulers lie outright that the economic problems in Nicaragua come from the Sandinistas not participating fully in this "free market system." The *real* fundamental problem with the Sandinistas was that their program was *not* one of decisively breaking Nicaragua from the whole structure of imperialist domination that was forced on the country by the U.S. Rather, the Sandinistas tried to get new terms with the U.S. under the same, overall relationship. One look at Nicaragua's neighboring countries shows that this whole structure and relationship of dependence is rotten and must be completely overthrown and smashed if the people are to break all their chains.

"Thanks in part to sustained U.S. aid levels to Central America, . . . first one country then another [has made] a remarkable recovery from near disastrous circumstances."

U.S. Aid Would Strengthen Central American Economies

Elliott Abrams

Elliott Abrams was assistant secretary for Inter-American Affairs in the Reagan administration. In the following viewpoint, Abrams states that the U.S. should give economic aid to Central America to help stabilize the economies and support the region's democratic governments. American efforts brought democracy to Central America, Abrams maintains, and American aid can now ensure that democracy flourishes in the region.

As you read, consider the following questions:

1. How are democracy and human rights related, according to Abrams?
2. Why does the author believe there has been little investment in Central America in recent years?
3. What does Abrams think the success of Costa Rica proves?

Elliott Abrams, testimony before the U.S. House of Representatives Appropriations Committee's Subcommittee on Foreign Operations, April 22, 1988.

This hemisphere—our immediate neighborhood—is of great strategic importance; in fact, critical to our national security. We cannot deal effectively with challenges to our interests in other parts of the world if we are unable to cope with problems closer to home. Historically, our ability to project power in the world, in part, has been based on the absence of threats closer to home.

Unfortunately, many of our allies in Latin America and the Caribbean do not have the resources to provide simultaneously for their own security and the basic economic needs of their people. Because we know they must do both if they are to survive and prosper, and if democracy is to be given a chance to flourish, we must help to make up the shortfall.

In the past, many Latin Americans seemed to view democracy as just another form of government to be tried and discarded if it resulted in no apparent immediate benefits. The current trend of democratization has been accompanied by some interesting and promising political developments that have helped the new democracies break out of the old patterns.

Many Latin Americans now believe that open societies are superior to closed ones and that democratic institutions are, therefore, worth building and strengthening. Accompanying this has been the formation of an informal but strong mutual support network among democratic leaders. . . .

Democracy and Human Rights

Respect for human rights has shown improvement in all the non-Marxist and nondictatorial states of Latin America. The marked reduction in the number of human rights abuses in recent years parallels the spread and consolidation of democracy: where democratic government has taken root, the human rights situation has changed dramatically for the better.

The security of the United States and the security of all free countries of this hemisphere benefit from the region-wide movement toward democracy. We have supported this trend not only because it is in accord with our deepest values but also because we believe it is in our interest. . . . Latin America's growing political maturity is demonstrating that we can enjoy the most constructive long-term relationships with countries where government is founded on the consent of the governed.

For these reasons, we emphasize democracy in our political relations with our neighbors. The modest assistance levels we have requested aim to provide the resources needed to support our quest for sustained democracy in this hemisphere. A reversal of the movement to democracy anywhere will be rejected by us as it will be by all the democracies in the region. . . .

Certain economies of Central America—particularly El

Salvador's—have been severely damaged by guerrilla-inflicted destruction as well as by a lack of investor confidence due to political and social instability and turmoil. The large exodus of capital, particularly during the early 1980s, has resulted in little new investment throughout this area, except in Costa Rica.

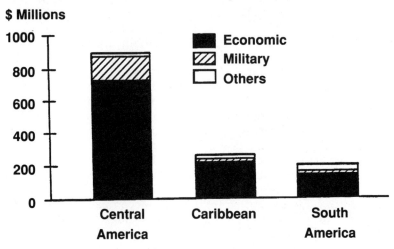

FY 1989 Assistance Request

Other: Includes Peace Corps and international narcotics.

Department of State Bulletin, October 1988.

It is clear that our friends need help to overcome their economic difficulties, to defend themselves, and to keep alive their faith in freedom and democracy. With foreign assistance, they have a chance to manage their own affairs and find their own way out of their present troubles. We should have no higher priority. Neither the communists nor the drug dealers are interested in strengthening the security, political systems, or economies of these countries. It is to us that our neighbors look for cooperation and support. It is in our interest that we respond. . . .

Development assistance is project support used for education and management training and some small business development. It also funds private sector and agricultural development and health and nutrition programs, primarily to increase the incomes of poor rural families to meet their basic needs.

Food for Peace, commonly called PL 480, provides food from U.S. Department of Agriculture stockpiles to those nations that are too poor to feed all of their people adequately. The food provided alleviates hunger and malnutrition and improves health. One of our most successful programs, it also generates local currency in some countries that is recycled to fund agricultural development, infrastructure improvements, rural education, and health programs. . . .

Remarkable Recoveries

Thanks in part to sustained U.S. aid levels to Central America, this half-decade has seen first one country then another make a remarkable recovery from near disastrous circumstances. Now freely elected civilian governments are offering their people the chance for a better future in El Salvador, Honduras, and Guatemala. Costa Rica continues to enjoy freedom and the rule of law, as it has for many years. . . .

Throughout Central America, it is in the U.S. interest to strengthen democratic institutions and the administration of justice and to support existing regional institutions to foster increased cooperation among the Central American democracies. As we support and encourage the development of the region, we should assist those existing regional institutions that contribute to improving the economic and social well-being of the citizens of these countries.

The regional program for Central America is designed to complement and to supplement U.S. bilateral assistance programs. It complements those programs by promoting on a regional basis what is also being done individually, with the objective of improving regional cooperation. It supplements the bilateral programs where it is more logical and cost-effective to implement projects on a regional basis, thus avoiding costly duplication. This regional program is managed partly from an office based in Guatemala City and partly by the U.S. Agency for International Development in Washington, D.C.

El Salvador and Guatemala

El Salvador is one of our closest allies in Central America. U.S. policy interests in El Salvador are to advance the cause of democracy; improve economic conditions; promote peaceful change; prevent hostile, antidemocratic forces from gaining a strategic foothold; and prevent the Soviet Union from increasing its influence through its support for the Salvadoran insurgents. The Government of El Salvador is critically dependent on U.S. support in its efforts to consolidate democratic government and rebuild its economy in the face of guerrilla sabotage and destruction.

U.S. policy promotes the consolidation of constitutional democracy in El Salvador by assisting the government to defend itself against a determined Marxist insurgency. . . . It addresses the socioeconomic roots of the insurgency and its historic political bases by continuing support for democratic development, judicial reform, respect for human rights, and responsive public institutions. It also helps stabilize the war-torn national economy and stimulates revitalization and growth. . . .

Aid Strengthens Democracies

Democracy is fragile, particularly in countries ravaged by years of corrupt and inefficient management. In countries such as these, a vote is not enough: We must now support democracy with assistance so the new governments can stabilize their economies, grow, and allow the benefits of that growth to be felt by the population as a whole. There must be assistance over time for the institutions of democracy to strengthen, take hold, and flourish.

Bernard W. Aronson, Speech before the Subcommittee on Foreign Operations of the House Committee on Appropriations, March 19, 1990.

Guatemala's size, proximity to the United States, large population, and regionally important economy make its stability and development important to the interests of the United States. Over the past 20 years, Guatemala has faced a lingering Cuban-supported insurgency that fed on the neglect and poverty of the nation's Indians, some 50% of the population. A succession of military governments attempted to put down the festering insurgency, but at great cost in human life and widespread human rights abuses. The violence led to a cutoff of U.S. military assistance in 1977.

In late 1985, Guatemalans freely elected a new civilian government, ushering in an era of new expectations for growth and democracy. The government, led by Christian Democrat Vinicio Cerezo, faces a continued but weakened Marxist insurgency, serious economic problems inherited from previous regimes, and an upsurge in common crime fed by unemployment. Undermanned and poorly trained police and criminal justice forces have had trouble controlling the increase in crime. The government, nevertheless, has made steady strides in ending human rights abuses, promoting economic growth, and in creating the conditions for greater citizen participation in government.

Military Assistance

U.S. Government assistance provided in the past to the Guatemalan Armed Forces has demonstrated our support for an important institution in Guatemala's democratic society. The assistance has addressed only the most pressing material needs of the Guatemalan Armed Forces, while enhancing professional competence.

138

The primary U.S. objective in Guatemala is the promotion of a democratic government that is friendly to this country, respectful of human rights, capable of dealing effectively with the Marxist insurgent threat, and responsive to the economic and social needs of its people. It is clearly in our interest that Guatemala adopt policies that strengthen democratic institutions, promote real economic growth, curb repressive practices, and thereby eliminate popular support for extremist solutions. . . .

Honduras is a key democratic ally of the United States . . . . As the poorest democracy in Central America, Honduras requires substantial assistance if it is to make difficult but necessary economic reforms in support of economic development and democracy.

U.S. security assistance to Honduras is a tangible demonstration of our commitment to this key ally's defense and development. The Azcona Administration has consistently formulated and implemented economic stabilization reform programs since it took office in January 1986. These accomplishments are particularly noteworthy when viewed in the regional context of instability and declining prices for primary exports and the destabilizing effect of quick profits provided by the illegal drug trade. . . .

Costa Rica's Weaknesses

Despite its long democratic tradition and the promise of the Guatemala accord, Costa Rica remains vulnerable to regional tensions. In sharp contrast to heavily militarized Nicaragua, its northern neighbor, Costa Rica maintains no standing army. The civil war in Nicaragua and the totalitarian orientation of the Sandinista regime have driven 150,000-250,000 Nicaraguans into exile in Costa Rica. This massive influx of refugees strains the country's public resources and social infrastructure.

The Costa Rican economy continues its slow recovery from the severe problems of 1981-82. When coffee prices fell and petroleum costs skyrocketed in the late 1970s, Costa Rica postponed economic adjustment by borrowing massively from abroad. Falling export revenues forced the authorities to halt interest payments on international loans. Commercial banks refused to provide new financing, plunging Costa Rica into economic crisis. The collapse of the Central American Common Market in the early 1980s was another blow to the Costa Rican economy. The economy contracted, forcing down real incomes. U.S. economic aid played a key role in helping Costa Rica overcome these serious problems. However, the country is still burdened with a high level of per capita debt.

U.S. assistance to Costa Rica seeks to promote economic

growth and the strengthening of the country's democratic institutions. Costa Rica provides convincing evidence that social and economic progress go hand in hand with democratic values in Central America. . . .

A Regional Focus

The Latin America and Caribbean regional program supports a variety of social, economic, and political development needs best addressed on a regional basis. In addition, several projects affect some countries—Mexico, Brazil, and Colombia, for example—where there are no bilateral AID [Agency for International Development] programs. The regional program focuses on administration of justice and human rights, education and training, health, agriculture and agribusiness, and private-sector support.

Individual projects in these areas are designed to reinforce the interdependent U.S. policy objectives of strengthening democracy and improving the living conditions of people throughout this hemisphere. . . .

The democratic ideal is universal; its practice is increasingly the stuff of life and politics throughout Latin America. Most of Latin America's democrats know they can count on U.S. support now; it is imperative that they be able to count on our support in the future.

"Billions of dollars in U.S. economic aid have flowed to Central America, yet there has been no economic development nor improvement in the conditions of the poor."

U.S. Aid Would Not Strengthen Central American Economies

Tom Barry and Deb Preusch

U.S. economic aid to Central America has hurt the region's economies and increased the poverty of most Central Americans, Tom Barry and Deb Preusch argue in the following viewpoint. They believe the U.S. uses economic assistance as a tool to punish enemies and reward friends, not to help the poor. Because aid is channeled through governments rather than social agencies, Barry and Preusch contend, most of it ends up in the hands of wealthy, pro-U.S. Central Americans. Barry is the chief writer and analyst for The Inter-Hemispheric Education Resource Center, a research and policy institute in Albuquerque, New Mexico. Preusch is the Center's executive director. They coauthored *The Central America Fact Book.*

As you read, consider the following questions:

1. How do AID programs alter Central American economies to benefit the U.S., according to the authors?
2. What measures do Barry and Preusch believe must be taken to promote equal economic development in Central America?
3. What conditions do the authors feel the U.S. should establish before it gives aid to a Central American government?

Tom Barry and Deb Preusch, *The Soft War: The Uses and Abuses of U.S. Economic Aid in Central America.* New York: Grove Press, 1988. Copyright © 1986 by The Resource Center. Reprinted by permission of Grove Weidenfeld.

The political foundations of U.S. economic aid policy are transparent—probably more so in Central America than anywhere else in the world. The Kissinger Commission recommended that U.S. military aid programs form a "shield" behind which U.S. economic assistance could go about solving the region's economic and political problems. But the distinction between military aid and economic aid has become increasingly muddled in Central America. Like military aid, nonlethal assistance is mainly used to stabilize "friendly" governments, back counterrevolutionary armies, and contain popular rebellion. Like military aid, U.S. economic support is used to reward friends and punish enemies.

Self-Interested Aid

Another key trait of the U.S. foreign aid program is its self-interested nature: the aid serves the "national interest" of the United States. Instead of considering a long-term global reordering, the national interest is defined over the short term and designed to benefit narrow economic, political, and military sectors in the United States. A country's voting pattern in the United Nations, its openness to U.S. investment, and its willingness to host military bases are the criteria Washington uses to determine who should get aid and how much.

The self-interested motivation of U.S. economic aid can be easily observed in the way AID [Agency for International Development] uses its assistance to push for alterations in a nation's economic policies. AID-imposed stabilization programs loosen restrictions on imports, decrease the price of exports, encourage foreign investment, and establish debt repayment schedules. In this manner, the agency serves as the self-appointed guardian of the private sector and the international banking community. AID uses its development assistance in similar ways—funding projects that promote the production of cheap exports to the United States, facilitate foreign investment, and encourage the purchase of U.S. products. While foreign aid does undeniably benefit the U.S. economy in some ways, a foreign aid policy based on a broader and more long-term conception of U.S. national interest would also benefit U.S. citizens. It could mean a lower tax burden, and such a policy could result in more productive and politically stable third world countries that would purchase more U.S. products. Fewer families would migrate from these developing nations, and the higher wage rates would mean that fewer U.S. factories would be closing down to seek cheap labor outside U.S. borders. Most economic aid comes boomeranging back to the United States.

The fact that U.S. assistance bolsters the elites in recipient countries is consistent with the U.S. government's practice of supporting those who back U.S. foreign policy and corporate investment. It is not surprising that Washington has found its most enthusiastic supporters, measured by a commitment to unrestricted private enterprise and to counterrevolution, among the members of the business elite. By channeling aid through governments that serve this privileged class, AID contributes to the strengthening of established power structures. This is as true on a local level as it is on a national one. Because AID makes little effort to direct its assistance to independently organized community groups, its funds generally flow into the hands of the most privileged members of a community. Those with the most commercial experience, education, and experience with government institutions are the ones who usually derive the greatest benefits from AID's development programs.

EL SALVADOR

Before U.S. Aid...

After U.S. Aid...

© 1982 Ed Fischer.

At the same time that U.S. assistance strengthens the Central American elite, it undermines the power of the popular sectors. It does this by sponsoring organizations like AIFLD [American Institute for Free Labor Development] to keep the labor movement weak and disorganized. AID also finances the formation of government-linked cooperatives that compete with independently organized peasant and worker groups, which seldom receive AID funds. A lack of resources hampers the influence of grassroots organizations while government repression decimates their ranks. In contrast, business associations, whose interests are often diametrically opposed to those of the popular sector, receive generous U.S. support and benefit from alliances with the government and military.

143

A more accurate label for AID might be the Agency for International Dependency. In its view, the path to development in the third world must be outward-oriented. Through its aid agreements and policy dialogues with recipient nations, AID encourages countries to look outside their borders for capital, investment, technology, and markets. AID also pushes countries to open up their economies to imports (especially those from the United States) and to prime their economies for increased export production (especially to the United States). It pressures them to adopt technology, consumption patterns, and diets that make them ever more dependent on the United States.

This abuse of economic aid clearly enhances U.S. corporate interests. It keeps Central American nations always looking to the developed countries for economic solutions instead of searching within their own country and region for development options. Their indigenous material and human resources are exploited by outsiders rather than harnessed for domestic advantage. Development strategies that call for increased exports and liberalized imports argue that countries must follow the dictates of comparative advantage. In the case of Central America, this means producing cheap exports based on cheap labor and importing manufactured goods from the industrialized world. While countries do need to be cognizant of their comparative economic advantages, it makes little economic sense to orient production exclusively toward foreign markets at a time when those markets are shrinking, commodity prices are falling, and new protectionist barriers are being erected. Only in boom times would this course of development possibly work—and even then it would mean relying on a low-paid, repressed work force. And even when traditional and non-traditional exports do increase, the income flows to a small elite, not the poor. The main condition for real economic progress is the increase in the income levels of the poor majority, making them consumers as well as laborers.

Ensuring Destabilization

In Central America, AID contends that its contributions are helping to stabilize the region. Yet the injection of large sums of aid, while providing short-term stability, is deepening the region's dependency on outside capital. When this aid dries up, it will leave economies and governments weaker than ever. AID's stabilization strategy is doing more to ensure the long-term destabilization of Central America than it can possibly achieve in steadying the region in the short term.

Yet another aspect of AID's dependency-building behavior is its preference for bilateral instead of multilateral or regional links. This emphasis on bilateral aid keeps countries divided and competing with one another. AID encourages each small nation to devise its own development plan rather than using the assistance as an instrument to create regional economic solutions. In its bilateral agreements with recipients, AID obligates countries to follow certain economic policies dictated by Washington. These policies not only serve the perceived interests of the United States but also those of global capital. In some cases, AID has withheld its assistance until countries comply with austerity and monetary measures recommended by the IMF and World Bank. These measures, while purported to be in the best interests of the countries themselves, are thinly disguised efforts to protect the loans and trade of the international banking community and private sector. Austerity policies invariably squeeze money out of the poor majority while leaving the elite relatively unscathed.

"Trickle-Down" Doesn't Work

U.S. foreign aid has not addressed the key obstacle to economic development in Central America: the extreme inequality keeping most people too poor to be customers in a market economy. U.S. aid has been based on a "trickle-down" thesis: by putting most of our assistance into the hands of generals, politicians, and business leaders it will be invested in ways that will create broad social benefits. The truth is that little of our aid trickles down to the poor—the majority in Central America. Unless people have money to spend, market forces cannot operate effectively. While touting market principles, U.S. aid policies have done little to address the major constraint on market development: the widespread poverty that limits demand.

Kevin Danaher, Phillip Berryman, and Medea Benjamin, *Help or Hindrance? United States Economic Aid in Central America*, September 1987.

During the 1970s, AID and the IFIs [international financial institutions] responded to criticism of development aid by adopting new rhetoric and by launching new types of development projects. AID embarked on a strategy to promote economic growth and help distribute the benefits to the poor. Its programs in integrated rural development formed part of this new effort. In response to increasing unemployment, AID supported food-for-work projects and financed industrial parks to attract labor-intensive manufacturing plants.

AID can point to some improvements in socioeconomic conditions since the launching of the new programs. Overall, however, the relative economic position of the poor declined. In most cases, Central American societies have experienced an absolute decline in income of the poorest sectors since 1970. The central reason for this failure is that AID does not recognize the phenomenon of unequal development. Unless there are measures taken—such as strong labor laws, agrarian reform, state control over certain areas of the economy, progressive taxation, international agreements to guarantee fair prices for commodity exports—economic growth for some will mean continued impoverishment for most.

Since 1980, billions of dollars in U.S. economic aid have flowed to Central America, yet there has been no economic development nor improvement in the conditions of the poor. While economic aid has soared to higher levels each year, regional trade has ground almost to a halt, exports continue to decline, the numbers of unemployed or underemployed approach 40 percent in most countries, and per capita income is sinking every year. The distorted priorities of AID contribute to this lack of development. Yet even with altered priorities, development aid would have few positive results in the conditions of war that exist in Central America.

An Obstacle to Development

In Central America, there are no ready-made solutions to underdevelopment. Economic aid, instead of being an answer, has proved to be a serious obstacle to broad-based development. True growth must come from within; it can never be imposed from the outside. Likewise, meaningful development cannot come from the top down, but must start with grass-roots initiatives. Trying to meet basic needs with international charity is not a lasting solution. Supporting popular organizations that are struggling for land reform, more government services, and better labor laws would yield far more beneficial long-term results. If economic aid is to stimulate development, it needs to be an instrument of empowerment, not one of dependency and pacification. If foreign donors are truly concerned about helping the poor, assisting small farmers, and creating equitable growth, then their aid should primarily flow to those governments that share those priorities. Aid should come with conditions that countries enforce agrarian reform, guarantee human rights and the right to organize, and seek to broaden income distribution.

Similarly, economic aid should go first to those countries struggling to establish their economic independence. As it is, funds are usually cut off as soon as countries take measures to reduce their dependency on U.S. trade, investment, and financing. AID rails against import-substitution schemes that aim to reduce imports through domestic manufacturing. Yet import-substitution, especially when it involves the production of basic goods and the use of local materials, is a necessary element in development, recognized even by AID itself in its younger days.

146

Economic aid could be put to better use on regional investment projects that produce necessary items like fertilizer and chicken feed than on those that grow snow peas or assemble jeans for export.

The Economic Colonization of Central America

External dependence in the form of subsidization of the Central American economies is growing rapidly. Whereas during the 1970s it was the growth of these economies which was subsidized, now larger amounts are required every year merely to slow the pace of economic contraction. The United States is the primary source of aid to Central American countries. . . . The political consequences of this financial involvement further aggravate the economic squeeze, leading to a process of economic recolonization or to the establishment of informal protectorates. . . .

The heavy economic dependence, and the loss of sovereignty it implies, are most pronounced in El Salvador and Honduras, but a similar phenomenon obtains in Costa Rica, under the combined economic pressure of the International Monetary Fund (IMF) and the United States, as well as in Panama, owing to the IMF and the U.S. military pressure. The fact that Guatemala was unsuccessful in maintaining IMF support and is now receiving substantial U.S. aid marks its first advance into the ranks of informal protectorates in Central America.

Xabier Gorostiaga and Peter Marchetti, in *Crisis in Central America: Regional Dynamics and U.S. Policy in the 1980s*, 1988.

Unfortunately, there are few examples of official economic aid that are not self-serving. Foreign aid projects backed by the governments of the Netherlands and the Scandinavian countries come closest to supporting economic independence, self-reliance, and popular empowerment. Among private donors there are more examples of foreign aid being used to meet local development priorities. The Oxfam organizations are models in this regard. Union-to-union solidarity, like that exhibited for the Coca-Cola workers in Guatemala, also serves as an example of beneficial foreign support. The most effective private development groups are those that try to avoid paternalism while seeking to instill dignity, promote self-sufficiency, spur critical thinking, and support independent organizing. Groups like Pueblo to People, which enhance cooperatives through the marketing of Central American crafts, show that development assistance does not have to be paternalistic, but can instill dignity and promote self-sufficiency.

The U.S. national interest needs to be redefined to allow room for economic aid programs that support empowerment not pacification, self-determination not dependency, and development for the many not just the few. Overhauling the U.S. foreign aid program should be part of this redefinition process. Central America is a good place to start. Both sides of the aisle in Congress have justified their support for increased U.S. economic aid on the grounds that this assistance promotes democracy and development. But the facts are otherwise. In the politically tense atmosphere of Central America, U.S. economic aid, like military aid, is essentially interventionist and counterrevolutionary. It throws money at our "friends" while trying to control the hearts and minds of the popular sectors. It is used to back low intensity conflicts that are in fact very high intensity for those who live in the region. Economic aid is not, as widely believed, addressing the root causes of the crisis in Central America. It is, instead, a misuse of tax revenue, an abuse of U.S. citizens' goodwill, and a less prominent but perhaps more destructive side of the war in Central America.

Recognizing Deceptive Arguments

People who feel strongly about an issue use many techniques to persuade others to agree with them. Some of these techniques appeal to the intellect, some to the emotions. Many of them distract the reader or listener from the real issues.

A few common examples of argumentation tactics are listed below. Most of them can be used either to advance an argument in an honest, reasonable way or to deceive or distract from the real issues. It is important for a critical reader to recognize these tactics in order to rationally evaluate an author's ideas.

a. *categorical statement*—stating something in a way that implies there can be no argument

b. *deductive reasoning*—the idea that since *a* and *b* are true, *c* is also true, although there may be no connection between *a* and *c*

c. *generalization*—using statistics or facts to generalize about a population, place, or thing

d *patriotic appeal*—using national pride to sway the reader into favoring a position which flatters one's own culture

e. *personal attack*—criticizing an opponent *personally* instead of rationally debating his or her ideas

f. *scare tactic*—the threat that if you don't do or don't believe this, something terrible will happen

g. *slanter*—to persuade through inflammatory and exaggerated language instead of reason

h. *strawperson*—distorting or exaggerating an opponent's ideas to make one's own seem stronger

The following activity can help you sharpen your skills in recognizing deceptive reasoning. The statements below are derived from the viewpoints in this chapter. *Beside each one, mark the letter of the type of deceptive appeal being used. More than one type of tactic may be applicable. If you believe the statement is not any of the listed appeals, write N.*

1. U.S. economic support is used to reward friends and punish enemies.
2. Thanks to sustained U.S. aid levels to Central America, this decade has seen first one country then another make a remarkable recovery from near disastrous circumstances.
3. Latin Americans seem to view democracy as just another form of government to be tried and discarded if it results in no apparent immediate benefits.
4. Fidel Castro is an egomaniacal tyrant.
5. Without American military aid, the government of El Salvador would fall into the hands of bloodthirsty Marxist guerrillas.
6. Capitalism acts like the kind man who said, "I'm so fond of poor people that it seems to me there are never enough of them." In Brazil alone, capitalism kills 1,000 children a day by disease or starvation.
7. A strong free-market economy is the only secure base upon which a prosperous and just society can be built.
8. Nicaraguans must search garbage dumps for anything edible or usable because of ten years of contra war and U.S. embargo.
9. Millions of Central Americans blame the U.S. for the region's political and economic problems.
10. The predatory Cubans take advantage of Central America's oppression and poverty to further their goal of communist world domination.
11. The bloody handprints of the U.S. are all over the economic crisis in Nicaragua.
12. Poverty and starvation are the order of the day for oppressed people in the U.S. empire.
13. It is clear that our friends in Central America need U.S. help to overcome their economic difficulties, to defend themselves, and to keep alive their faith in democracy.
14. The Sandinista defeat can be read as a falling out of the "anti-gringo" sentiment that has plagued Latin America. After all, the Nicaraguan people elected the candidate openly endorsed by the president of the U.S.
15. Ronald Reagan was an ignorant and uninformed leader, as his policies toward Central America proved.
16. The world knows that America's only goal is for Central Americans to experience the democracy and freedom enjoyed by citizens of the U.S.
17. All Nicaraguans who love their nation will join the Sandinistas in protecting Nicaragua from U.S. imperialism.

Periodical Bibliography

The following articles have been selected to supplement the diverse views presented in this chapter.

Stephen Baker, Bill Javetski, and Ruth Pearson — "Ortega Could Be Winning Much More than an Election," *Business Week,* February 26, 1990.

Henry R. Breck — "Rain Forests for Rent?" *Newsweek,* December 5, 1988.

Steve Burkholder — "U.S. Endowment's Useless Meddling," *The Progressive,* February 1990.

George J. Church — "The Check Is Not in the Mail," *Time,* May 14, 1990.

Alexander Cockburn — "Beat the Devil," *The Nation,* December 19, 1988.

Deirdre Fanning — "Another Panamanian Headache," *Forbes,* November 13, 1989.

John Greenwald — "Bitter Cup of Protest," *Time,* May 28, 1990.

Tony Jenkins — "The Unmaking of Doña Violeta," *The Nation,* February 26, 1990.

James J. Kilpatrick — "United States Can Afford to Help Panama," *Conservative Chronicle,* January 10, 1990. Available from *Conservative Chronicle,* PO Box 11297, Des Moines, IA 50340-1297.

Andrew Liberman — "Salvadoran Coffee, Go Home," *The Progressive,* May 1990.

The Nation — "Money-Go-Round," April 16, 1990.

The New Republic — "Foreign Fade," April 23, 1990.

Eva Pomice — "A Capitalist Requiem for Old Karl Marx," *U.S. News & World Report,* December 25, 1989-January 1, 1990.

Paul Craig Roberts — "Don't Push Central Planning on the Third World," *Business Week,* July 18, 1988.

Linda Robinson — "The Plan to Rebuild Panama," *U.S. News & World Report,* January 15, 1990.

Zachary Schiller and Mark Landler — "P & G Can Get Mad, Sure, but Does It Have to Get Even?" *Business Week,* June 4, 1990.

Douglas Waller — "Foreign-Aid Follies," *Newsweek,* April 16, 1990.

Lawrence Weschler — "The De-Meaning of Humanitarian Aid," *The Nation,* February 27, 1988.

What Role Does Christianity Play in Central America?

Chapter Preface

The Catholic Church has long been an influential institution in Central America. The Church's role has become more controversial in the last few decades because of the interpretation by some of its members of the basic Christian tenet of helping the poor.

In the 1970s, more and more religious workers in Central and South America began to argue that their Christian duty of helping the poor required examining why people are poor. Such an examination, they believed, would lead to solutions that would end poverty. When they looked at Central America, they saw a region characterized by vast economic disparities. Jon Sobrino, a Jesuit priest in El Salvador, is one of several who saw a symbiotic connection between great wealth and great poverty. "Wealth and power cannot exist," he wrote, "if people do not suffer in powerlessness and poverty and without dignity." Sobrino and others argued that in this situation, the Church must side with the poor and advocate that wealth be more equally shared. This idea, termed "liberation theology," challenged the very structure of many Latin American societies.

Others do not see Christian duty toward the poor in this light. Liberation theology was criticized, for example, by the Congregation for the Doctrine of the Faith, the institution within the Catholic Church that is charged with protecting and promoting Catholic beliefs. The Congregation argued that liberation theology focuses too much on "liberation from servitude of an earthly and temporal kind" rather than liberation from sin. Liberation from sin is the central message of the Gospels, according to the Congregation, which also maintained that the Gospel's poor are not simply those who lack money, but also those broken in spirit and lost to sin. The Congregation said liberation theology suffers from "a disastrous confusion between the poor of the Scripture and the proletariat of Marx [the founder of communism]." Advocating that wealth be shared is adopting Marxist ideas, the Congregation stated. Bringing those ideas into the Church makes it a church primarily concerned with class differences and excludes people who do not view Christian duty in the same way.

In Central America, where so many people are both Christian and poor, clearly this debate on what the Church should do for the poor is important. The following viewpoints debate the role of Christianity in Central America.

"We bring good news to the poor. The good news includes democracy, a democracy that, first and foremost, means the right to eat."

Christians Help the Poor in Central America

Blase Bonpane

In the following viewpoint, Blase Bonpane supports the actions of church groups in Central America. He argues that many church members have been harassed or killed because their support for Central America's poor challenges an unjust social order. These true Christians, Bonpane states, work for justice for all people, not just the wealthy or those in power. Bonpane worked as a Maryknoll priest in Central America before he was expelled from Guatemala for his political activism. He directs the Office of the Americas, an educational foundation and peace organization, and is a professor at the University of California in Los Angeles. He has written the book, *Guerrillas of Peace: Liberation Theology and the Central American Revolution.*

As you read, consider the following questions:

1. Who is labeled a communist in Central America, according to Bonpane?
2. How have traditional church teachings prevented people from being politically active, according to the author?
3. What point does Bonpane make by describing his decision to stop baptizing starving babies?

"Liberation Theology as a Force for Change," by Blase Bonpane in *Central America: Democracy, Development, and Change,* John M. Kirk and George W. Schuyler, eds. (Praeger Publishers, an imprint of Greenwood Publishing Group, Inc., Westport, CT, 1988), pp. 143-148 passim, © 1988 by John M. Kirk and George W. Schuyler. Reproduced with permission.

These observations are based on many years of experience as a Maryknoll priest in Guatemala, from where I was expelled when I began to denounce the horrific realities of life and death there. In Guatemala when the poor attempt to organize, they are called communists. Many people whom I served as a priest in Guatemala died because they were called communists. I once asked a death squad leader why one of our most promising students had been selected for torture and death. "Because he is a communist," was the reply. When asked how that was determined, I received a second answer: "We heard him say he would give his life for the poor." According to these standards, Jesus is a communist in Guatemala. We cannot say the Lord's Prayer and fail to do the will of God on earth. In Guatemala today, a new person is being formed. This new, revolutionary person insists that human values be applied to government. This leads to a ruthless reaction from government. Important freedoms are lost, and undesirable "freedoms" are acquired. Children should not be free to die of malnutrition. No one should be free to die of polio or malaria. Women should not be free to be prostitutes. No one should be free to be illiterate. The loss of these "freedoms" is essential for a people to make their own history. An important tool in bringing these changes about is the theology of liberation—the kind of theology that made the early Church an immediate threat to the Roman Empire. . . .

What Democracy Is

Forty thousand people died today of violence, principally by starvation. We should note that they died in places that have freedom of the press. Ironically, many of them couldn't read. Most of them would have enjoyed the freedom of the press—if they had owned the printing press. In light of these facts, we can appreciate the great many myths about what democracy is, or isn't. Democracy enshrines the right to be free of the violence of starvation, and that right is an important one. Liberation theology in Central America needs to state this clearly and unequivocally—despite the confrontation (and church censure from certain quarters) that will result. To avoid one's responsibility in so stating is to be a poor Christian. . . .

The theology of liberation contrasts with what can be called the "theology of empire." What does empire want of people? It wants first and foremost, nonaction. It wants people to do nothing. It wants conformity. It wants people to let some authority figure make decisions. It wants to pacify everybody. Much of theology has been oriented toward pacification. First and foremost, the wholesaling of guilt ("You are very evil"), to be compensated for gradually by the retailing of forgiveness, very slowly. This accompanies the skillfully crafted sermons heard in most of our churches: first of all perfect yourselves, then someday you'll be able to change someone else. So, we don't do anything today because we're not perfect yet, and the same is true for tomorrow, and so on. By waiting until we are perfect before doing anything, inaction goes on forever.

James Yang. Reprinted with permission.

Liberation theology, on the other hand, maintains that people are on this earth to make history. They are not here as spectators at a football game; they are here to participate in the football game. The future created will depend on each of us. We are co-creators with the Almighty. The creative force of God is with us.

When we go out to evangelize, we bring good news to the poor. The good news includes democracy, a democracy that, first and foremost, means the right to eat. That right is beautifully crafted into the Nicaraguan Constitution, together with the right to a job, a decent house, free medical care, and free education. It's incredible what poor countries can do. Why can't the United States do the same?

On the Side of Justice

Liberation theology knows that God is on the side of justice and when injustice is done, that is un-Godly. We know that God is on the side of peace. We know what side God is on and we can make the necessary judgments. Don't fall into the liberal trap, saying both sides are the same. No, they are not the same. I have been observing the Central American revolution in one form or another for some twenty-five years. The two sides have nothing in common. They are not the same at all. One side works for the children of Central America. The other side practices rape and torture and summary execution. Look at them, and learn to discern. . . .

We Should Build the Kingdom

Jesus was never seen promoting the building of churches, nor did He travel around promoting church attendance terribly much. We should therefore ask ourselves: should we build the church as we know it as an institution, or should we build the kingdom? The answer, of course, should be to build the kingdom. Let's build clear signs of peace. In the United States, where has the kingdom been? It's been in the streets, in the civil rights movement, in the peace movement: these are movements whose people have been crucified. Look at the example embodied in the assassination/crucifixion of Martin Luther King. He opposed the Indochina war, and he said that our country was on the wrong side of these revolutions. We should be with these revolutions around the world, he claimed—and he was right.

For liberation theologians, the New Testament is much more meaningful in our times. We should not allow any institutions —including the churches—to oppress or to enslave. We should not allow them to instruct us about what to do with our conscience. The individual has to make those decisions. To do that, we must free ourselves from the stifling bureaucratic side of organized religion; we can then become free persons and participate in some of the rites that we loved, and appreciate them more than ever. In Guatemala I decided one day, after baptizing a few scraggly-looking babies, near Chichicastenango, not to baptize any more hungry babies. Before anything else, these children needed vaccinations. After that they needed to be assured of food, and after they looked healthy, and were healthy, then we could talk about baptism. Until then it would simply be an empty exercise.

Liberation theology is divisive, pitting friends and relatives against each other. Far from being unhealthy, though, these divisions are absolutely essential: they were essential for Martin Luther; they are essential now. You have to decide who represents the truth—someone who speaks in the name of power from the episcopacy or a few peasants who gathered together to read the Gospel. Was the former Archbishop of Managua who defended the Somozas because "all authority comes from God" to be believed, or the *muchachos* who fought against *somocismo?*

Revolution really begins the moment people read and discuss the Gospel and come to decisions on what they are going to do about their lives.

Defining Real Sin

In the case of Central America, liberation theology, the struggle for peace and social justice—what many understand as the revolution—exists to help bring about the Kingdom of God. We can achieve this goal. It's not simply a matter of the glorification of a specific political struggle, but rather of saying that people have the *right* to that specific political struggle, and of our seeking to understand—selflessly and objectively—their goals. As Christians, though, we need to stop simply thinking of our personal sins, of being shocked by four-letter words and not nuclear missiles. We have to define what sin is, and we have to identify the real sins. A real sin is the fact that 40,000 children died today who did not have to die—that's a sin. The real sin is that there are diseases that are tolerated in El Salvador, while hundreds of millions of dollars are spent in military aid. That is a crime. As we begin to attack the visible real devils of the world we live in (and not the false ones our governments, the media, and the churches present before us), we'll discontinue the practice of reciting silly little personal peccadillos to the clergy—and become more holy in the process.

*"If [U.S. church people had denounced
Marxism] . . . ten years ago, the poor of Central
America would now be at peace."*

Christians Naively Support Oppression in Central America

Michael Novak

Some of the most vocal critics of U.S. policy in Central America
have been church groups. Michael Novak, the author of the following viewpoint, criticizes the actions of these church groups.
Novak maintains that these groups do not work on behalf of the
poor or for human rights, as they claim, but naively support
Cuba's Communist government and Communist rebel movements. If church people truly wanted to help Central Americans, he argues, they would support the efforts of the U.S. and
moderate, democratic forces in the region to establish peace.
Novak, a philosopher and journalist, directs social and political
studies at the American Enterprise Institute, a think tank in
Washington, D.C. He is also a former ambassador and presidential adviser. His books include *Confession of a Catholic*, *The Spirit
of Democratic Capitalism*, and *Will It Liberate?*

As you read, consider the following questions:

1. Why does the author believe many U.S. Christians support
   the wrong side in El Salvador?
2. Why are the churches vulnerable to the actions of leftists,
   in Novak's view?

Michael Novak, "Subverting the Churches." Reprinted by permission of *Forbes* magazine,
January 22, 1990, © Forbes, Inc., 1990.

Many U.S. church people hate to be called "Marxists." All they want, they say, is to "side with the poor." That in itself is noble. Why, then, don't they denounce Marxist violence in Central America—Cuba, Nicaragua and Salvador—violence whose burden falls most heavily on the poor?

Naive Church People

If they had done this ten years ago, the poor of Central America would now be at peace. Instead, they argue as Cuba argues at the U.N. [United Nations]. They support the same forces and oppose the same enemies as Cuba. They may not share all of Fidel Castro's values, but, politically, they do his work. The interpretation many naive church people give of El Salvador, for example, is that the U.S. supports an "oligarchy" that brave church people, solely interested in "helping the poor," must oppose.

I remember the famous story from Journalism 101 about the reporter who cabled that the hand of God smote Johnstown with a devastating flood. His editor cabled back: "Forget flood. Interview God." If the rulers of El Salvador are a small, permanent oligarchy, why aren't they being interviewed and profiled? Why can't we at least see their photos? No journalist seems to have found any "oligarchy" to interview.

A Voice of Moderation

In the weeks before his death, Father Ignacio Ellacuria, the brutally murdered rector of the Jesuit University, publicly warned the rebel leaders, some of whom had been his students, that they lacked popular appeal, that their acts of terrorism had turned many people against them and that their dream of a popular insurrection was fantasy. Father Ellacuria's polling showed they had less than 10% popular approval.

Publicly, the good father urged support for President Alfredo Cristiani's efforts to reach a negotiated peace. Father Ellacuria was a voice for moderation and, in this instance, for giving U.S. policy a chance. Thus his cruel murder, with five of his fellows, was not only morally barbarous but (if done by anyone supportive of the government) politically stupid as well.

During the violent uprising, the rebels announced that within three days they would control the capital and on the fourth day topple the government. They intended to penetrate President Cristiani's home and seize or murder him. In fact, the poor of El Salvador, as Father Ellacuria predicted, refused to accept the arms the Farabundo Marti de Liberacion Nacional (FMLN) offered them.

During this urban assault, a reporter for *The Washington Post* recognized union leaders and human rights workers with weapons in their hands, shouting from the barricades: "Now we are not a front. We are the FMLN." This goes far beyond "helping the poor." Reports also persist that several unit leaders of the guerrilla uprising were foreigners from Europe and elsewhere.

Chuck Asay, by permission of the *Colorado Springs Gazette Telegraph.*

In Costa Rica, the five Central American presidents declared the FMLN illegitimate and denounced its dependency on foreign support. Even Nicaraguan President Daniel Ortega sold out his Salvadoran friends.

Who, then, does support the leftists seeking the violent overthrow of the legally elected Salvadoran government? A good many otherwise well-intentioned Americans. Lobbyists for the National Council of Churches, the U.S. Catholic Bishops and other religious bodies are besieging the U.S. State Department, the Congress and their captive congregations in a campaign to denounce not the FMLN but the same Cristiani government that the Central American presidents endorsed and defended. Pro-guerrilla American activists pressured the Nestlé company into refusing to buy Salvadoran coffee, a craven corporate surrender to a noisy minority.

How has the left so thoroughly seized the symbolic organs of the Christian churches? It was easy. Nearly all the churches have since World War II created ever larger central bureaucracies of activists and lobbyists, dedicated mainly to left-wing interpretations of the political world. This is an entirely "new class" in the churches. Most are neither pastors nor religious workers but political professionals. They are good at what they do, and their power is unchecked.

While the rest of the world is rejecting the Marxist social ideal, many of them still cling to it. For 40 years some have avoided showing compassion for the martyrdom of Eastern Europeans under communism. While their ideal seems to be neither Stalinism nor Castro's Cuba, they have entrusted their own moral credibility into the hands of the Sandinistas in Nicaragua and the FMLN, both faithful students of Fidel.

Clinging to a Dying Doctrine

Their commitment to Marxist Christianity in Central America is obvious. If that Marxism fails, that commitment will be shown as utterly misplaced. In defiance of the collapse of Marxism elsewhere, they cling to their faith. Try to give them argument, and you will see.

"[Liberation theology] addresses both the inner concerns of each person's relationship with God and the outward concerns of forming a better, more just society."

Liberation Theology Promotes Justice in Central America

Robert McAfee Brown, interviewed by *U.S. Catholic*

Robert McAfee Brown is professor emeritus of theology and ethics at the Pacific School of Religion in Berkeley, California. He is a former contributing editor to the magazine *Christian Century* and has written several books, including *Theology in a New Era: Responding to Liberation Themes, Unexpected News: Reading the Bible with Third World Eyes,* and *Spirituality and Liberation.* The following viewpoint is excerpted from an interview with Brown in the monthly magazine, *U.S. Catholic.* In it, he argues that liberation theology grew out of Latin American Christians' experience of poverty and violent oppression. Liberation theology seeks to raise the standard of living and end the violence in Central and Latin America, Brown states.

As you read, consider the following questions:

1. How has liberation theology changed traditional Latin American Christianity, according to Brown?
2. Why does the author disagree with the charge that followers of liberation theology encourage violence?
3. How does the author respond to the argument that liberation theology is Marxist?

Excerpted, with permission, from a *U.S. Catholic* interview of Robert McAfee Brown in the April 1989 issue. Published by Claretian Publications, 205 W. Monroe St., Chicago, IL 60606.

How did a white, middle-class male from California get involved in liberation theology?

Two events, in particular, were very important in introducing me to this movement. In the early 1970s I was asked to read and comment on a book called *A Theology of Liberation* (Orbis Books, 1973) written by Father Gustavo Gutiérrez, who was then a little-known Peruvian priest. As I read the pages of Gutiérrez' book, I was flabbergasted. "This is a blockbuster," I said to myself. "This is a whole new way of getting at things—a whole new method of dealing with the issues. If he's right in what he's saying, I've got to start again at square one." In one of the few prescient comments I've ever made, I said in the blurb on the dust jacket of the book that *A Theology of Liberation* might be the most important book of the decade. Sixteen years later I'm still sure it is the most important book written on liberation theology.

A New View

That was my intellectual conversion. I had to start looking at the world through other than white, North American, male, middle-class, Protestant eyes. I had to see through the eyes of the victims of what our middle-class North American community has done to Third World peoples for generations.

On a more personal level, I was made more aware of liberation theology through our daughter, who went to Chile for a year after high school through the American Field Service program. This was in 1973, just three months after Augusto Pinochet had staged his bloody, CIA-backed coup and ousted the socialist government of Salvador Allende. Naturally, we were concerned about our daughter going into such a situation, but we were assured that she would not be put in danger. Fortunately, she was placed in a home where the mother was sympathetic with Allende and she got a sense of what the Chileans had been trying to do. In the space of a few months, our 18-year-old girl grew up; she became a woman. She also saw horrible things.

The house where she stayed was often a refuge for people trying to escape Pinochet's hatchet men. Our daughter would meet young people at the house, and then the same people would be found in a ditch with their throats slit a few weeks later. She saw what terrible risks people must take when they attempt to free themselves from political and economic oppression.

Thus, through our daughter our family got an immediate understanding of how awful the situation in Latin America really is and why themes of liberation are not just intellectual exercises but matters of life and death for the poor of Latin America. Of course, we also made the discovery that many of the repressive governments in Central and South America were in office thanks to U.S. foreign policy. So, we realized that liberation theology addressed issues that were not simply issues to be dealt with "down there" but touched us closely in North America as well.

What is liberation theology?
There is no easy answer to this question. When Gutiérrez wrote *A Theology of Liberation,* it wasn't as if he said, "Listen, I've got top-notch, formal training; and now I'm going to create a theology for the masses." Liberation theology came from below, from the underside of history, from the poor and oppressed people of Latin America who tried to relate their own personal experiences to similar biblical experiences and the message of Jesus. Like all true theologies, it addresses both the inner concerns of each person's relationship with God and the outward concerns of forming a better, more just society, in such a way that the supposed distinction simply disappears.

Before this movement, theology had come from folks on top—the people with degrees who knew six languages and could situate themselves in great centers for learning and create new theories. Gutiérrez received the traditional training: Louvain, Rome, Lyons—but when he got back to Peru, he discovered that his scholarly training didn't really fit the situation.

A Different Situation

Why not?
Because in Central and South America the majority of the people struggle against seemingly insurmountable odds to get rid of very repressive governmental regimes. They have suffered terrible injustices and indignities. Yet, for hundreds of years, they were conditioned by all the authorities, including the church, to accept their lot in life without complaint. The crucifix, which is the major symbol of Christian faith in Latin America, was interpreted in such a way that it became a teaching instrument for passivity and acquiescence. People were told, "See the Son of God up there on the cross? Is he crying out? Is he trying to rock the boat? Is he trying to organize a labor union? No, he's accepting God's will for him. Who are you to think that you have a right to complain? Your situation may be difficult, but how much more difficult was Jesus'—to have suffered and died on the cross for the redemption of the world?"

These are the kinds of things the people heard for centuries. But, little by little, in the last 25 years or so, a handful of people began thinking, "No, what's going on here is terribly wrong." They looked at the crucifix and said, "What a horrible thing to have happened there. How could it be that somebody who tried to love the world should have been treated in such a way by society? We've got to see to it that such brutality doesn't keep happening. We've got to see to it that we have a society where those who try to give of themselves in love to others are not destroyed."

How did liberation theology begin to take shape?

166

Small groups of Christians began forming what became known as base communities, where members without any particular academic training or skills—some of whom were illiterate—met and talked about the problems they were facing. They would then relate their experiences to what was happening in Jesus' ministry or in other biblical times. So, what is being called the liberation-theology movement continues to grow out of these small communities of the disadvantaged. Priests and theologians are sometimes involved, and they help to bring order to the stories the people tell of their experiences and then try to relate the events to faith. Often small groups of laypeople meet in someone's home or in a church and in what we Protestants would call Bible study, where they make connections between their plight and that of Jesus of Nazareth. They see clear connections between their own situation and that of the disciples gathered around Jesus. The crucifix, for example, has become a catalyst for realizing that someone suffering on the cross is not the picture of life that God intends to be the final story of human existence.

Persecuted for Serving the Poor

This defense of the poor in a world deep in conflict has occasioned something new in the recent history of our church: persecution. . . . There have been threats, arrests, tortures, murders, numbering in the hundreds and thousands. As always, even in persecution, it has been the poor among the Christians who have suffered most.

It is, then, an indisputable fact that our church has been persecuted. But it is important to note why it has been persecuted. Not any and every priest has been persecuted, not any and every institution has been attacked. That part of the church has been attacked and persecuted that put itself on the side of the people and went to the people's defense.

Oscar Romero, Address at the University of Louvain, February 2, 1980.

Why do you think this movement caught on?
It started, as we've been discussing, out of the situation of oppression in which people found themselves. But there is also another factor. This may be where my inherent Protestantism comes to the fore, but it seems to me that the most important resource these people have developed for reflection on their situation is the Bible. I used to think that one reason liberation theology developed was that Catholics had rediscovered the Bible, but I think that it's truer to say that they *discovered* the Bible. The Bible was not that important in traditional Spanish

Catholicism. It's only been since *Divino afflante Spiritu,* an encyclical on the Bible in 1943, and most of all out of Vatican II that Catholics began to take Bible study very seriously.

So, because the Bible became a real instrument for discerning God's will, the biblical story brought an incredible new vitality to Catholics, especially in Latin America. The old stories speak of the liberation of a people in bondage, and people who are part of the contemporary liberation movements are getting nourished by liberation themes in Isaiah and Amos and Jeremiah. The Exodus story is now seen as a liberation paradigm. When critics charge that liberation theology is nothing but warmed-over Marxism, they need to be reminded that a person doesn't have to go to Marx to discover that there's injustice in the world; Isaiah does that very well, as do all the biblical prophets.

The Bible's Meaning for Latin Americans

How does the Bible speak differently to Latin Americans?

Because their own story of extreme poverty and oppression has forced them to deal with injustice in the world, Latin Americans are energized and fortified when they discover that fighting injustice has been a continual struggle throughout history. In fact, the whole biblical story is the story of this struggle. The biblical God is on the side of widows and orphans and the oppressed. The God of the Bible tries to enlist all humankind into sharing in that struggle. As people share in the struggle, they find resources from God to help them continue. They know it's not going to be easy or simple or risk-free, but they discover through biblical stories that it was never easy or simple or risk-free. Yet, they are reassured by the fact that these ancient people carried on and put themselves on the line and realized that the concerns of God were tilted in their direction rather than in some other direction.

This method of biblical reflection is a basic contribution of liberation theology. Liberation theology is not so much a new content as a new method. The method consists of starting where people are in the midst of the struggle, engaging in that struggle, and then reflecting on that struggle in the light of Christian tradition. Gutiérrez defines this process very nicely. He says that theology is always "the second act." The first act, he says, is commitment—and by that he means commitment to the poor. As people begin to engage in the struggle to help the poor, then theology gives them a framework to help them reflect on what they're doing. . . .

Why does liberation theology make North Americans nervous?

The two biggest perceptions, which are really misperceptions, are that supporters of liberation theology are violent and

Marxist. Let me say a word about each. On the violence charge: I think critics are talking a cheap shot. People committed to liberation nowadays have to face the issue of violence—not because they're raising the issue, but because they live in societies that are already violent. Moreover, violence is not taking place only when somebody is getting stabbed or raped or shot. The countryside can be very peaceful, but violence can be all over the place if the people in the countryside are starving to death. This understanding of violence is a very important breakthrough in theological and ethical thinking. Theologians are now saying that it's just as much an act of violence if a child dies of starvation or is permanently brain damaged by malnutrition as if you had stuck a bayonet in that child's stomach.

The Example of Jesus

In Jesus the poor see the one who carries on a practice calculated to transform an oppressive society into a communion of sisters and brothers, a society of justice in conformity with the ideal of the reign of God. . . . Jesus' death on the cross, his execution as an alleged blasphemer and subversive, is seen in Latin America, where Latin Americans too are slaughtered as blasphemers and subversives, as the most authentic demonstration of Jesus' quest for the transformation of his society—of his love not only for the individual, poor or rich, but for the masses of the poor—as the demonstration, therefore, of a political, liberative love as well.

Jon Sobrino, *Spirituality of Liberation*, 1988.

This kind of violence, which is sometimes called structural or institutional violence, is present everywhere; so those in the liberation struggle have to decide how to deal with it. Staging armed revolution or physical violence is way down on the list of real responses to the oppression people endure. In fact, in most situations armed revolution would be morally irresponsible. Look who's got all the guns. Not the starving peasants. But there sometimes are extreme cases where resorting to violence becomes necessary—just as it became necessary to go to war to stop Hitler or to engage in a revolution to overthrow Somoza.

What about Marxism?

Although very few Christians adopt a Marxist worldview, some of them do discover that sometimes it helps to look at the world with the help of certain Marxist categories to understand particular situations more clearly. The best example is class struggle. Marx didn't invent class struggle. He only noticed it. He saw there was a ruling class and a subjugated class; and the small group of people with most of the power dominated and oppressed the masses of people who had almost none of the power.

There is no question that that state of affairs describes most of the Third World. It isn't much help here in the United States because we don't have such tidy class distinctions, but it is useful to Third World countries in discovering what their situation really is and how to begin to break out of such a painful, brutal cycle.

A person doesn't have to invoke the name of Marx to make that kind of analysis; but in Latin America, when liberation theology began to develop out of the experiences of the poor, there were many Marxists who were working with the poor. Catholic priests had a difficult time with this fact at first because Marxists had always been presented as the church's enemy. Eventually, however, the involved clergy saw that these presumably dreadful Marxists were actually doing what the church should have been doing in the *barrios*, namely, helping the poor get organized and to work for genuine social change. Many priests and nuns realized that for years they had been catering only to the elite of society. They saw that taking food baskets to the poor at Christmastime, while it needed to be done, was not enough and that a Band-Aid operation was not what Jesus meant by doing justice.

A Community Working for Change

So what does doing justice look like for Latin American Christians?

The first thing they try to do is help one another survive. That's a full-time job—surviving the death squads and the poverty. That can take almost all of the energy the people have, but somehow small groups of fifteen or twenty people keep finding the time to get together at their tiny base communities. Here they are reminded that they remain totally powerless on their own. Being alone is not only inefficient, it is not Christian. There's no such thing as a solitary Christian. Christians are always in community; therefore, these small groups of people decide that they must get the community involved in making change. They begin to analyze what's wrong with the city government and how power is being abused, and they discover that people who rock the boat disappear. They decide that it's time to stage rallies or marches and make more demands on the government, and they write and preach and try to persuade people to build up a significant enough social force to be taken seriously and effect change. Little by little, change does come.

*"Liberation theology . . . wonderfully serve[s]
interests of very concrete political forces—[the]
Marxist Left, and most particularly the int[erests]
of the Soviet Union and Cuba."*

Marxist Ideas Corrupt Liberation Theology

Humberto Belli

Humberto Belli was a Marxist and a member of Nic[aragua's]
Sandinista movement until he became a Christian in 19[77. From]
1979 to 1982, he was an editor at the daily newspaper, *L[a]*
In 1982, Belli moved to the U.S. He has written *Ni[caraguan]*
Christians Under Fire and *Breaking Faith*. He also teache[s theol-]
ogy at the Franciscan University in Steubenville, Ohio[. In the]
following viewpoint, Belli argues that communists hav[e allied]
with advocates of liberation theology, a doctrine which e[mphasizes]
solidarity with the poor. Belli believes this combin[ation of]
Christianity and communism threatens democracy in the[region.]

As you read, consider the following questions:

1. What events does Belli believe contributed to the loss [of]
   Catholicism's traditional hostility toward communism[?]
2. In the author's view, what ideas make liberation theol[ogy]
   Marxist?
3. How have liberation theologians transformed organiza[tions in]
   Nicaragua, El Salvador, and Guatemala into Marxist gr[oups,]
   according to Belli?

Humberto Belli, "Liberation Theology and the Latin American Revolutions," in *Th[e Politics]*
of Latin American Liberation Theology, Richard L. Rubenstein and John K. Roth, ed[s.]
Washington, DC: The Washington Institute Press, 1988. Excerpted with permissio[n of the]
Washington Institute for Values in Public Policy.

171

Revolutions in Latin America are taking place in a largely Christian environment. That the fate of these revolutions is entwined with dynamics of that environment is a safe assumption. At any rate, that became the explicit assumption of one of the most influential revolutionary leaders of Latin America, the legendary Che Guevara. He once said: "When the revolutionary Christians dare to give an integral testimony, that day the Latin American revolution will be irreversible.". . .

Insightful leaders such as Guevara had the intuition that in order to win or at least to neutralize the non-Marxist forces in the region, Latin American Marxists had to devise new strategies.

Religious Anticommunism

Fear of communism among large segments of the traditionally Roman Catholic and agrarian societies of Latin America posed a formidable obstacle. The Roman Catholic church, influential as it was in the education establishment, among the upper and middle classes, and among the peasantry, militantly and almost unanimously preached against communism. Several papal encyclicals and church documents explicitly and unambiguously condemned it. As early as in 1846, Pope Pius IX had called communism an "infamous doctrine."

Leo XIII had defined communism as "the fatal plague which insinuates itself into the very marrow of human society only to bring about its ruin."

Even more stern were the expressions of Pius XI. In his famous encyclical, *On Atheistic Communism*, he referred to "the most persistent enemy of the church," "a satanic scourge," which used a "propaganda so truly diabolical that the world has perhaps never witnessed its like before." Pius XI concluded that "Communism is intrinsically wrong, and no one who would save Christian civilization may collaborate with it in any undertaking whatsoever."

The ban on any collaboration between Christians and Communists became official church policy in 1949, under Pius XII, when a decree of the Holy Office forbade Catholics to join the Communist party or encourage it in any way. Before theological relativism and pluralism were acceptable in Latin America, Vatican views were taught and understood as possessing near-absolute authority. . . .

Landmarks of change in the Christian world were Vatican II and the Latin American Bishops' Conference at Medellín, Colombia (1968). Although neither of these events explicitly questioned the traditional teachings of the church about communism, they brought significant changes in emphasis and style, together with some new openings that set in motion long-dormant forces and launched proposals with unforeseen conse-

quences. A discussion of whether these and similar results were a faithful reflection of the spirit and intent of those who framed Vatican II falls outside the scope of this analysis. Suffice it to say that in the wake of the council, changed circumstances made it easier for new theological interpretations to gain a foothold within the church. . . .

Liberation Theology

For a variety of reasons, interpretations of those who tended to view Marxism as a friendly set of ideas found very fertile soil among Latin American theologians and religious who had studied or were studying in Europe, and who had been influenced by different European liberal theologians, especially Germans like Jürgen Moltmann, Rudolf Bultmann, and Johannes Metz. Many of these Latin American theologians became co-authors and advocates of what is known as liberation theology, particularly after the Peruvian priest, Gustavo Gutiérrez, published a book in 1971 in which he expounded systematically the key tenets of such a theology.

A Disastrous Confusion

In its positive meaning the "church of the poor" signifies the preference given to the poor, without exclusion, whatever the form of their poverty, because they are preferred by God. The expression also refers to the church of our time, as communion and institution, and on the part of its members, becoming more fully conscious of the requirement of evangelical poverty.

But the "theologies of liberation," which deserve credit for restoring to a place of honor the great texts of the prophets and of the gospel in defense of the poor, go on to a disastrous confusion between the poor of Scripture and the proletariat of Marx. In this way they pervert the Christian meaning of the poor, and they transform the fight for the rights of the poor into a class fight within the ideological perspective of the class struggle. For them, the "church of the poor" signifies the church of the class which has become aware of the requirements of the revolutionary struggle as a step toward liberation and which celebrates this liberation in its liturgy.

Congregation for the Doctrine of the Faith, *Origins*, September 13, 1984.

The originality of Gutiérrez and his followers' views was not their call for social justice or their call for political involvement on behalf of the poor—as it is often assumed in less-informed church and journalistic circles in the developed world. Such concerns had been present among Christian Democrats and among socially minded Christians in the tradition of Jacques

Maritain and Pierre Teilhard de Chardin. The magisterium of the church, as expressed in several encyclicals such as Leo XIII's *Rerum Novarum* (1891), had also upheld the rights of workers to demand just wages and had issued calls on behalf of social justice.

A Marxist Perspective

New in Gutiérrez's thought, however, was his adoption of the idea of class struggle as framed by Marx: that society is divided into two irreconcilable social classes, the oppressed and the oppressors; that conflict—not reconciliation—between the two must lead to a classless, harmonious society once the private ownership of the means of production is abolished; and that all views and institutions (theology and the church included) respond to either the class interests of the oppressed or to the interests of the oppressors.

Gutiérrez provides an explicit summary of the movement's adoption of Marx's perspectives:

> Only a class-based analysis will enable us to see what is really involved in the opposition between oppressed countries on the one hand and dominant peoples on the other. . . .
>
> [The] people must come to power if society is to be truly free and egalitarian. In such a society private ownership of the means of production will be eliminated because it enables a few to expropriate the fruits of labor, . . . generates class division in society, and permits one class to be exploited by another. . . .
>
> Only by eliminating private ownership of the wealth created by human labor will we be able to lay the foundations for a more just society. That is why efforts to project a new society in Latin America are moving more and more toward socialism.

Even a superficial acquaintance with Marxist doctrine readily suggests that these views are indistinguishable from those espoused by Communist and Marxist organizations around the world. But in fact, the liberationists' originality was their attempt to express the idea of class struggle in Christian terms, or, that is to say, their effort to provide theological legitimacy for many of Marx's key ideas. Sin was identified, for practical purposes, with unjust social structures, namely, capitalism and Western imperialism. Deliverance from sin, salvation—oftentimes made synonymous with liberation—was to be achieved by revolution. The revolutionary cadre, the party, was to be the Moses or the Messiah, leading the people away from oppression into the promised land, or into the kingdom of God—oftentimes identified with socialism. That society was divided into the oppressed and the oppressor meant that Christians had to take sides with the former as against the latter. No neutrality in this regard was possible, either for the individual Christian or for

174

the church. Both had to take an "option for the poor"—usually identified as the oppressed or the proletariat—which necessarily meant entering the conflict-ridden arena of politics and embracing the projects of the poor. The catch here is that by "the poor" liberationists meant, practically and theoretically, the revolutionary poor, those aware of their class interests and actively seeking the overthrow of capitalism. . . .

Although allowance should be made for a certain diversity of positions among the liberationists, the centrality of revolution (the belief that revolutionary political action against the ruling socioeconomic order is the way to make Christian love for the poor truly effective) became the distinguishing mark of the theologians who are either identified or who identify themselves with this perspective.

Marxist Indoctrination

When I was working as a Jesuit priest, under the orders of my superiors, we utilized Marxist-Leninist ideology, and worked with the poor, in order to influence the poor to opt for a road of violent revolution. We were perfectly capable of indoctrinating minds with the theology of liberation and Marxism-Leninism. . . . Using our authority as priests, we were successful with the poorest masses.

Luis Pellecer, quoted in *Washington Inquirer*, January 12, 1990.

Deprived of two characteristics, however, the primacy of political action and of revolutionary goals, liberation theology would be difficult to distinguish from other Christian stands. Keep the option for the poor and take away political militancy and one gets Mother Theresa of Calcutta. Keep political militancy and take away revolution and you get Christian democracy or reformism.

Liberationists also shared among themselves and with the Latin American Marxists the belief that the basic—although to some of them not the exclusive—source of the misfortune and oppression of the poor in Latin America was to be found in the dependency of the economies of the subcontinent or their subjugation under the yoke of Western imperialism.

In view of the basic premises of liberation theology and of their justification in religious terms, it is easy to see how it provided for the first time a means to build a bridge between Marxists and Christians, and how it could help to achieve the type of integration of Christians into the revolutionary process of which Che Guevara had once dreamt a feat of portentous consequences. . . .

The first country to use the Marxist-Christian alliance on a significant scale was Nicaragua. The results were awesome. Two liberationist priests, Fathers Ernesto Cardenal and Uriel Molina, who were enchanted by the Cuban revolution and founded the first two Christian base communities (CEBs) in Nicaragua, were approached by Sandinista leaders in 1969 and 1971. The priests felt honored by these overtures and began working in coordination with the Sandinistas. Their key role was to teach the basics of liberation theology to mostly middle-class Catholic young people. Part of the instruction was a conscientious effort to wash away the students' possible misgivings about communism and to teach them the virtues of "Marxist analysis.". . .

The Contribution of New Recruits

For the Sandinistas the revolutionary Christian recruits that Father Molina was educating in his base community in Managua proved to be an attractive discovery. As mostly upper-class youngsters, the revolutionary Christians were able to provide the Sandinistas with some key logistical support (cars, farms, homes, and so on). But they offered far wider opportunities also. Its association with the revolutionary Christians gave the FSLN [Sandinista National Liberation Front] an air of greater legitimacy and increased its appeal domestically and abroad. . . .

Young converts to liberationism flocked to the Sandinista Front, while internationally a handful of Catholic priests involved with the Sandinista revolutionaries championed the Sandinista cause and even made appeals in the United States Congress to cut off aid to Nicaragua's dictator, Anastasio Somoza. Simultaneously committees of solidarity with the people of Nicaragua appeared around the world, oftentimes under the auspices of church-related groups. . . .

The Nicaraguan revolutionaries did not face the potential problem of democratic allies who could become disillusioned on discovering their true politics, or who would attempt to wrest control for themselves. Significantly, the Nicaraguan Marxists soon found that they had nothing to fear from the Christian liberationists. The dynamics of their theology was such that with the passing of time many adherents totally embraced the cause of Marxist Leninism, including its atheistic aspect. In a set of interviews with the North American Marxist Margaret Randall, Father Fernando Cardenal confessed how many of the converts to liberation theology ended up abandoning their Christian faith, an experience also undergone by the twelve student founders of Father Molina's first base community. And even if some converts did not follow the entire process, the way they defined key religious concepts was such that they all fit, without representing a challenge, into the Marxist ideological framework. This was evident with some of the priests who admitted that one could not be a Christian without being a

Marxist. . . .

On July 19, 1979, the Sandinista revolution triumphed. Its leaders knew that a key ingredient of their success had been the participation of Christians. In the words of a communique of the Sandinista Front, Christians had taken part in the revolution "to a degree unprecedented in any other revolutionary movement in Latin America and perhaps in the world. This fact opens new and interesting possibilities for the participation of Christians in revolutions elsewhere.". . .

Liberation Theology Revitalized Marxism

By the early eighties the multifold political advantages that liberation theology was offering to the radical Left were becoming apparent. A most important advantage was its contribution to weakening the old barrier that religion had represented for the advancement of communism. In this regard, liberation theology not only has tried to make Marxism acceptable to Christians but has in a way "baptized" most basic Marxist concepts. Another related contribution has been to provide a medium through which Marxist ideas can be presented to the public, using a terminology that, because of its reliance on biblical and theological terms, does not alienate the faithful. This new, "edited" version of Marxism, has also helped to revitalize it among some segments of the Western intelligentsia, at a time when its prestige was fading. Liberationism provides new ground for political utopianism, although one which is now less sociologically based than it is theologically inspired—thus making it more immune to scientific refutation.

The effectiveness of this approach is complemented by the fact that it is often promoted by religious personnel, who are more likely to be trusted than are traditional political activists. In this regard, the bulk of the Marxist political message—revolutionary class struggle against Western capitalism to impose collectivistic socialism—has gained access to a vast pool of human resources strategically located in the societies of Latin America. . . .

What was done in Nicaragua involving some basic Christian communities and agricultural organizations like CEPA [Center for Agricultural Education and Training] has been done in several other countries. In El Salvador FECCAS (Federation of Christian Peasants of El Salvador) was transformed into a militant organization that later joined the BPR (Revolutionary People's Bloc), which was linked to the guerrillas. According to Phillip Berryman, "there is a direct line from basic Christian communities' pastoral work to the popular organizations to a Marxist guerrilla organization."

A similar process has been followed in Guatemala, with the CUC (Committee for Peasant Unity), an outgrowth of the pastoral agents of the Justice and Peace Committee; in Brazil, where some of the basic Christian communities work with the Marxist (Workers' party); and in several other countries. . . .

The undisguised joy of communists at the phenomenon of liberation theology could be a cause of potential embarrassment for some liberationists, which may have been one of the reasons behind recent attempts of some of these theologians to deny the Marxist character of their theology and the movements they support. Father Ernesto Cardenal candidly admitted in an interview that "some liberation theologians maintain that they are not influenced by Marxist philosophy at all. In this case it is necessary to discern whether they say this for tactical reasons, so as not to be compromised politically." Yet, it is also plausible that some liberationists may feel uncomfortable with the real possibility of becoming agents of totalitarian political ideologies, and that they are now trying to work for a distinguishable Christian liberation. To what extent this effort should be recognized as a genuine one will depend largely on the theologians' willingness to renounce the Marxist myth that class struggle is the road to a classless society—as was the Vatican's instruction on liberation theology in 1984; on their capacity to develop a more specific—and democratic—agenda of social change; and on their readiness to denounce oppression from either the Left or the Right, implying their willingness to sever ties with, or distance themselves from, Marxist dictatorships. As long as these criteria are not met, it will be legitimate to consider liberation theology as an ideology that, independently from the original motivations of its framers, wonderfully serves the interests of very concrete political forces—the Marxist Left, and most particularly the interests of the Soviet Union and Cuba.

A Trojan Horse

As the cases of Cuba and Nicaragua indicate, the tactical blurring of the revolutionaries' true goals has been a decisive element in their victories. Liberation theology has come to enrich their arsenal of tactics, providing not only a means to cancel out the potential obstacles of the religious factor, but a way to harness it in behalf of the revolutionaries' agenda. In some respects, it may not be out of proportion to refer to the prevailing type of liberation theology as a true Trojan horse, whereby the aged and relatively decadent Marxist-Leninist ideology has found a new capacity to penetrate the Christian churches and the West—this time in religious garments.

What it takes to confront such a challenge is something to be answered by serious study and effort. The first step, however, is to realize that the challenge is very serious.

178

"[Evangelicals] regard violence as deeply repugnant. They're not going to engage in any revolutionary movement that involves violence."

The Evangelical Movement Benefits Central Americans

David Martin, interviewed by Tim Stafford

David Martin is a sociologist who teaches at the London School of Economics and at Southern Methodist University in Dallas. His book, *Tongues of Fire,* details the growth of evangelical Protestantism in Latin America. The following viewpoint is excerpted from an interview Martin gave to Tim Stafford, a senior writer at the magazine *Christianity Today.* Martin argues that evangelical Christianity has grown in Central America because it meets the spiritual needs of the people. It offers people comfort in a region torn by war, he contends, and redefines Christian duty in a more meaningful and positive way than traditional Catholicism.

As you read, consider the following questions:

1. Why does Martin disagree with the argument that evangelical religion is imported from North America, not a religion indigenous to the region?
2. What do the new religions teach about family life, according to the author?
3. In Martin's view, what are the political attitudes of the evangelicals?

From "The Hidden Fire," by David Martin, interviewed by Tim Stafford, *Christianity Today,* May 14, 1990. Reprinted with permission.

You have used the term revolution *to describe what is happening in Latin America today. Why that word?*

Well, it is a revolution. This has been the most Catholic region in the world, and people have assumed that it's never going to be anything else unless it turns toward secular radicalism, and particularly toward Marxism.

What nobody took into account, and what is quite revolutionary, is this enormous growth of what I call radical primitive Protestantism. Perhaps 10 percent of Latin Americans are now Protestants. If you take into account that the number of people actively involved in the Catholic church may not be more than 15 percent of the population, you have a situation where the active adherents on either side are not so very different in number. There would be some parts of the continent where those people who are involved in the church are more Protestant than Catholic.

Now that is a revolutionary situation. Nothing like it had been anticipated. It's as extraordinary in its way as the growth of Islamic fundamentalism, or the totally unanticipated events that have occurred in Eastern Europe.

An Unreported Phenomenon

While we have read a good deal about those phenomena, most Americans have not heard much about the growth of Pentecostalism in Latin America. Why is that?

People tend to believe that the only things that matter are political events. What they don't look at are the changes that have been going on underneath. These are often utterly unreported.

That's one element. The other element is that lots of North American and European intellectuals, including Christian intellectuals, have a view of the future in which liberation theology plays the central role. So there is a kind of incapacity to see what is actually happening on the ground.

I saw this while going around Guatemala in a bus full of intellectuals of one kind or another. The most obvious thing to me was that we were passing a storefront church every 200 yards. Yet when the guide pointed out that something like 66 percent of Guatemalans were Catholics, nobody bothered to ask where the other 34 percent could be. These scholars showed a combination of visual blindness plus an utter lack of curiosity.

Is that partly because Pentecostalism or Protestantism in Latin America has been assumed to be socially irrelevant, that it's a sort of North American transplant?

There is this feeling that Protestant converts are making off in the wrong direction and are in some way giving up their cultural inheritance for a mess of North American pottage. But I believe that is a misapprehension of the actual situation.

People tend to look at the fact that the televangelists are active in Latin America. "The 700 Club," Jimmy Swaggart, and Oral Roberts beam their programs all over the continent, from Jamaica to Argentina. People also tend to note the economic support that comes from the North American versions of these churches.

Changing Society for the Better

Scientific explanations recognize the ways in which becoming evangelical helps a person get control of his or her life and ultimately change society for the better. Latins who become evangelicals frequently better their lives by acquiring personal disciplines (reinforced by their new community's values) that make them marketable employees. As John Maust, editor of *Latin America Evangelist,* points out, these converts no longer participate easily in Latin America's culturally sanctioned corruption; they become honest, industrious, and thrifty. . . .

These changes in personal lifestyle translate into increased prosperity for families and communities, as entrance into nonhierarchical Christianity provides opportunities for developing indigenous leadership and organizational skills.

David Neff, *Christianity Today,* May 14, 1990.

But when you look at what is actually happening on the ground, you see that when these churches become indigenous—and some of them have been indigenous for pretty well the whole of the century—one of the things that helps them to take off is the degree of their independence. . . .

Not only that, these groups are extremely fissile. They're always breaking off one from the other. So there's no question of some kind of central control from North America. In many countries, there are anything up to 350 separate groups working. So you have a completely open market in religious offerings and many of them are very, very localized. Whatever the marginal influence that the power and attraction of the United States may be, whatever the help provided by intermittent finance, especially in the area of communications, the basic reasons have to be sought in Latin America itself.

Creating a New World

What do you see as those basic reasons and aspirations in their culture?

They feel that the world in which they are living isn't giving them what they hoped for. It doesn't offer them betterment. And they come to feel that everything associated with that world is reprehensible. That includes the Catholic church. So they walk out.

It doesn't really matter whether the Catholic church at this particular juncture is saying that it's in favor of social change, or whether it's allied with the landowners or the military. That's not the political level at which these people are thinking. They are asking, What kind of commitment, here and now, in my locality, will allow me to rope myself together with other people so that we can start creating our own free social space? They're trying to create a new world inside the New World.

For example, they are tied to the old system through the commitments of godparents. There are a whole set of complex obligations to those whom they take as godchildren. These are constantly tying them in to the old system. The same is true of the fiestas. You have to make certain expenditures as part of your contribution. Now all that belongs to the *status quo ante*, and what these people do is to walk out, and reconstitute themselves as brothers and sisters in Christ—that's their phraseology.

Meaning that they do not continue to hold those old obligations.

That's right. They move out of those obligations, not straightforwardly because they are obligations, but because they tie them in to everything that was before.

Reconstituting Family Life

What about family life in Latin America? Is that also transformed?

Yes, that's an excellent point. Pentecostals and the other Protestant groups are very keen on reconstituting the family and also altering the psychology of the male. Those two things go together. I talked to one Protestant who said, "We try to explain that a real man is not a man who can bed three women and shoot three men, but the one who can cope with one woman for one whole lifetime." That is revolutionary in Latin American terms. It means giving a new kind of language to the male. This is the point made by a very interesting American anthropologist named Elizabeth Brusco. What she points to is the way in which the language of male preachers is full of the images of female nurture. There's a softening of the Latin American male.

It's important to recognize that the majority of Pentecostal and other evangelical groups are women, and quite a lot of them are abandoned women. They are creating a kind of female trade union, if I could put it that way, against the depredations of men. Within the church they find men who are better disposed toward them. There's a kind of coming together of well-disposed males, and of females who want to find well-disposed males. There's a kind of internal marriage market.

In the outside world they are very, very vulnerable. But within the disciplines of the church, they're much less vulnerable.

As a British sociologist, how did you become aware of the growth of Protestantism in Latin America?

I got interested in it because of my study of the growth of secularization worldwide, particularly in Christian countries. Although it is perfectly possible in many countries to chart a change from a religious faith to a more secular faith, in the Latin American case it looked as though something quite unusual was happening.

The other element of my interest was that, coming from a Methodist background, I was interested in the growth of the Methodist movement and its relationship to the English industrial revolution. That led me to ask, Could something rather similar be happening in Latin America?

An Indigenous Movement

Latin American Pentecostals are running a very successful indigenous movement, and they are able to do that without any American support whatever. Of course, they are to some extent drawn by images of betterment which have their major point of origin in the United States, but it is not clear to me why such aspirations should of themselves attract condemnation.

David Martin, *National Review*, September 29, 1989.

What similarities do you see?

One is that if you trace the ancestry of Pentecostalism, it leads back to Methodism. Most of the work on the origins of Pentecostalism lead back to holiness movements in the U.S., and those holiness movements are often breakaway movements within Methodism. So there is a line of ancestors there.

But the other more important connection is of a whole variety of effects associated with Methodism that apparently are being repeated in Latin America today.

Masses of world-shattering changes were going on in England in the mid-eighteenth century, and at the same time there was appearing a form of voluntary religiosity that was methodical —that's what the word *methodist* means. It provides a kind of discipline of the self and a discipline of time that would go well with factory discipline. It also would provide a kind of emotional release at the same time. So there's a double advantage—that you're methodical on Mondays, and you express yourself on Sundays.

This kind of religion, while breaking the historic church-state connection, was of a moderate democratic kind, not inclined toward revolution, but inclined to teach people ways of running their own show. It provided them with all sorts of skills. But it didn't lead them in a revolutionary direction. Whereas in France, for example, the breakup of the church-state relationship ended up in a very volatile, aggressive revolutionary situation.

Catholicism's Response

What about the Catholic church in its relationship to these changes? Does it perceive the growth of Protestantism as a threat?

It certainly is the case that the Catholic church sees these groups as a threat. From time to time the Catholic church publishes a report on what is generally called the problem of the sects. That's a rather pejorative way of putting it. The implication is that sects really have no right to be operating in what is fundamentally Catholic territory.

Many of the historic Protestant churches have actually respected that supposition. But the Pentecostals and the more strongly evangelical groups didn't. Their success has really shaken the Catholic church. Instead of being a monopoly, they are in a market situation. That means they have to compete and look at what it is that is providing the dynamic for Protestant expansion. . . .

You've painted a picture of a movement that is largely invisible to international experts, which has had a radical impact on about 10 percent of the Latin American population. Do you have any thoughts on what we can expect as time goes on?

I think in order to assess that you have to take the view that change in daily culture has very important effects on a wider scale.

Perhaps I could draw a comparison. The myriad black churches in America were quietist in their attitude toward politics. Nonetheless, they created a very large social space in which they could be themselves, in which they could decide what happens, and in which they learned certain skills of administration and speaking. Those capacities could be deployed outside the sphere of the church and could also emerge in movements, like the civil-rights movement. At some point you've built up a whole series of latent capacities, and then at a given juncture, that can emerge into the political realm.

Protestants' Impact on Politics

So you would anticipate that Pentecostalism or Protestantism will make a more public, political impact in Latin America.

Yes. Many people feel that Pentecostalism is either a form of nonpolitical quietism, or that it's actually utilized by dictatorial regimes of the Right. The first thing I want to say is that these people have nothing much to anticipate from the powers of the Right or the Left. In particular, they have nothing to anticipate from either left-wing violence or right-wing violence. Those things have simply meant, so far as they are concerned, grief and suffering. So one finds that they regard violence as deeply repugnant. They're not going to engage in any revolutionary movement that involves violence. That works itself out in various ways. For example, in Nicaragua they didn't oppose the government [of the Sandinistas] on the whole. But they did not want to be drafted into collective work, particularly military operations. That kind of reorganizing of society along military lines simply doesn't appeal to them, and they'll not get mixed up in that.

It's a shift outside of the system of violence, anything that involves the shedding of blood. Here they are related not simply to Methodism but to early Christianity. They have a deeply pacific view of the world. The development of a segment of the population that will have little to do with violence seems very significant to me.

Beyond that, most of the evidence suggests that they tend to behave rather similarly to other people of their status and situation. They are concerned with who can do something about the sewage, for example. Here the pastor acts like most of the other pressure groups. They go and talk to their political representative, saying, "Perhaps I can find you some useful votes from our church if you do something about the situation in our locality." It's traditional patronage politics that involves them rather the same way as it involves anybody else. . . .

A Fervent Movement

Do you anticipate that Protestantism will grow to be dominant in Latin American culture?

Here I go back to what I said about the effect it has on the Catholic church. The more the Catholic church feels itself under pressure, the more it may become like its competitors.

If you simply take the statistical trends, it would quite soon be the case that Guatemala is a Protestant country. The Brazilian trends also point to very extensive Protestantization. But it's usually the case that there is some self-limitation in a movement like this. If people are walking out of something, it becomes a little bit difficult when there is nothing left to walk out of. The drama has got a kind of built-in deceleration.

But I also want to add that whereas in previous situations the group has simply risen socially and become part of the culture, in this situation they constantly recover themselves by splitting. There is a deep suspicion of the kind of cooling off that will destroy their cutting edge. They have an amazing capacity to renew their fervor.

"Fundamentalist converts . . . 'often show little perseverance and normally fall into political or religious indifference.'"

The Evangelical Movement Harms Central Americans

Penny Lernoux

Penny Lernoux (1940-1989) was an award-winning investigative reporter based in Colombia. She was the Latin American correspondent for the magazines *The Nation* and *National Catholic Reporter*. Her books included *Cry of the People, In Banks We Trust,* and *People of God.* In the following viewpoint, Lernoux argues that the growth of evangelical sects in Central America is worsening the violence in the region. According to Lernoux, the evangelicals support right-wing military dictatorships and U.S. policies designed to keep the dictators in power. The growth of religious fundamentalism endangers those working for peace, human rights, and self-determination for Central America, she concludes.

As you read, consider the following questions:

1. How has the growth of evangelical fundamentalism affected Guatemalans, in the author's view?
2. Why does the author believe so many Central Americans have converted to the Protestant sects?

Two decades ago, when Protestant fundamentalists and evangelicals were regarded as religious "crazies" in many parts of Catholic Latin America, converts tended to keep their religion to themselves. "People didn't admit to being evangelical," recalled an evangelical pastor in Bogotá, "because they feared they would be rejected by their neighbors and employers."

Today when, in the pastor's words, there are "evangelicals everywhere," adherents not only openly proclaim their born-again conversion but actively seek recruits on buses, street corners and in parks. Such big-time evangelists as Argentine Luis Palau and U.S. television preacher Jimmy Swaggart pack city stadiums with tens of thousands of enthusiasts; only the pope draws larger crowds. Unlike the previous generation of evangelicals, today's conservative Protestants in Latin America are aggressively challenging Catholicism's religious monopoly—and succeeding.

The Catholic Church's own surveys show how serious is the challenge: every hour 400 Latin Americans convert to the Pentecostals or other fundamentalist or evangelical churches. One-eighth of the region's 481 million people belong to fundamentalist or evangelical churches, and in some countries, such as Guatemala, it is estimated that half the population will have switched into those churches by the end of the century. Not since the mass baptisms of Latin American Indians by the conquering Spanish in the 16th century has Latin America witnessed a religious conversion of such magnitude. . . .

Religious Tensions

Evangelical inroads into traditional Catholic territory have led to religious tensions throughout the region. For example, in Cotopaxi province in central Ecuador, a dispute between Catholics and evangelicals led to two deaths and nearly 100 injuries after two Indian evangelists denounced their Catholic brothers to the local military.

Chilean Catholics took umbrage at statements by televangelist Swaggart during his visit to Santiago in early 1987, after he defended the regime of General Augusto Pinochet and congratulated him for having expelled the devil—meaning the left—in the 1973 coup. The fundamentalists, who have converted approximately 10 per cent of the Chilean population, including 15,000 members of the armed forces, are called "Reagan cults" by Catholic critics because of their close association with such Reagan supporters as Swaggart, Pat Robertson and Jerry Falwell. But the fundamentalists are popular with the Pinochet government because of their political conservatism and emphasis on passive acceptance of authority—in contrast to socially activist Catholic groups inspired by liberation theology.

Tensions are particularly severe in Central America where the religious war has coincided with a shooting one. On the one hand there are U.S. and Central American Catholics who oppose Washington's policies in the region; on the other, fundamentalists who support them. Thus the competition for souls has strong political overtones. The most serious clashes have occurred in Nicaragua, where a pro-Sandinista "popular church" composed of Catholics and mainline Protestants is at odds with the anti-Sandinista fundamentalist churches, and in Guatemala, where one-quarter of the people have converted to the fundamentalists.

Persecuting Catholics in Guatemala

In the 1970s and early '80s, Guatemala's Catholic Church suffered severe persecution under a succession of military regimes because of its defense of human rights. During the 1982-83 administration of the born-again General José Efraín Ríos Montt, for example, several Catholic priests and hundreds of catechists were murdered. While Catholics were being slaughtered, U.S. fundamentalist churches, including Ríos Montt's church, the California-based Gospel Outreach, received the army's blessing to evangelize among the Indian population. Even after the military ousted him for abusing the principle of separation of church and state, Rios Montt continued to enjoy the support of Pat Robertson.

A Shift to the Right

The political sympathies of evangelicals shifted radically to the right by the 1960s. The rise of the pentecostals marginalized the mainline churches, pushing to the forefront a conservative theology that preached individual salvation and an imminent Second Coming. . . .

This rightward shift of evangelical politics has been encouraged and applauded by the U.S. government. While the extent of the collaboration in Latin America between the Religious Right and Washington is still unknown, Washington certainly has recognized the political power of evangelicals in the region.

The Resource Center Bulletin, Winter 1988.

Catholic bishops in Guatemala—as elsewhere in the region—resent the persecution by governments seen to be in league with U.S. fundamentalist missionaries. "The sects divide the community," said Guatemala City's Archbishop Próspero Penados, who argued that their growth has aided the Reagan administration in dominating the region partly by weakening Catholic unity. "The church is the only voice that defends the people" against persecution by governments allied with the United States, he said.

The results of such divisions can be tragic, as demonstrated by the desperate plight of the Guatemalan village of Semuy. The residents were forced to flee their homes in 1981 after a member of a fundamentalist sect denounced the village as "communist" to the local military command because the people would not convert from Catholicism. The sect's leader, with a bandana covering his face, led the army into the village and pointed out people he claimed were "subversives." Thirty-four villagers were taken away and never seen again; the rest fled into the mountains, where they hid for five and a half years. When they eventually emerged, under the protection of the local Catholic bishop, they found that Semuy was controlled by the same fundamentalists responsible for the 1981 raid.

Guatemalan fundamentalists remain unmoved by such suffering, for they believe the Indians are "demon-possessed" because so many of them are Catholics (at least nominally). And since demons are associated with communists, the Indians are subversives, too. Similarly, U.S. fundamentalists working in Guatemala agree with Swaggart that Catholicism is a "false cult" and the "doctrine of devils." A letter from the U.S. head of one fundamentalist group in Guatemala, for example, spoke of doing "battle in the heavenlies" against the pope and his priests so that God would "arise and scatter [Guatemala's] enemies and establish her upon the rock that is Jesus Christ." The tone of U.S. fundamentalist and Pentecostal radio programs, which blanket Central America, is equally aggressive. Indeed, the only point on which the fundamentalists agree with the Catholics is that the religious war is likely to get worse. "Guatemala could become another Northern Ireland," predicted an evangelical pastor in Guatemala City.

Funding the Contras

U.S. fundamentalists have also been deeply involved in the Nicaraguan contra war. Robertson's Christian Broadcasting Network has been among the biggest contributors, raising millions of dollars for food, medicine, clothing, vehicles and other aid for so-called Nicaraguan refugees who also happened to be contras, or for Miskito Indians drawn into the contra struggle. Although Robertson tried at first to pretend that CBN contributions were not meant for the counterrevolutionaries, his organization did not deny that the supplies were being shipped through intermediary groups with close ties to the Reagan administration or that they were being sent to the war-torn Nicaraguan-Honduran border, where the contras were headquartered. In contrast, such politically neutral refugee aid groups as the

Office of the United Nations High Commissioner on Refugees purposely located their Honduran relief camps at least 33 miles from the border to avoid involvement with the hostilities. That CBN's refugees were indeed contras was confirmed by Mario Calero, the brother of contra leader Adolfo Calero, who said that the counterrevolutionaries were an army of refugees. "Some of the refugees are freedom fighters," he said, adding that he considered himself one of them.

Aggressive Evangelicals

Part of the concern in Latin America about this U.S.-inspired proselytism stems from the often militaristic phrasing used by aggressive evangelists. Mission literature bristles with references to establishing beachheads in certain areas, spiritual warfare, winning a country for Christ, joining God's Army, and victory campaigns. The "onward Christian soldiers" enthusiasm of many U.S. missionaries does not sit well with Latin Americans all too familiar with U.S. imperialism and military intervention.

The technological power of the evangelicals and their colonizing mentality have also evoked Latin American fears and defensiveness. Mission societies commonly talk of mounting campaigns to evangelize the continent's "hidden" or "unreached peoples." Evangelical literature refers to the heathen and pagan tribes of the third world. Missionaries are encouraged to reach out to the "frontier" peoples, as if the center of the world were the mission centers of southern California.

The Resource Center Bulletin, Winter 1988.

Fundamentalists' humanitarian aid served two purposes: it freed other funds for the purchase of military hardware, and it was enlistment bait for the Miskitos, thousands of whom had crossed the border after periodic clashes with the Sandinistas. Hungry and penniless, the Indians often had no choice but to join the contras, although they hated them at least as much as they did the Sandinistas. "It's clear that the border relief programs are not designed to meet the long- and short-term interests of the Miskitos, but rather are designed for political purposes as a conduit of aid to the contras," a relief official said.

God's Plan

Robertson never hid his feelings on the matter. He frequently likened the contras to freedom fighters, and when the U.S. Congress balked at providing more aid in 1985 he went on television to denounce the "craven submission of our leaders and Congress to the demands of communism, [which] makes you sick to your stomach." Robertson also visited a contra training

190

camp in Honduras to preach his fundamentalist gospel and distribute good cheer. "I think God is in favor of liberty and justice and He is against oppression," he told the troops, comparing the contra struggle to the American Revolution. "If we can do something to help these men fight for freedom, I think it is perfectly in God's plan." The visit, which was later shown on U.S. television, shocked some religious leaders because of the way Robertson seemed to be saying that the contras had God's blessing. Richmond's Bishop Walter Sullivan, among the most out-spoken Catholic opponents of U.S. aid to the contras, was so outraged that he publicly criticized Robertson, saying "I cannot imagine Jesus reviewing troops." Robertson furiously replied that he had not been reviewing troops and that, if Sullivan didn't watch his words, he might be in trouble for "libel and slander.". . .

Many fundamentalists . . . [believe] in a "God-is-an-American" religion that dismisses any challenge to U.S. hegemony as the work of the devil. "You can make a strong case for saying the American way is synonymous with Christianity," claimed William Murray, a U.S. evangelical active in the fundamentalists' contra-aid operations.

Catholic critics claim that the primary attraction of the "American way" is the money lavished on religious converts by their U.S. sponsors. But while poor Latin Americans agree that gifts of food, clothing and other handouts are an incentive to convert, many say that the gifts are less important than the welcoming religious atmosphere in fundamentalist churches. Most are small and neighborly, with the pastor living in the same block as his congregation. They also respond to the people's yearning for religious symbols, or "popular religiosity," through dancing, popular songs and physical gestures such as raising arms to heaven. In contrast, traditional Catholic churches serve vast numbers of people who have little or nothing in common, and they are often impersonal "supermarkets for the sacraments," as some liberation theologians call them. Rituals frequently seem remote and cold, and community relations, so important to the impoverished urban newcomer, are virtually nonexistent.

Christian Base Communities

While the Catholic "supermarket" offers little challenge to the fundamentalists, the church's Christian base communities are a different matter. Like the fundamentalist churches, the communities are small—usually 15 to 20 families per group—and composed of people from the same village or neighborhood. The overwhelming majority are poor, and many are strengthened by communitarian traditions. Like the born-again churches, the base communities offer a more personalized religious environment, solidarity, a sense of equality and a means to express popular religiosity. Indicative of their appeal, the base community

191

movement has grown from a single village in rural Brazil to more than 100,000 communities throughout Latin America.

The time span for this development—two decades—parallels the explosion of fundamentalism. However, religious and sociological studies demonstrate that wherever a base community flourishes, fundamentalists are unlikely to gain a foothold, because the community meets the religious needs of the people. And whereas the fundamentalist church supports the status quo, the base community is a force for social and political change. It also leads to a new, more mature and enduring faith, in contrast to that of fundamentalist converts who, as liberation theologian Pablo Richard has pointed out, "often show little perseverance and normally fall into political or religious indifference."

The Church Fears Democracy

But while experience shows that the Catholics' answer to the fundamentalists lies in the base communities, only a minority of bishops have strongly pushed for them because of the Vatican's frequently voiced concern that they are too "horizontal"—meaning that they are a democratic influence on a hierarchical church —and liable to become involved in social and political issues. The Roman Curia is also suspicious of the communities because they are a popular expression of liberation theology. Thus, although the church has the means to meet the fundamentalists' challenge, it is afraid to apply it.

a critical thinking activity

Evaluating Sources of Information

When historians study and interpret past events, they use two kinds of sources: primary and secondary. Primary sources are eyewitness accounts. For example, the diary of a church worker in Honduras describing her experience there would be a primary source. A book about religion's role in Honduras that used the worker's diary would be a secondary source. Primary and secondary sources may be decades or even hundreds of years old, and often historians find that the sources offer conflicting and contradictory information. To fully evaluate documents and assess their accuracy, historians analyze the credibility of the documents' authors and, in the case of secondary sources, analyze the credibility of the information the authors used.

Historians are not the only people who encounter conflicting information, however. Anyone who reads a daily newspaper, watches television, or just talks to different people will encounter many different views. Writers and speakers use sources of information to support their own statements. Thus, critical thinkers, just like historians, must question the writer's or speaker's sources of information as well as the writer or speaker.

While there are many criteria that can be applied to assess the accuracy of a primary or secondary source, for this activity you will be asked to apply three. For each source listed on the following page, ask yourself the following questions: First, did the person actually see or participate in the event he or she is reporting? This will help you determine the credibility of the information—an eyewitness to an event is an extremely valuable source. Second, does the person have a vested interest in the report? Assessing the person's social status, professional affiliations, nationality, and religious or political beliefs will be helpful in considering this question. By evaluating this you will be able to determine how objective the person's report may be. Third, how qualified is the author to be making the statements he or she is making? Consider what the person's profession is and how he or she might know about the event. Someone who has spent years being involved with or studying the issue may be able to offer more information than someone who simply is offering an uneducated opinion; for example, a politician or layperson.

Keeping the above criteria in mind, imagine you are writing a paper on Christianity's role in Central America. You decide to cite an equal number of primary and secondary sources. Listed below are several sources that may be useful for your research. *Place a P next to those descriptions you believe are primary sources. Place an S next to those descriptions you believe are secondary sources.* Next, based on the above criteria, *rank the primary sources, assigning the number (1) to what appears to be the most valuable, (2) to the source likely to be the second-most valuable, and so on, until all the primary sources are ranked. Then rank the secondary sources, again using the above criteria.*

P or S		Rank in Importance
_____	1. A speech by the Archbishop of El Salvador, criticizing the military for threatening priests.	_____
_____	2. The book *Christians and Central America: An Analysis,* written by a member of the organization American Atheists.	_____
_____	3. Viewpoint one in this chapter.	_____
_____	4. An editorial in the *Los Angeles Times* by a professor who argues that the Jesuits are encouraging violence.	_____
_____	5. An interview with a Pentecostal missionary working in El Salvador.	_____
_____	6. A documentary series on public television about the controversy raised by the growing evangelical movement in Guatemala.	_____
_____	7. Viewpoint four in this chapter.	_____
_____	8. A Miami reporter's story on the visits of church groups to Nicaragua.	_____
_____	9. A book by a British graduate student, titled, *The History of Evangelism in Central America.*	_____
_____	10. A 1980 speech by a U.S. senator criticizing El Salvador's military.	_____
_____	11. Transcripts from the Puebla conference on liberation theology. Conferrence participants included many Central American religious workers and advocates of liberation theology.	_____
_____	12. A position paper drafted by an association of wealthy Guatemalan land owners, titled, "The Church and Subversion in Guatemala."	_____

Periodical Bibliography

The following articles have been selected to supplement the diverse views presented in this chapter.

Phillip Berryman	"El Salvador's National Debate," *Christianity and Crisis*, December 12, 1988.
Christianity and Crisis	"Reflections: Liberation Theology Here and Now," June 12, 1989.
Merrill Collett	"The Cross and the Flag: Right-Wing Evangelicals Invade Latin America," *The Progressive*, December 1987.
Crisis	"Salvadoran Lessons I," January 1990.
Alfredo Cristiani	"In El Salvador, a New Arena Party," *The New York Times*, March 15, 1989.
Dinesh D'Souza	"Cry of the People," *Crisis*, April 1990.
Don Feder	"Into the House of Bondage," *National Review*, March 5, 1990.
J. Bryan Hehir	"We Must Do More than Deplore the Killings We Finance," *Los Angeles Times*, November 24, 1989.
Patrick Lacefield	"Can This War Ever End?" *Commonweal*, March 23, 1990.
David Martin	"Speaking in Latin Tongues," *National Review*, September 29, 1989.
Maryknoll	"Oscar Romero: Martyr's Spirit Lives Among the Peoples of Central America," special issue, March 1990.
Michael Novak	"Structures of Virtue, Structures of Sin," *America*, January 28, 1989.
Peter O'Driscoll	"Letter from El Salvador," *America*, April 16, 1988.
Daniel Pilarczyk	"Bishops in White House Meeting Discuss El Salvador," *Origins*, January 4, 1990.
David Oliver Relin	"The Church of the Powerless," *Scholastic Update*, February 9, 1990.
John K. Roth	"How Latin American Liberation Theology Sees the United States and the USSR," *The World & I*, May 1988.
Robert A. Sirico	"Replacing Liberation Theology," *Reason*, June 1990.
Jon Sobrino	"The Ecumenism of Blood and Love," *Sojourners*, February/March 1990.
David Stoll	"A Protestant Reformation in Latin America?" *The Christian Century*, January 17, 1989.

Is Peace in Central America Possible?

Chapter Preface

The yearning for peace in Central America is made more poignant by Central America's modern history of violence and instability. Most Central American countries have known only brief periods of peace in the last two centuries.

The 1800s and early 1900s were marked by the efforts of the newly independent Central American nations to establish governments. This process was often violent. Between 1820 and 1965 there were forty-five coup d'etats in the five Central American countries of Guatemala, Honduras, El Salvador, Nicaragua, and Costa Rica. Unfortunately, the coups established a destructive pattern and divided the nations' peoples into camps bitterly opposed to each other. This pattern has continued to the present. For example, in the 1980s, Guatemala experienced five changes of government, three of these changes being violent coups.

Whether Central America's tumultuous history can be overcome is hotly debated. The following viewpoints consider whether and how the nations of Central America can establish peace.

"The violence of the past must be recognized, but so too must the dangers and futility of violence in the future."

Peace in Central America Is Likely

James D. Riley

In the following viewpoint, James D. Riley argues that the countries of Central America are becoming peaceful and stable nations. The violence and upheaval of the last two centuries are part of a normal process, according to Riley. He argues that Central American nations will follow Mexico's path, a country with a violent past that is now stable and at peace. Riley teaches history at the Catholic University of America in Washington, D.C. He specializes in Central American, Latin American, and Mexican history.

As you read, consider the following questions:

1. According to the author, what factors cause Central America's upheavals?
2. What historical and current events does Riley use to support his explanation of Central America's conflicts?
3. How did Mexico make the transition from violence to peace, according to Riley?

From James D. Riley, "History, Politics, and Nation-Making in Central America," in *Culture, Human Rights, and Peace in Central America,* George F. McLean, Paul Molina, and Timothy Ready, eds. Lanham, MD: University Press of America, 1989. Reprinted by permission of the publisher.

The troubled politics of most Central American nations have been poorly understood by many observers and subjected to a range of ideological interpretations. To those of the Left, the upheavals are perfectly described by dependency theory and seen as the result of foreign economic domination—mainly by the U.S. In alliance with local allies, this is seen as attempting to prevent legitimate reforms and the rise of strong national states which could contest its economic control of the region. To the Right, the situation is a textbook case of Marxist intrigue in which the Soviet Union, using its surrogate, Cuba, supports violent revolution and stirs the troubled waters formed of legitimate social grievances and inevitable economic problems. Its attempt is both to create trouble for the United States, and to establish docile satellites in the affected region. What joins these two views is a belief that the most significant causes of instability come from outside the region.

I would like to suggest another way of viewing the problems, one in which instability is the result of an internal dynamic of change. In each country this involves a struggle to cope with a changing sense of national identity which requires a redefinition of national purpose and a restructuring of national institutions to serve that purpose. The Central American states are, in effect, undergoing the same type of quest which was undertaken in the United States 200 years ago. Just as its constitution represents a uniquely American solution to its problems, so too will the Nicaraguan, Guatemalan, Honduran and Salvadoran solutions. (It would appear that Costa Rica has already found its own.)

Colonial Patterns

The concept of the Nation-State is a foreign import to Central America. During the pre-Colombian period, the Indian societies in Central America advanced little beyond the tribal or independent village level. At various times conquest kingdoms—the Quiche being the most notable of the local variant—developed, but they invariably disintegrated and left relatively untouched the basic loyalties of the people to their tribe, village or clan (calpulli-chinamit). Moreover, although the Indians of Guatemala and Honduras were intimately involved in the trade patterns of Meso-america because of the cacao which could be grown on the Pacific Coast, the result of commerce was not the growth of regional unity, but rather conquest. The Lingua Franca of Central America became Nahuatl, a vestige of the establishment of trading colonies of Teotihuacanos, Toltecs and, ultimately, Aztecs in the region.

The lack of any large scale regional confederations such as dominated central Mexico, combined with the disunity of

Spanish conquest groups, made the Spanish occupation of Central America both difficult and costly. First of all, rather than one conquest, there were several. The defeat of major groups such as the Quiche or the Cakchiquel did not pacify the region because they controlled relatively little territory; consequently, more *entradas* to deal with lesser tribes were necessary so that warfare extended for a long period of time. Moreover, the character of the Spanish conquest differed dramatically from that of Mexico. Competing groups assaulted Central America from both north and south. Finding no great kingdoms to be controlled or wealth to be distributed, they used the region's human and material resources for further exploits outside the region, particularly in the Peruvian campaigns. The fact that the conquistadores had no particular interest or concern in maintaining and nurturing the Indian groups—as they did, for example, in Mexico and Peru—gave the early conquest period its particularly rapacious character, numerous examples of which would grace the writings of Bartolomé de las Casas.

The Democratic Awakening

More than 100 years of pitiless dictators, injustice, and widespread poverty, precede the democratic awakening in Central America. Either to live in violence for another century, or reach a peace overcoming the fear of liberty; this is the challenge facing my little America. Only peace can write a new history.

In Central America, we are not going to lose faith. We are going to change history.

Oscar Arias Sanchez, in *Nobel Costa Rica*, 1989.

The ultimate result of the conquest combined with the short-lived boom in cacao demographically and socially to devastate the region. The wars, enslavement and forced movements of Indians, and disease combined to destroy populations. . . .

Destroying the Social Structure

The Indians who remained alive in the North as the sixteenth century closed were also in vastly different social and economic circumstances. Much of the pre-Colombian political and social structure had been destroyed. Obviously, the Spanish went about the task of dismantling any political organization which could rival them; consequently, any nobility above that of the village disappeared. The social structure within the villages also changed. Spaniards relied on local nobles—caciques—as intermediaries between the Spanish and the Indian worlds, but economic pressures from both above and below soon reduced this

200

nobility to the level of the *macehuales*. Consequently, the villages became an undifferentiated economic mass and in governance tribal chiefs were replaced by elders.

The consequence of the century of tragedy was to destroy the pre-Colombian cultures and any basis for reestablishing the pre-conquest unities which had existed. In addition, the new societies which were created by the Spanish presence had only the most ephemeral unity and inter-community contact. While Spaniards searched for the "produit moteur" which would bring them prosperity, great demands were made on the Indian communities—forcing them to relate to the outside world and to engage in a larger market economy. But by the middle of the seventeenth century, the search for valuable commodities had been shown to be a failure and Central America lapsed into a period of somnolence which by and large would last until the late nineteenth century. . . .

No Formal Unity

In practice, the formal political unity of Central America was non-existent. Indian communities were self-governed and, except when it was unavoidable, turned only infrequently to any outside political authority. In the Ladino regions of Costa Rica, Honduras, El Salvador, and Nicaragua, political life revolved around the cabildo of the dominant town. With little possibility of appeal to Santiago because of distance and poverty, necessary political and judicial decisions were made at the town level. The politics of the cabildo and *corregimiento* were also of interest because, in societies which lacked any economic bases for status, possession of office (both civil and ecclesiastical) offered not only a small salary and some economic opportunities, but also prestige. This is reflected in the colonial rivalries which would plague areas such as Nicaragua after independence.

The ultimate situation, to quote Murdo Macleod, was a Central America that was:

> rural, self-sufficient, poor for the most part, fragmented politically and economically, and culturally introverted. It was during this period that the basis was laid for the modern . . . political and economic divisions of the area, and for the cultural cleavage between 'Indian' and 'Ladino' which hampers Guatemalan nationhood to this day.

Central America achieved its independence as an afterthought. When Mexico obtained its independence in 1821, Spanish authorities in Guatemala, in effect, simply left. Initially, Central America fell into the Mexican "Empire," but in 1823 declared its independence, forming a Federation. Each of the modern nations was a state of that federation. . . .

In the 1840s the Central American Federation formally broke

201

apart and the states became nations. Governors were now presidents; but again very little thought was given to political organization and there was no real concept of the "Nation" and its purpose.

Living in Peace

I believe that through joint effort and through partnership, the day will come when in all nations of the Americas the rule of law prevails, human rights are respected, the strong are just, the weak are secure, and the people live in peace.

James A. Baker III, Speech before the Council of the Americas, May 1, 1989.

The difficulties of modern times stem in part from the attitudes and concerns of the political elites of that time. Thus, in order to consider the failures of "Nation-Making" and how and why elites created systems which excluded the mass of the population, it behooves us to consider the period since 1840 in more detail. However, because an individual consideration of each country is beyond the scope of a short essay of this sort, I would like to select a single country—Guatemala—to illustrate the basic point I am trying to make. . . .

Problems of Nation-Making

Throughout the history of Guatemala there had been a division between Indian and Ladino. After independence the Ladino elite dominated the institutions of the state and conducted a series of policies in line with their perceptions of the interest of the nation. This provoked no violence from the Indian community, not because they were not capable of violence—their support of Rafael Carrera belies that—but because they had no interest in the "Nation" and did not perceive Ladino control and policies as fundamentally dangerous to things they considered important. They were used to exploitation in the form of labor levies and taxes; they had had long centuries of experience with outsiders making demands on them. But they had developed a series of methods for dealing with the demands of outsiders which moderated exploitation and allowed them to maintain the essentials of their world as they saw fit.

Within the Ladino community, political power was exercised by a small elite and usually in an authoritarian manner. The regimes of Justo Rufino Barrios and Jorge Ubico had much in common with those of the colonial governors. Political stability within the Ladino community was the result of essentially satisfied expectations. However, modernization created a middle sector in Guatemala which increasingly desired participation in national institutions. It is these groups—intellectuals, small entrepreneurs, urban workers and bureaucrats—who provided the basic support for the Ladino reform movements of Juan Arevalo and Jacobo Arbenz. Thus in the 1940s and 1950s, conflict increasingly emerged not only between Ladinos and Indians, but also within the Ladino community itself. Violence erupted because the old style of politics could neither incorporate the new demands of the Ladino community, nor deal with the protests of the Indians. The contending parties had no traditional way of talking to each other or of resolving peacefully the problems of each group. . . .

The approach of the military and the old elites will not work. Short of exterminating the entire Indian population (50 per cent of the total population), and totally alienating the middle sectors, violence is not able to bring peace. Conversely, it is rather doubtful that the guerrillas can succeed in exterminating the dominant Ladino groups. Rather, the contending parties have to find a way of incorporating their interests and cultures into a common political system—one which might not be democratic in character —and a shared sense of nationhood. If there is no other basis for nationhood, one might be found in shared distrust with a recognition that the other is not going to go away. Certainly no one can rewrite Guatemalan history to say that the Indian and Ladino communities share a common past and bond of brotherhood. The violence of the past must be recognized, but so too must the dangers and futility of violence in the future.

The Lack of Nationhood

I have dwelt upon the Guatemalan situation because the lack of nationhood and the polarization of the communities is so apparent. But, while the dynamic is different in each case, the same constitutional issue and historical process is operative in Honduras, Nicaragua and El Salvador.

In Nicaragua, for example, the basis for conflict is not ethnic, but rather a traditional political system based on family rivalries. Even during the colonial period, elite families of Leon and Granada vied for control of local offices because, in a money-poor environment which lacked any economic basis for prestige, governmental office provided the only employment and the only way in which elites could distinguish themselves. After independence, these elite families would label themselves Liberal and Conservative, but the labels had little ideological content and their feuds little meaning. The vast majority of the Ladino population lived in rustic isolation as subsistence peasants and ignored these petty feuds.

In the latter nineteenth century, however, the United States intervened for its own purposes and the game became more seri-

203

ous as the financial opportunities stemming from office holding increased. Unwittingly, in its pursuit of its own security and believing that it was fostering democracy, the United States gave one of the players—Anastasio Somoza Garcia—a tool to end the competition.

The *Guardia Nacional* with its monopoly on force stopped the petty warfare, but the political attitudes of the elite remained unchanged. Possession of office brought no concern for the public welfare beyond the welfare of the elites occupying the posts. Despite development, that attitude did not change. As in Guatemala, the emergence of the middle classes during the 1950s and 1960s created tensions when peasants, heretofore outside the process, began to lose their lands to outsiders and to be forced into the cities as laborers.

The Ultimate Consequence

The ultimate consequence of the economic process was that new groups desired a role in the political processes in order to protect their own interests. Instead of being granted entry, however, exploitation increased and became more arbitrary when Anastasio Somoza Debayle took power. He fell because his rapacity alienated even those elites who had supported his father.

The Spirit of Freedom

As a region, Central America is in mid-passage from the predominantly authoritarian patterns of the past to what can, with determination, with help, with luck, and with peace, become the predominantly democratic pluralism of the future. That transformation has been troubled, seldom smooth, and sometimes violent. . . . But the spirit of freedom is strong throughout the region, and the determination persists to strengthen it where it exists and to achieve it where it does not.

National Bipartisan Commission on Central America, January 1984.

The success of that revolution did not resolve the problem of political structures. The parties which combined as anti-somocistas—the FSLN [Sandinista National Liberation Front], the traditional elites, and the newly emerged peasants—still have not found a constitutional system or political process which could incorporate all their interests. Thus, the civil war continues.

My point is that this is a uniquely Nicaraguan problem that must be solved by Nicaraguans. The fact that Costa Rica is not involved and is at peace, despite having much the same colonial heritage, ethnic situation and environment, proves this point. Costa Ricans found a system growing out of their own unique tradition.

Is there any historical precedent for negotiations and compromise between social groups without a shared sense of nationhood and a constitution culturally and politically acceptable to all important groups in the society? In my estimation, the answer is yes: Mexico went through precisely these struggles in the early twentieth century and its constitution of 1917, with subsequent political interpretation from 1917 to 1940, offers an instructive case of how contending groups, while disdainful of each other, can find a constitutional *modus vivendi*.

Political Implementation

The Mexican case is instructive in several ways. First, prior to 1910 the existing constitutional system as well as its political implementation failed to recognize the legitimate interests of an Indian sub-culture. The elites who wrote the constitutions of the nineteenth century were urban, secular and Creole (white) in origin and considered it irrelevant—or regressive—that the majority of the country was rural, intensely Catholic, and Indo-mestizo. As in Guatemala, political relations were characterized by disdain for the others' traditions, and on the part of the dominant creole class, an attempt to exterminate those traditions. Nevertheless, between 1917 and 1940, this dominant creole elite found a way of coming to terms with traditions it abhorred.

Second, while exploitation and considerable disparities in the distribution of income continue (Mexico has the most maldistributed income of any country in Latin America), political scientists report that there is wide acceptance of the political system and very little interest in violent revolution.

Third, the process of developing these compromises on which political peace was based was a very violent one, and one which the United States labeled as "Communist"—actually Bolshevik —and tried to stop.

Finally, Mexico's solution to its problem produced a political system which both functions as a modernizing force and can be seen as compatible with the political traditions of the older communities. Rather than following a North American model totally, or a European ideology such as Socialism or Corporatism, it probably can be described best as an authoritarian democracy. It is an eclectic solution and works precisely because Mexicans ignored foreign entanglements, both ideological and political, and came up with pragmatic solutions to problems which reflected Mexican realities and Mexican traditions.

This final point is my basis for believing that the Central American states can do likewise.

"The prospects for the emergence of long-term peace in El Salvador and Guatemala are very dim."

Peace in Central America Is Unlikely

John A. Booth and Thomas W. Walker

Author John A. Booth is a professor in the political science department at the University of North Texas in Denton. He is the author of *The End and the Beginning: The Nicaraguan Revolution* and chairs the Latin American Studies Association's Task Force on Scholarly Relations with Nicaragua and Central America. Thomas W. Walker is professor of political science and director of the Latin American Studies Program at Ohio University in Athens, Ohio. He wrote *Nicaragua: The Land of Sandino*. In the following viewpoint, Booth and Walker predict that Nicaragua, El Salvador, and Guatemala will continue to be plagued by war. The authors maintain that the repressive policies of powerful elites will cause the region to remain violent.

As you read, consider the following questions:

1. According to Booth and Walker, how do the political situations in each country differ?
2. Why do the authors believe peace is so difficult to achieve in Central America?
3. What factors have prevented peace in Central America in the past, according to Booth and Walker?

John A. Booth and Thomas W. Walker, *Understanding Central America*. Boulder, CO: Westview Press, 1989. Excerpted with permission.

The problem of reducing and ultimately eliminating violent conflict in Central America can be viewed from both a short- and a long-term perspective. In the long run, lasting peace will be achieved only through the creation of more just societies, ones in which economic disparities are reduced and something approximating genuine democracy, based on avenues for free and meaningful participation by the majority of the citizenry, becomes a reality. The history of the five major Central American countries makes this point quite clear. The countries plagued by endemic violence—Guatemala, El Salvador, and Nicaragua—are precisely those that not only suffer from tremendous economic inequities but also have been ruled traditionally by powerful elites that have stubbornly refused to allow effective grass-roots participation or meaningful social and economic reform. The other two countries—Costa Rica and Honduras—though very different from each other, enjoy relative peace precisely because they were free of one or both of the violence-producing characteristics of their neighbors.

Historical Observations

Since the time of the Spanish Conquest, Costa Rica was set apart from the others by the fact that it had a relatively more just society, higher levels of meaningful participation, and a normally flexible elite willing to bend and make accommodations when necessary. Out of this mixture, genuine democracy and responsible government eventually emerged quite naturally. Honduras, though even poorer and more socially backward than its three immediate neighbors, perhaps for that reason never developed the type of unbending and cruelly exploitative elite that emerged in Guatemala, El Salvador, and Nicaragua. In this sense, backwardness may have been a blessing, for instead of using violence and repression as the preferred tactic for dealing with grass-roots mobilization and accompanying demands for social justice, the relatively weak elites of Honduras normally have been forced to rely on tolerance and the rhetoric of reform. Though meaningful democracy is still a distant dream for Honduras, violence at least has been kept at relatively low levels.

If we are correct in these historical observations, it would seem reasonable for us to predict that Costa Rica is likely to continue to enjoy domestic peace, Guatemala and El Salvador will probably undergo continuing conflict or periodic spasms of violence, whereas Honduras and Nicaragua could go either way. Let us take a closer look.

Costa Rica—The probability of violent conflict in Costa Rica would appear to be remote. Elite flexibility, a participatory democratic system, and a relatively egalitarian society make violence both unattractive and unlikely. We should warn, however, that nothing is certain. Should these conditions change, violence might well emerge. If, for instance, the already fragile economy were to deteriorate abruptly and popular unrest were to increase, the elites might be tempted to use force rather than compromise. The potential instrument of that force has been emerging in recent years. Technically, Costa Rica abolished its military in the 1940s. However, the Reagan administration, intent on pressuring the Sandinistas, persuaded the Costa Rican government to modernize and strengthen its Civil Guard. To date, U.S. military aid has trained small border units and increased the Civil Guard's firepower and equipment. The security forces remain small by Central American standards, and Costa Rican observers report little apprehension about an impending militarization. However, if the absence of a military establishment in the past has been a factor favorable to democracy in Costa Rica, any military resurgence should be viewed with concern. . . .

National Security Doctrine

The growth in size, firepower, and professionalism of the Central American armies has been accompanied by an ideological assimilation of the Doctrine of National Security. This Doctrine, which inspired the short-lived tyrannical military dictatorships in Argentina and Brazil and the . . . dictatorship of General Augusto Pinochet in Chile, asserts that the army is the exclusive judge of what is good for the nation. The armed forces have consequently replaced the oligarchies as the controllers and manipulators of the economy and the society, a status of privilege that they understand they enjoy as long as they implement political and economic policies determined by the United States. The recent substitution of civilian presidents for military dictators in Guatemala, El Salvador, and Honduras has not changed the reality. Ultimate power still stays with the armed forces. The civilian regimes exist at the will of the military which determine the parameters within which they can function.

Gary MacEoin, *Central America's Options: Death or Life*, 1988.

Honduras—The future of Honduras is less clear. It has only one of the two characteristics that seem to be most essential for domestic tranquility. That characteristic, the relative flexibility of its elite class, has contributed significantly to its largely non-violent past. The other ingredient, social justice, is missing. Honduras is the poorest of the five countries we have studied. It has the worst social conditions. That those conditions have not generated the levels of unrest that would lead to widespread violence is due largely to the willingness of the elite to allow, rather than repress, grass-roots organizations and to pay lip service to, rather than openly resist, programs of reform. If the already bad economic situation were to deteriorate even more and the elites (backed by their burgeoning U.S.-supplied military) were to opt for force rather than accommodation, the spiral of violence might well begin. However, if past patterns of elite flexibility continue, the levels of violence exhibited in neighboring countries may be avoided for some time. Honduras has developed a disturbing pattern of death squad killings and security force human rights abuses since the early 1980s. These suggest at least some potential for the emergence of a terrorist demobilization campaign like those witnessed in Guatemala and El Salvador. In the long run, the best guarantee for peace in Honduras, as elsewhere, is social justice. For the poorest of Central America's countries, the possibility of genuine improvement in that realm seems remote.

The Sandinista Revolution

Nicaragua—Ironically, Nicaragua in the first several years after the Sandinista revolution had embarked on precisely the type of change needed to bring true stability. As we noted earlier, the new government had encouraged and supported grass-roots organizations, had responded positively to their demands, and had institutionalized input from such organizations into decision-making at all levels. With the volunteer labor of members of the grass-roots organizations, the government had also embarked on a variety of programs in education, health, food distribution, social security, agrarian reform, and housing that had begun to narrow the social gulf between rich and poor. Finally, opposition was generally tolerated, within fairly broad limits, and state-sponsored terror—a fact of life in Guatemala and El Salvador—had become a thing of the past in Nicaragua. Accordingly, on their various visits to Nicaragua during that period, the authors observed an open and peaceful society in which the possibility of civil conflict seemed much reduced.

The end to that brief period of tranquility was externally imposed. Though a handful of right-wing guerrilla bandits had harassed the country prior to 1981, smuggling cattle and killing literacy crusaders, they were a trivial nuisance. After Ronald Reagan was inaugurated in Washington, however, the situation changed radically. A U.S.-organized, U.S.-trained, U.S.-equipped, and U.S.-advised contra army was disgorged into Nicaragua from across both of its borders, and millions of dollars of CIA [Central Intelligence Agency] and National Endowment for Democracy funding were pumped into non-Sandinista media, party, and interest groups in order to maximize domestic internal polarization. The result was considerable death and destruction, a rapid reversal of previously improving economic conditions, and the imposition of various state-of-emergency restrictions on civil and political rights.

© Boileau/Rothco. Reprinted with permission.

As this was being written, it appeared that the contra war was winding down. An agreement signed in El Salvador at the February 1989 Central American presidential summit provided for the dismantling of contra bases in Honduras. Even so, the damage the war had already inflicted on the economy, daily life, social programs, institutions, intra-elite trust, and the human rights situation in that troubled country would, at best, take years to mend. Accordingly, the possibility of returning to the type of domestic peace that obtained in the period prior to the contra war was by no means certain.

Guatemala and El Salvador—The prospects for the emergence of long-term peace in El Salvador and Guatemala are very dim. Both of the conditions that, in any society, seem to be important for domestic tranquility—a relatively egalitarian social structure (or public policy that at least attenuates the worst effects of poverty) and a flexible elite willing to allow and accommodate grass-roots participation—are starkly absent in those two countries. It is doubtful that the formal holding of elections during, or in the wake of, bloody programs of demobilization will contribute in the long run to lasting domestic tranquility, even if those elections are technically clean, as they were in Guatemala in 1985. Regardless of the formal nature of government, the old and violent cycles of protest-mobilization-repression, protest-mobilization-repression, are likely to continue in both countries unless a firmer foundation for social peace is established.

Prospects for Peace

Having discussed the long-term prospects for peace, let us now turn to policies or procedures that might end the current situation of violent civil strife in several countries, at least in the short run. One tactic for short-term peace that has been employed in various parts of the world, including Guatemala and El Salvador, is to try by the use of state terror to demobilize the opposition completely. It is true that if they are willing to be sufficiently brutal, governments can sometimes so terrorize a dissatisfied civilian population as to achieve temporary peace. The Salvadoran *Matanza* of 1932 provides a grisly Central American example: it politically demobilized a whole generation of Salvadorans. However, we would argue that such a tactic is not only morally reprehensible but also extremely short-sighted; peace achieved in this way is seldom permanent.

We believe that the best means for the reduction of tensions and the achievement of peace is negotiation leading to compromise and accommodation. We are not alone in this belief. Almost immediately after the Reagan administration came to power and began issuing bellicose statements about Central America, certain European and Latin American countries started calling for negotiated settlements of the conflicts there, rather than military confrontation. The response of the Reagan administration was a secret, but subsequently leaked, National Security Council planning document for Central America, which, among other things, observed, "We continue to have serious difficulties with U.S. public and congressional opinion, which jeopardize our ability to stay the course. International opinion, particularly in Europe and Mexico, continues to work against our policies.". . .

In late 1986 the Iran-Contra scandal broke, plunging U.S.

211

Central American policy into disarray and seeding grave doubts among Central American leaders about the future of U.S. actions, especially the administration's ability to keep funding the contra war. In the resultant vacuum of U.S. initiative, the peace process sputtered on into 1987. Early that year, president Oscar Arias Sánchez of Costa Rica began drafting a peace proposal. Late that summer Ronald Reagan, anxious to renew military aid to the contras and to lift U.S. policy out of its doldrums, enlisted Speaker of the House Jim Wright as a cosponsor of a "peace plan" for Central America. . . .

Prospects for Development

In the late 1980s, the possibilities of economic growth, human development, and meaningful democracy in Central America were being held hostage by the continuing turmoil in that region. Over the previous decade, the devastation and other expenses of the war had caused a significant decline in per capita income and a diversion of public resources away from social programs in those countries most affected. What is more, civil and political liberties had been restricted in the name of wartime national emergency. Logically, then, a continuation of the armed conflicts appeared likely to cause further decay and deterioration in these conditions.

John A. Booth and Thomas W. Walker, *Understanding Central America,* 1989.

The Wright-Reagan plan was announced just days before the presidents of Central America were scheduled to meet in Esquipulas, Guatemala, to discuss the Arias plan. Proposed by the United States virtually without prior consultation with the Central American countries or the contras, the Wright-Reagan plan apparently so alarmed and offended the Central Americans that it gave them the final incentive they needed to sign their own agreement. On August 7, 1987, all five presidents of Central America initialed a revised version of the Arias proposal, the Procedure for the Establishment of a Strong and Lasting Peace in Central America (also known variously as the Central American Peace Accord, the Esquipulas accord, or the Arias Peace Plan). With provisions designed to promote national reconciliation, cessation of hostilities, democratization, free elections, cessation of assistance to irregular forces, the nonuse of national territory for irregular forces attacking other states, international and internal verification, the 1987 peace accord caught the Reagan administration temporarily off balance, won worldwide acclaim, and earned Oscar Arias a Nobel Peace Prize. Speaker Wright quickly broke ranks with the White

House and enthusiastically endorsed the Central American accord, thus undercutting the White House ploy for contra aid. . . .

Sabotaging the Peace Process

The peace plan itself included provisions for the international monitoring of its own implementation. An International Verification and Follow-Up Commission composed of representatives of the United Nations, the Organization of American States, all eight countries of the Contadora and Contadora Support groups, as well as the five Central American countries, were to monitor the process and meet and report their findings in January 1988. Unfortunately, there was one fatal flaw: the five Central American countries (all of them parties to the conflict and four of them allies of the major foreign actor in the regional drama) had reserved to themselves the right to veto any objectionable aspect of the report. Just prior to the plenary meeting of the commission, the representatives of the UN [United Nations], the OAS [Organization of American States], and the eight Contadora and Contadora Support countries to the International Verification and Follow-Up Commission met and unanimously approved an initial report that tended to be far more critical of the U.S. government and its four Central American allies than it was of Nicaragua. Among other things, the draft prepared by the Verification Commission included the statement (Paragraph 21):

> Despite the appeals made by the Central American Presidents, it remains the policy and practice of the United States Government to provide assistance, particularly military assistance, to irregular forces operating against the Government of Nicaragua. The definitive termination of such assistance is still an indispensable prerequisite for the success of peace efforts and the success of the Procedure as a whole. . . .

In conclusion, though we may shock many self-styled foreign policy "realists" in the United States, we would argue that a U.S. policy toward Central America that is genuinely "kinder and gentler" would almost certainly prove to be wiser and more pragmatic. As long as the U.S. government remains a de facto ally of the privileged minorities of the region, acquiescing or aiding in programs of bloody demobilization, it will simply be underwriting continuing instability. Only a very different policy—one that actively supports and promotes free and open grassroots economic, social, and political participation—will provide for long-term stability in Central America.

"U.S. military assistance to El Salvador, as with Guatemala, has not only promoted Central American stability but also provided policy leverage for promoting human rights advances."

U.S. Policy in Central America Promotes Peace

Tom Cox

Tom Cox is a policy analyst specializing in Latin American affairs at The Heritage Foundation, a think tank in Washington, D.C. In the following viewpoint, Cox argues that U.S. economic and military aid to the Central American democracies will suppress any chances of Soviet-backed revolutionary groups reaching power. He believes that upholding these democracies will promote peace.

As you read, consider the following questions:

1. According to Cox, how has U.S. intervention affected Central America?
2. Why does the author argue that Central America is so important to the U.S.?
3. What further measures does the author suggest the U.S. should take to maintain peace and stability in the region?

Tom Cox, "The Cold War Endgame in Central America." This article appeared in the May 1990 issue and is reprinted with permission from *The World & I*, a publication of The Washington Times Corporation, © 1990.

Longstanding East-West tensions in Central America are melting away at a stunning pace. At Malta, President Bush cited Soviet military aid to the Sandinistas (totalling more than $2 billion under Mikhail Gorbachev) and the export of revolution by Cuba and Nicaragua as "the single most disruptive factor in the [U.S.-Soviet] relationship." By recognizing Violeta Chamorro as the legitimate victor in a "free and fair election" in Nicaragua, however, the Soviet Union has taken a giant stride toward transforming the June 1990 meeting between Bush and Gorbachev into the most successful superpower summit in the postwar era.

Meanwhile, Hungary and Bulgaria broke from the socialist bloc to provide the decisive votes for passage of a UN [United Nations] measure condemning Cuban human rights abuses.

Soviet Aid

Yet, although Gorbachev is clearly hard-pressed to spend an estimated $10 billion—more than one-fourth of Moscow's total hard currency earnings—on military expeditions in Afghanistan, Angola, Ethiopia, and Vietnam, he has not given up on any of them. The recent Soviet delivery of six Soviet MiG-29 fighter-bombers to Cuba provides a clear indication of Moscow's reluctance to relinquish its status as an aggressive superpower.

Soviet support for these Third World outposts is no longer a peripheral Cold War concern; it is the leading issue on the super power agenda. The rising momentum of democracy east of Berlin and the declining prospect of military conflict in Europe only magnify the strategic importance of Central America. As long as Marxist FMLN [National Liberation Front] terrorists threaten El Salvador's fragile democracy and Cuba serves as a Soviet aircraft carrier in the Caribbean, Cold War tensions will remain.

Unfortunately, U.S. containment strategy in the region has traditionally focused on averting disaster rather than on achieving decisive victory in the battle against political instability and economic stagnation. U.S. geopolitical priorities emphasizing Central Europe and the Middle East have relegated Central America to a peripheral role in U.S. foreign policy.

The Reagan Doctrine

The Reagan Doctrine succeeded in realigning U.S. strategy in the region toward a more assertive posture. The 1985 U.S. trade embargo raised the cost of Sandinista subversion of neighboring countries and weakened Daniel Ortega's control over domestic opposition in Nicaragua. Moreover, by supporting freedom fighters in Afghanistan, Angola, and Nicaragua, President Reagan put the Soviets on notice that their free ride for global subversion was over. The policy was a bargain. Soviet military aid to the Sandinistas was nearly 25 times greater than U.S. military aid to the Contras.

A more assertive U.S. effort to support democratic development in the region is reaping significant benefits. Anti-Yanqui
rhetoric by public officials notwithstanding, Latin American citizens have welcomed U.S. help in fulfilling their democratic aspirations in Grenada, Panama, and Nicaragua. An unprecedented opportunity now exists to promote market-oriented development in Central America. Liberation theology, which
equates the socialist model with economic development, is ir-
reparably damaged. Pope John Paul II, by declaring (in 1987) individual economic initiative to be "an inalienable right" and urg-
ing citizens of the region to "make the greatest possible use of
private enterprise," is now the pope of economic liberty. Newly
elected leaders, including President Alfredo Cristiani of El
Salvador and Rafael Calderon of Costa Rica, have likewise embraced free-market policies.

Establishing Liberty

The history of the Americas can be read as a record of the effort
to escape tyranny and establish liberty. Our forebears came to
this hemisphere in search of freedom from oppression and hardship. Simon Bolivar defined our vocation: to resolve here in the
Americas the "great problem of mankind, the problem of how to
live in freedom."

That effort—to solve the problem of liberty—continues to this
day. It dominates the politics of our world, and especially the
lives of the people of Central America. In Central America today
there is a momentous struggle between two conceptions of human life—two conceptions of culture, economics and politics.
Each conception has its distinctive end, its distinctive method.
One leads to tyranny; its method is violence. The other leads to
freedom; its method is consent. There never has been as much
evidence as today that the way of freedom leads to peace, creativity, development and well-being, and that tyranny leads to violence, economic stagnation and war.

Jeane Kirkpatrick, *Central America and the Reagan Doctrine*, 1987.

Yet, despite the growing strategic significance of the region
and the prospects for U.S. success in promoting democracy and
market-oriented development in Central America, a popular in-
clination to minimize or scale back American involvement remains. Central America claims less than 4 percent of U.S. military assistance to foreign countries, and economic assistance to
the region is declining. U.S. economic aid to Latin America to-
talled $941 million in fiscal year 1990, roughly half of the U.S.
total for 1985. U.S. economic support funds for Central America
took the brunt of U.S. aid cuts, falling by more than 30 percent

216

from commitments for fiscal year 1989.

U.S. economic assistance to emerging democracies in Panama and Nicaragua may serve as a prelude to a renewed commitment to the region. In order to eliminate Cold War tensions and exploit opportunities for economic development and stability in Central America, Washington should take the following steps:

• Bolster fragile democracies and reduce the potential for Soviet- or Cuban-sponsored instability by promoting market-oriented development and political security in the region.

• Apply political and economic pressure against Soviet proxies in Central America. The pressure of economic failure and political isolation has been the primary catalyst for democratic reform within the Soviet bloc.

• Foster indigenous political opposition to totalitarian regimes.

Nicaragua is still the key battleground in a Central American crisis marked by political instability and economic stagnation. The humiliating election defeat suffered by the Sandinistas on February 25, 1990 not only may remove a longstanding security threat to the U.S. and Central America but also may provide the anchor for a stable and prosperous Central America that fosters new trade and investment opportunities for U.S. businesses. But Washington must defend and nurture Nicaragua's democratic renaissance with sound aid policies and strong political backing.

The U.S. definition of an "acceptable" political settlement in Nicaragua that permits normal diplomatic and economic relations should follow the criteria outlined by Reagan on April 4, 1985: Sandinista compliance with their formal pledge to the Organization of American States on July 12, 1979, to establish a "broad-based democratic government," a "mixed economy," and freedom of expression and worship in Nicaragua; termination of Sandinista-sponsored subversion of neighboring countries; removal of Soviet-bloc military and intelligence personnel; and the reduction of Nicaraguan military forces to parity with those of neighboring countries.

A Plan for Nicaragua

The following steps are necessary to foster democracy and promote economic development in Nicaragua:

• The 8,000 Contras encamped in Honduras should not be forced to return until Sandinista Defense Minister Humberto Ortega and his 65,000 troops submit to President-elect Chamorro's political authority. Similarly, secret police chief Tomas Borge must renounce his pre-election pledge that the Sandinistas "are not going to give up at the polls what we achieved through arms."

• U.S. emergency assistance should be directed at relieving social and political pressures on the new UNO [National

Opposition Union] government. Food, clothing, and medical supplies are high priorities. Nicaragua's need for farm machinery, herbicides, and fertilizers is even more immediate. Nicaragua's bean, cotton, corn, and other crops must be planted in May. State-owned farmland—roughly 40 percent of all arable land in Nicaragua—is largely idle. Tractors and farm machinery parts are scarce. Poor crop harvests in the fall season would make cash-starved farmers more hostile toward UNO-sponsored measures to cut the national budget and combat inflation.

Peace in Central America

We fully support the Esquipulas, Tesoro Beach, and Tela accords as a lasting framework for peace in Central America. Uniting all these accords is a fundamental commitment to democracy and the democratic process. We continue to work with other nations to translate the promises in those agreements into a permanent reality—whether through El Salvador's five elections since 1982, the Nicaraguan election, or the Panamanian election that exposed Manuel Noriega's corruption to the entire world. We seek the support of all governments for peace and the democratic process in Central America. . . .

The U.S. record is clear; we have been active over the past year in bilateral and multilateral efforts to strengthen the prospects for peace across the globe.

James A. Baker III, Speech before the Senate Foreign Relations Committee, February 1, 1990.

- U.S. financial aid to Nicaragua should help cover the transition costs to a free market. Such costs include the substitution of inflated currency (cordobas) issued by the Sandinista government with a new, stable currency; unemployment compensation for displaced government bureaucrats and soldiers; and hard currency to pay Nicaragua's short-term credit obligations and purchase oil, new machinery, spare parts, and basic consumer goods to revive the economy. Nicaragua's cash shortage is acute. Export earnings fell from $680 million in 1978 (the last full year of Anastasio Somoza's reign) to $210 million in 1989.
- Congress should designate Nicaragua as a beneficiary of the Caribbean Basin Initiative, which suspends or liberalizes U.S. import restrictions on goods imported from that region. Washington can help Nicaraguans help themselves by opening the U.S. market to Nicaraguan goods. The Bush administration should strongly urge Congress to reduce current U.S. tariffs on imported textiles, clothing, leather goods, and shoes. U.S. sugar import quotas—which allow U.S. producers to corner roughly

90 percent of the domestic sugar market—should be raised. Sugar imports from Caribbean Basin countries in 1989 were 73 percent lower than average annual imports from 1975-1981.

Debt Relief

• Washington should press for Nicaraguan debt relief, especially debt cancellation or write-downs by Western European governments and debt-equity swaps by commercial banks. Nicaragua's per capita debt is nearly twice that of Mexico. Congress should lead the way by waiving Nicaragua's arrearages to the U.S. Agency for International Development (AID).

Western government creditors can encourage development of Nicaragua's private sector by trading their share of Managua's $6.8 billion foreign debt for an equity stake in a newly created Nicaraguan Development Fund. This fund would buy state-owned food distribution and foreign trade companies at a discount and sell them to workers in these enterprises or to other domestic investors accepting cordobas, which are overabundant, as partial payment. Debt could be taken back by the fund to pay for the remainder of the cost of the enterprises.

• The administration should establish a joint AID-Nicaraguan team (including representatives from UNO and the Superior Council for Private Enterprise [COSEP]) to investigate how to promote grass-roots local banking and capital markets through deregulation and economic reforms in Nicaragua. By diverting credit to inefficient state enterprises, Sandinista officials dried up credit for productive private producers. Credit is crucial for the recovery and expansion of small businesses in light manufacturing, food processing, carpentry, and other crafts.

• The United States must establish criteria to determine if its aid is contributing to Nicaragua's progress toward a free-market economy. The UNO government can attract desperately needed cash from abroad and demonstrate its long-term commitment to economic development by cutting taxes and government spending, selling state-owned enterprises, guaranteeing the security of private property and contracts, deregulating the private sector, and lifting restrictions on foreign investment. If these reforms are enacted, subsequent U.S. aid could be dispersed through a private, nonprofit Enterprise Fund for Nicaragua administered by UNO and COSEP representatives and American businessmen selected by Bush. With this fund, the United States could lend capital to private businesses in Nicaragua. (Congress has allocated roughly $300 million to similar funds for Poland and Hungary.)

U.S. assistance to the new Chamorro government should provide a framework for more efficient and productive U.S. aid programs throughout Central America. Washington has frequently squandered opportunities to foster market-oriented development in the region. Land reform in El Salvador, for example, is touted as an AID "success story," yet coffee production—El Salvador's main export—fell by more than 50 percent during the 1980s. Farmers were forced to sell their coffee to a government monopoly at less than one-third of the world market price. Inefficient state-run agricultural cooperatives relied on more than $100 million in AID handouts to survive. U.S. aid programs during the 1980s failed to spur a dramatic shift toward market-oriented development in Central America. For the region as a whole, the ratio of private investment to gross domestic product fell from 16 percent in 1980 to 11 percent by 1986. Central American commodity export earnings in 1988 failed to exceed the 1980 total of $4.9 billion.

The synergism between U.S. economic and military assistance is clearly evident in El Salvador. Sabotage by Marxist FMLN terrorists has caused more than $2 billion in economic damage in El Salvador since 1980. U.S. economic assistance to the Cristiani government, totalling $315 million for fiscal year 1990, is nearly three times greater than U.S. military aid. Although some U.S. lawmakers and issue groups seek to reward the latest FMLN offensive by cutting off U.S. aid to the newly elected Cristiani government and accepting FMLN power-sharing demands as a starting point for peace negotiations, the tide of this decade-long war has clearly turned against the FMLN. FMLN base camps in Nicaragua are on the brink of extinction, and the failed November 1989 offensive in El Salvador only reconfirmed the movement's lack of popular support.

U.S. military assistance to El Salvador, as with Guatemala, has not only promoted Central American stability but also provided policy leverage for promoting human rights advances. The bloodiest periods in Central America's history—1977-79 in Guatemala and 1979-1980 in El Salvador—occurred after the Carter administration halted such aid in response to human rights abuses. . . .

U.S. Dedication

U.S. dedication to market-oriented development and the application of political and economic pressure against Cuban- and Soviet-sponsored instability in the region will open the door for U.S. trade opportunities and close the book on what may be the final chapter of the Cold War. At stake is the fate of fragile democratic institutions in El Salvador, Panama, and Nicaragua —and a better future for all of Central America.

"The road to a negotiated settlement of the conflict in Central America has been a long and tortuous one. Such efforts . . . foundered on the opposition of the United States."

U.S. Policy in Central America Inhibits Peace

Sandor Halebsky and Susanne Jonas

Sandor Halebsky is a professor of sociology at Saint Mary's University in Halifax, Nova Scotia, and the author of several books, including *Cuba: Twenty-Five Years of Revolution*. Susanne Jonas teaches in the Latin American Studies program at the University of California at Santa Cruz. She also edits *Contemporary Marxism* and has written several books on Central America, including *Guatemala*. In the following viewpoint, Halebsky and Jonas argue that throughout the 1980s, the United States actively tried to prevent peace in Nicaragua by interfering in a long series of negotiations. The authors also contend that U.S. intervention in the Nicaraguan peace process was merely the most recent example of the U.S. inciting war in Central America.

As you read, consider the following questions:

1. What was the significance of the Contadora peace process, according to the authors?
2. What obstacles to peace do the authors believe remain in Central America? How can they be overcome?
3. What specific methods has the U.S. used to disrupt the peace process in Central America, according to the authors?

"Obstacles to the Peace Process in Central America," by Sandor Halebsky and Susanne Jonas in *Central America: Democracy, Development, and Change,* John M. Kirk and George W. Schuyler, eds. (Praeger Publishers, an imprint of Greenwood Publishing Group, Inc., Westport, CT, 1988), pp. 167-176 passim, © 1988 by John M. Kirk and George W. Schuyler. Reproduced with permission.

The road to a negotiated settlement of the conflict in Central America has been a long and tortuous one. Such efforts began as early as the summer of 1981 in Managua, but have foundered on the opposition of the United States to anything short of the destruction of the Sandinista government.

The search for peace during the 1980s has made clear the differences in the meaning and importance of negotiations to Nicaragua and the United States. For Nicaragua, successful negotiations are a means of putting an end to death and destruction. They offer the opportunity to move ahead with development efforts and the creation of a better life for the Nicaraguan people. For the United States, negotiations are a problem in public relations. They reflect the need to appear to be a nation open to reason, one seeking peace while continuing to wage war. Negotiations also serve to placate Congress and manipulate public opinion. It is in response to the intransigence of the United States that the Latin American, and ultimately, even the Central American nations, had to take a number of unprecedented initiatives toward a settlement of the conflict.

The Search for Peace

The search for peace has been pursued through a number of channels. It has included the unsuccessful efforts of Nicaragua to negotiate directly with the United States, the elaborate Contadora process, and the August 1987 Esquipulas Accords of the Central American presidents. The following discussion describes each of these approaches.

The present account necessarily focuses on the peace process in Central America. To understand fully the obstructive role played by the United States in that process, however, one must see the Reagan administration's obsession with Nicaragua and their opposition to a negotiated settlement in terms of the broader global strategy represented by the so-called "Reagan doctrine." The current administration developed this strategy in response to the weakening of U.S. hegemony following its defeat in Vietnam and the heightened domestic opposition to involving U.S. troops in foreign adventures. The doctrine seeks to reverse revolutionary or communist "advances" almost anywhere in the world where American power can be more or less safely projected by aiding counter-revolutionary forces, as in Angola; or by the direct application of U.S. troops where their role and number can be controlled, as in Grenada. As former Under Secretary of Defense Fred Iklé has pointedly remarked, "containment has been outflanked . . . it doesn't work in the Third World." He denounced any effort to "contain communism within Nicaragua" as a "terrible idea." What is sought is not the containment of change but its reversal. The choices, in his apocalyptic world view, were between "appeasement" and "freedom." Similar sentiments have been echoed in the rhetoric of the president. Nicaragua thus finds itself as the prime test case for the Reagan doctrine of aggressively seeking the rollback of any national change identified as communist or even suspect in its loyalty to the United States. . . .

© Christian/Rothco. Reprinted with permission.

American unwillingness to negotiate became increasingly clear from 1982 on as U.S. representatives essentially rebuffed initiatives by Nicaragua and other Latin American countries. By the spring of 1982, the administration policy had clearly hardened. In February, the efforts of Mexican President José López Portillo to outline peace terms were perceived as an annoyance by the Reagan administration. In response to the Mexican initiative, however, it felt compelled to offer an 8-point proposal in early April. When Nicaragua responded on April 14 with a 13-point proposal for discussion, it evoked little interest or action by the United States. The Nicaraguan proposal sought to meet U.S. concerns over security and arms shipments and offered to negotiate all disagreements without preconditions. They also requested the participation of Mexico in the discussion as a "moderator" or "witness." The United States stalled and avoided actual negotiations. A September effort by Mexico and Venezuela to initiate talks was greeted with "great interest" but in effect was turned aside by the Reagan administration.

In 1983, Nicaragua continued its efforts to engage the United States in negotiations. Its proposals attempted to meet U.S. concerns in the region. In April, however, the United States turned down the Nicaraguan request for talks with the United States and Honduras, with United Nations Secretary General Pérez de Cuéllar, serving as mediator. Then, on July 19, 1983, the fourth anniversary of the overthrow of Somoza, Nicaraguan President Daniel Ortega, reversing earlier Nicaraguan reluctance and responding to American demands, announced Nicaragua's willingness to participate in multilateral talks and to accept verification by the United Nations of any accords reached. He outlined a wide-ranging 6-point peace plan to end hostilities, arms shipments, and military assistance in the region. Foreign bases were to be prohibited, and on October 20 Nicaraguan Foreign Minister Miguel d'Escoto delivered to Washington four draft treaties reflecting and extending the earlier July announcement. They addressed all U.S. security-related concerns and fell within the framework for peace developed by Contadora, including a provision for the Contadora nations to monitor compliance.

On December 1, 1983 Nicaragua also provided the Contadora mediators with a draft proposal dealing with a freeze on arms, the size of armies, and the development of democracy and representative political institutions in Nicaragua and Central America. This followed an announcement two days earlier by Interior Minister Tomás Borge, who stated Nicaraguan agreement to the withdrawal of all Cuban military advisers if a regional agreement were reached. During the last two months of 1983, the Nicaraguan government also initiated liberalization measures within the country—among them amnesty, the announcement of forthcoming elections, and easing of press censorship. In effect, the Nicaraguans indicated a willingness to meet United States strategic, military, and security concerns, as well as some of its demands regarding internal political forms. . . .

Beating Back Contadora Initiatives

The United States also responded negatively to the Contadora initiative. Mexico, Panama, Venezuela, and Colombia, nations more or less bordering on Central America, initiated this effort on January 8, 1983. It reflected their concern with achieving stability, security, and peace in the region, and their determination to buttress the principles of self-determination and nonintervention by foreign powers. The destabilizing effects of the Reagan doctrine and continuing warfare in Central America

—and potentially within their own states—heightened these concerns.

In September 1983, the Contadora nations secured the agreement of Costa Rica, El Salvador, Guatemala, Honduras, and Nicaragua, to a 21-point "Document of Objectives" in the areas of security, economic cooperation, and politics. In January 1984, working groups began drafting a formal accord, and on September 7, 1984 finally presented a draft treaty. It prohibited arms smuggling and support for guerrilla movements, the presence of military advisers and foreign military bases, the importation of arms, and the holding of military exercises. It provided for a verification commission to go anywhere in Nicaragua, and required the holding of free elections. In effect, it met many of Washington's concerns.

A Profound Crisis

The national economies of Central America are experiencing a profound crisis. The primary reasons are the extreme inequality that keeps the majority in poverty, and war. Policies of the U.S. government have exacerbated the crisis by striving for a military defeat of the government of Nicaragua and opposition movements in other countries.

Kevin Danaher, Phillip Berryman, and Medea Benjamin, *Help or Hindrance? United States Economic Aid in Central America*, September 1987.

At first, the United States appeared to respond positively. It began to raise objections, however, when Nicaragua unexpectedly signed the agreement on September 21; and then launched a successful effort to torpedo the draft treaty—a proposal which capped nearly two years of work by the Contadora countries. In October, the administration could congratulate itself on having once again subverted an effort at a negotiated settlement of differences, even while proclaiming its support for negotiations and the Contadora efforts. Thus, in a secret October National Security Council document, revealed by *The Washington Post* on November 6, the NSC proudly proclaimed that "we have effectively blocked Contadora group efforts to impose the second draft to the Revised Contadora Act. . . . We have trumped the latest Nicaraguan-Mexican effort to push signature of an unsatisfactory Contadora agreement." The United States thus rejected a treaty that would have ended hostilities with Nicaragua while meeting its own stated concerns. The treaty failed to win American acceptance because it did not satisfy the real American objective—the destruction of the government of Nicaragua.

Given the preceding events, it is not surprising that in spite of considerable efforts by Contadora after 1984 the United States continued to block a negotiated settlement of their differences with Nicaragua. The opposition persisted even when the "Support Group" of Argentina, Brazil, Peru, and Uruguay added their support to the Contadora initiative, thus bringing nations with 90 percent of the Latin American population behind these efforts. The Contadora effort had become a Latin American-wide initiative. It signaled an even more fundamental Latin American initiative (evidenced in the 1986 and 1987 meetings and pronouncements of the eight nations' heads of state in Rio de Janeiro and Acapulco) to establish an organizational presence and policies independent of the United States.

The Contadora process weakened in 1985 because of U.S. pressures, but peace efforts revived early in 1986 at Caraballeda, Venezuela. Foreign Ministers of the Contadora and Support Group nations met on January 12 and reiterated a number of previous proposals that addressed the Nicaraguan need for peace and security. The Caraballeda declaration also included a plea for "national reconciliation" in Nicaragua, which could be interpreted as talks between Nicaragua and the Contras. On February 10, in an attempt to secure the American return to negotiations, the eight Foreign Ministers of the Caraballeda Group travelled to Washington and presented these proposals to Secretary of State George Shultz. They were rejected. . . .

Changing Trends and the Peace Process

Early in 1987, attention focused on a new proposal, from Costa Rican President Oscar Arias Sánchez. Initially, the Arias Plan was seen as an alternative to Contadora, one that would be acceptable to (and controlled by) the United States. The Arias Plan, however, has developed a dynamic of its own, particularly since August 1987 when the Central American presidents signed Peace Accords based largely on the plan. What began as an alternative to Contadora has become, in some respects, its continuation.

The four pro-American presidents braved open and intense U.S. opposition to sign the Peace Accords with Nicaraguan President Daniel Ortega in Guatemala City on August 7. Unlike the Contadora proposal, the Accords provide for domestic changes within the Central American countries (ceasefires where there are armed insurgencies, internal dialogue with unarmed opposition groups, amnesty, national reconciliation commissions, democratization measures, guarantees to returning refugees)—as well as a cut-off of foreign assistance to the Nicaraguan Contras and other insurgent movements, and an

226

agreement by each country not to serve as a base for attacking neighboring countries.

The Accords initiated a fluctuating and contradictory peace process but they reflect profound changes now taking place in Central America—including a redefinition of relations with the United States. The fresh peace efforts also reveal the bankruptcy of the Reagan administration's Central American policy. These emerging trends are becoming clear to actors and observers throughout Central America and internationally. . . .

Building Peace

We cannot even begin to build a more human society in Central America until a way is found to stop the slaughter and engage in a political search for a new equilibrium. That, in turn, cannot happen until the United States abandons its determination to impose its will on these neighbors, in violation alike of international law and the principles it professes.

Gary MacEoin, *Central America's Options: Death or Life,* 1988.

Regional peace implies the revival of economic integration and increased trade among all five countries, and offers concrete benefits to governments plagued by years of economic crises. It is increasingly difficult for these governments to achieve their major domestic objectives—which are conservative—without regional stability, and hence a redefinition of their stance toward current U.S. policy. . . .

During the implementation of the Peace Accords, there have been increased U.S. maneuvers, pressures, and retaliations. These can retard, but they cannot permanently reverse, the growing tendency of each Central American government to act in its own interests, whether or not those coincide with the interests of the United States. These are signposts of what many regard as a long-range, structural shift in Central American (and Latin American) relations with the United States—a redefinition of the terms of U.S. hegemony and an assertion of "relative autonomy."

The agreements make official what was already an explicit and pervasive view in Central America (and, for that matter, virtually everywhere in the world outside the United States): the Contras are both discredited and nonviable; and as long as U.S. funding keeps them alive, the chances for peace in the region are greatly reduced. Furthermore, Costa Rican President Oscar Arias clearly disagrees with the Reagan policymakers —the Contras are the problem, not the solution in Nicaragua. It is the Contra war that has increased tensions between Nicaragua and its neighbors and made democracy more difficult to achieve in Nicaragua. . . .

By early October 1987, the Sandinistas had taken concrete measures to reopen *La Prensa* and Radio Católica, and to declare a ceasefire. Further concessions, including direct negotiations with Contra leaders (something the Sandinistas had vigorously and repeatedly rejected) and a broader amnesty law, were also offered in January 1988 as evidence of their commitment to the peace process by the Nicaraguan government. These actions bear out their repeated promises to implement the provisions of the Accords ahead of schedule, as a sign of good faith. They have also begun a campaign of public education based on the theme that the implementation of the Accords is the program and the priority of the FSLN [Sandinista National Liberation Front] for the coming period of time. Debates have been held in the National Assembly and there is widespread discussion in the base-level mass organizations.

None of this surprises Central Americans as much as it does North Americans. Certainly there is a spectrum of views about Nicaragua, ranging from great skepticism, to pragmatism, to firm trust that Nicaragua will implement the Accords. What is strikingly absent from most discussions in Central America is the extreme ideological demonization of the Sandinistas or "Sandinista-bashing" that characterizes the discourse even of many Contra opponents in the United States.

Will the Peace Process Succeed?

Does the above mean that the peace process will succeed? Not necessarily—and certainly not unless the terms of the Accords are applied by the other Central American governments—and respected by the United States. In many significant respects, these governments are much farther than Nicaragua from meeting the standards set by the Accords for both peace and democratization. . . .

Although the United States cannot achieve its active goal (overthrow of the Sandinistas), it does retain considerable power to torpedo the Peace Accords—by continuing to fund the Contras, by preventing Honduran compliance, by constantly upping the demands on Nicaragua, or by attempting to reconstitute the "Tegucigalpa Group" (the other Central American governments minus Nicaragua). It is for this reason that the battle must still be won *in the United States*, as a precondition for a lasting peace in Central America.

By late 1987, the initial thrust for peace in Central America had been weakened by the unrelenting U.S. assault on the peace process (directly and indirectly). Internal conflict within the Central American countries also remained unresolved.

"Each country in Central America is struggling to define its own national identity and its own strategies of problem solving."

Central America Must Choose Its Own Path Toward Peace

Carlos Fuentes

In the following viewpoint, Carlos Fuentes asserts that the United States has no right to interfere in Central America's political situation. Instead, he argues, Central Americans should ally to establish peace and find internal solutions to economic and political problems. Fuentes is a former Mexican ambassador to France and an acclaimed Mexican novelist and poet whose works include *Christopher Unborn, The Good Conscience, Old Gringo, Constancia and Other Stories for Virgins,* and *The Death of Artemio Cruz.*

As you read, consider the following questions:

1. How has U.S. policy toward Central America affected that region, according to the author?
2. What policies does the author suggest to satisfy both the U.S. and Central America?
3. What role does Fuentes suggest the U.S. should play in Central America?

"Uncle Sam, Stay Home," by Carlos Fuentes, *Harper's Magazine,* January 1989, © 1989 by Carlos Fuentes. Reprinted by permission of Brandt & Brandt Literary Agency, Inc.

This is a good time to look back on mistakes and lost opportunities in Latin America, so as not to repeat the former and so as to recapture the latter.

Recent Failures

The primary reason for these recent failures is the United States' unique obsession with events in Central America, particularly in Nicaragua. The last administration—despite eight years of feverish activity, rattling rhetoric, and millions of dollars spent—failed to overthrow the government in Managua. The administration also failed to defeat the rebels in El Salvador. Moreover, the Reagan approach failed to bend the independent will of President Oscar Arias of Costa Rica or to pressure him into abandoning either his own territories or his policies favoring the use of diplomacy over the use of force. It should be noted, too, that all the rhetoric and military spending failed to prevent violent outbreaks against the U.S. presence in Honduras; and in Panama, the Reagan administration put forth a blundering policy which, instead of overthrowing General Manuel Noriega, has overthrown the Panamanian economy. . . .

The Bush administration must seriously ask itself what it wants in Latin America: peace through security arrangements, diplomacy, and cooperation with independent governments; or war through proxy armies, subservient governments, and alienated populations. And it must ask with whom it is most likely to achieve what it wants.

We share a hemisphere of enormous contrasts and vast inequalities—not the least of which is the asymmetry of power between Latin America and the United States. This is why we in Latin America have sought mightily to arrive at diplomatic arrangements that would equalize our relationships with other countries and limit the power of the United States within mutually acceptable bounds. Each country in Central America is struggling to define its own national identity and its own strategies of problem solving. Change is the name of the game, and there is more to come. We are not your enemies; we simply know the ground better than you do; we remember more than you do.

A New Latin America

We live in a Latin America of paradox and crisis. A region of simultaneous stagnation and unchecked growth; one where reforms are no sooner initiated than they are postponed. But despite this crisis we are moving toward a new Latin America that looks beyond the tripod of Iberian conquest, a society dominated by church, army, and oligarchy. We are moving toward a new economics and a new politics—a democracy, but one drawn from Iberian, not Anglo-Saxon, traditions. New institutions wrought not just through elections but through revolution and evolution, through mass movements and insurgency. Our crisis has spawned a new model of development and, along with that, a new approach to our international relationships.

All of this marks the present reality of Latin America. Latin America is becoming at once more independent and more unified—in spite of economic crisis, political change, and an erosion of inter-American relations—as our role in the world diversifies and the influence of the United States shrinks in our region.

The United States, for example, now accounts for only one-quarter of all foreign investment in Latin America, down from three-quarters thirty years ago. And U.S. aid is proportionally down from 70 percent twenty years ago to 30 percent today, while investment and aid from Japan and Western Europe are growing exponentially. Trade between Japan and Latin America has increased by a factor of twenty since the late 1960s, and Japanese capital is fueling the development of Mexico's industrial ports, its Pacific resorts, its industries, and its debt-for-equity schemes. We are preparing to enter the Pacific Basin community, and upper- and middle-class Mexicans now send their children to learn not French or English but Japanese in our high schools. Today more than half of the world's trade is transacted in the Pacific. Latin America hopes to participate in this great commercial expansion.

We are also looking toward Western Europe. Speaking at Harvard University, the Prime Minister of Spain, Felipe Gonzalez, reminded his audience that the New World, whose quincentenary we will be celebrating in 1992, was first the Iberian New World. Only later did it also become the Anglo-Saxon New World; but in any case, no other region of the world outside Europe resembles Europe so much as the Americas. Gonzalez proposed that Western Europe join both Americas, Ibero-America and Anglo-America, in a trilateral partnership, whereby we would cooperate more closely, cushion our hemispheric differences through European mediation, and pool our resources.

Cooperation, Not Subjugation

This leads me to the question of Latin America's place in the world, and its place alongside the United States, in cooperation, not subjugation. Today multilateralism shapes our international outlook. It is imperative that we strengthen international organizations and insist on adherence to the rule of law in international relations.

We, in Latin America, know that our best shield against the excessive power of the United States has always been the law. Our problem is getting the United States to join us, the weaker neighbors, in respecting the laws, treaties, and institutions that we've mutually agreed upon. We have done it before, we can do it again.

In fact, this has been the only successful hemispheric policy. The Good Neighbor Policy guided your actions when your presidents were Franklin Roosevelt and Harry Truman; your secretaries of state, Dean Acheson and George Marshall; your undersecretary of state, Sumner Welles; and your coordinator of inter-American affairs, Nelson Rockefeller. These kind of men exist today. They are simply not being employed. Or, if brought to government, they are chased out by ideology triumphant, which will not tolerate reason, compromise, and shared objectives. The ideologue banks on force; he achieves weakness. He demands dogmatic purity; he ends up with political measles. He prophesies disaster, and the prophecy is fulfilled.

No U.S. Sovereignty

The United States is no longer sovereign in this hemisphere. Latin America invites the United States to join in developing the legal, diplomatic, economic, and political relations appropriate to a new era in world affairs; and to give full attention to the key issues on which the future depends: debt, drugs, and migration.

Debt is stunting growth, depriving new Latin democracies of

legitimacy, and eroding the social fabric. Everyone in Latin America is convinced that as currently structured, the debt will not be paid. Nevertheless, intelligent solutions must be found, but this will happen only if we come together seriously and decide to pardon debt selectively, to lower interest rates, or to fix a multiyear target of external financing with an overall plan of internal reforms for each Latin American government. The purpose of such a plan would be to restore an economic growth rate of 5 percent regionally, avoid political crisis, renew public confidence in democratic governments, and move toward social justice.

New Nationalism

If we peruse U.S.-Latin American relations over the last ten to fifteen years, we will see some new trends. A new nationalism is visible with some signs of Latin American solidarity and a clear tendency to present a common front toward the United States. Witness the renegotiation of the Panama Canal Treaty in 1976-1977, the fall of Somoza in 1979, the Malvinas War [Falklands War] in 1982. Under these conditions, it seems unlikely there will be a return to the past. It may be that we see being defined a "new accord," the basis of a new order in U.S.-Latin American relations. Even though only the future will reveal what the eventual outcome will be, we can assert confidently that in this redefinition of old and bitter relations, Latin America will have a more independent and active role than before. It is hard to deny that what happens in Central America will decisively affect the mutual advantages visible in the outline of that new order.

Hector Perez-Brignoli, *A Brief History of Central America,* 1989.

Another task is the fight against drugs. Here we must redistribute responsibility so we can begin to focus on not only supply but demand.

And we must find a program to deal with the waves of migrants moving from south to north. This dilemma can be addressed only by acknowledging the interests of all countries involved and, above all, the interests of the migrants themselves.

We have lost a great deal of time recently that we must now recoup. What we're really entering is the world of the twenty-first century. In this world, Latin America expects to lead *itself* in Latin American affairs. We believe that the United States has more options in our region than simply either capitulating or going abroad in search of monsters to destroy.

We do not ask of you abstention or intervention—but rather cooperation, your civilized presence, your great moral and intellectual values, your essential adherence to systems of justice and human rights, your great economic resources, and above all, the capacity and value of your human capital.

Apply all of this to the reconstruction of our battered hemispheric system. We must all create a new policy based on rationality, consultation, mutual respect, mutual concessions, and the essential quid pro quo of inter-American relations. You give us non-intervention, we give you security assurances: we cooperate with each other.

How is it you can find so many solutions to your own internal conflicts through negotiation, patience, respect for the law, and an understanding of the other's point of view, and yet withhold these virtues when you deal with Latin America? Why can you so rapidly find solutions to conflicts with your enemies when they are strong and with your rivals when they are daring, but find it so difficult to reach agreement with your friends in this hemisphere? Your *friends*, not your satellites. *Our* hemisphere, no one's backyard, everyone's front entrance, the home of every man, woman, and child in the New World.

"We ask for an international response that will guarantee development so that the peace we are seeking can be a lasting one."

Central America Needs International Aid to Establish Peace

William Ascher and Ann Hubbard

In the following viewpoint, authors William Ascher and Ann Hubbard summarize the results of a study conducted by a task force of the International Commission for Central American Recovery and Development, a research organization that studies Central America. Ascher and Hubbard contend that Central America needs international aid to reshape the regions' economic, political, and social systems. Such aid can help promote peace in Central America. Ascher teaches public policy and political science at Duke University in Durham, North Carolina. He is also the director of Duke's Center for International Development Research. Hubbard is a law student at Duke University. She was the director of communications for the International Commission for Central American Recovery and Development.

As you read, consider the following questions:

1. How do Ascher and Hubbard characterize the relationship between economics and peace?
2. Why and how have past efforts to aid Central America failed, according to the authors?
3. What programs do the authors recommend to help Central America achieve peace and stability?

William Ascher and Ann Hubbard, eds., *Central American Recovery and Development: Task Force Report to the International Commission for Central American Recovery and Development.* Durham, NC: Duke University Press, 1989. Reprinted with permission.

> From the international community, we solicit respect and help. We have Central American roads to peace and development, but we need help to make them come true. We ask for an international response that will guarantee development so that the peace we are seeking can be a lasting one. We firmly reiterate that peace and development are inseparable.
>
> Declaration of Central American Presidents
> Esquipulas, Guatemala, August 1987

By signing the Esquipulas peace accords in August 1987, the five Central American presidents affirmed their governments' urgent desire for peace after eight years of civil war. The agreement called for not only an end to hostilities, but also democracy, economic development, regional cooperation on a broad range of issues, and economic assistance from the international community. The presidents put particular emphasis on the link between peace and development: without peace economic recovery cannot proceed; without equitable economic development peace cannot endure.

The Importance of Economic Factors

Central America's political and social struggles have propelled the region into the world spotlight, but economic factors form the antecedent for understanding the region's crisis. Central America's severe economic and social problems are not the result of grossly insufficient rates of economic growth; gross domestic product (GDP) grew at a healthy 5 percent per year between 1950 and 1980. The problems came because that growth was marked by harsh inequities and massive distortions. Large sectors of the population—women, subsistence farmers, indigenous peoples—were excluded from the benefits of growth. Their dissatisfaction has fueled the region's conflicts.

In the 1980s the economies deteriorated, and social tensions heightened. Three of the five Central American countries—El Salvador, Guatemala, Nicaragua—have been ravaged by military conflicts that have claimed the lives of 160,000 people since 1981 and seriously damaged the nations' infrastructure and productive sectors. All five countries have suffered from social and economic turbulence, exacerbated by the fighting in the region. Even Costa Rica, so often the bright exception to the region's problems of inequality and political instability, has felt the economic deterioration resulting from the collapse of intraregional trade and the burden of a large refugee population. For the region as a whole, efforts to reverse marked economic deterioration have not succeeded: in 1987 per capita income for the region as a whole had fallen to the level of two decades earlier. The region has grown increasingly dependent on external aid, but that aid has also helped promote polarization and support militarization.

Despite the obstacles to recovery, Central America clearly possesses the potential for growth. The region is endowed with sufficient natural resources relative to its current population, a favorable climate for agriculture, the human resources required for light manufacturing, and a geographical position well suited for trade and tourism. Through the signing of the peace plan and through ongoing efforts to forge closer regional economic and political ties, Central Americans have demonstrated their will for peace and economic development. The international community is showing an increased awareness of the need to provide the region with aid that is linked to lasting economic development, not just short-term economic stabilization and national security. The old model of political exclusion of large population segments, which exacerbated unbalanced economic growth and social and political polarization, is dramatically less viable as a strategy of political control. New actors such as political parties, non-governmental organizations, and religious groups are entering the political arena to press claims for their constituents and members. This certainly does not guarantee the stability required for economic development; in fact the mobilization of previously excluded groups has been an obvious element in the turmoil in the region. Yet *if* a more fully participatory Central America can find stable political formulas and workable models of sustained economic development, then democracy and equitable development can reinforce one another.

A Mutual Effort

It is important that the effort to achieve economic recovery and development in Central America be the result of mutual effort by both the Central American nations and the international community.

Colin I. Bradford Jr., *Central American Recovery and Development Task Force Report to The International Commission for Central American Recovery and Development*, 1989.

The region needs a coordinated regional economic strategy built on concerted international support. There is growing support for such a regional development plan in Central America and throughout the world. The United Nations Development Programme has drawn up a special plan for economic cooperation with Central America, based in part on the Central American Vice Presidents' Plan of Immediate Action. Above all, the Esquipulas peace accords have set forth the conditions for meaningful action on Central America.

The International Commission for Central American Recovery

and Development was formed in 1987 to help the Central American nations achieve their desire for equitable and sustained economic development. With forty-seven members from twenty countries in Latin America, North America, Europe, and Asia, the commission provides a forum for collaboration between Central Americans and the international community, whose assistance is a prerequisite for economic recovery and development. . . .

To help prepare the commission for its work, a Study Task Force was assembled in 1987 to analyze and suggest fresh prescriptions for a set of the most serious problems facing Central America. Members of the multidisciplinary task force include specialists in Central American development, economics, politics, and administration. . . .

The commission recognized from the outset that economic progress must go far beyond improvements in economic aggregates like the gross national product (GNP) and the balance of trade. Economic equity and poverty alleviation are not only of great intrinsic importance, they are also critical for the long-term prospects of political stability and the consolidation of democracy.

In the case of Central America, equity need not come at the expense of efficiency. Many of the obstacles to sustained economic development in Central America stem from poverty and the lack of access to resources by large segments of the populations. Agricultural development has been held back by lack of access to credit, general productivity has been constrained by low educational and health levels (except in Costa Rica), and home-market industrial expansion has been limited by the inability of many families to afford major manufactured items. Therefore, the work of the commission has emphasized the importance of exploring "growth with equity" strategies while not taking their success for granted. . . .

External Assistance

Central America will need external support if it is to recover. But underlying structural and institutional problems must be addressed before proposing a program for external assistance or trade openings. . . .

The Alliance for Progress began its life operating with a new development principle that stressed social reform and democratic political processes as much as economic growth. But in response to forces in the United States and in Latin America, the Alliance shortly became "just another aid program," promoting economic growth but following the recipient country's existing pattern of income distribution.

The Alliance approach also contained a largely unexamined

bias in favor of industrialization and manufacturing over agricultural development, which contributed to inequality and too-rapid urbanization by widening the rural-urban income gap. Ironically, the Alliance was noted for its emphasis on land reform, but this was a matter—albeit a very important one—of distribution *within* the rural sector. This unbalanced development also created barriers to an effective export orientation necessary to balance foreign trade and restrain foreign indebtedness. The waste and inequity involved in the Alliance for Progress boom reveal the pitfalls of major aid infusions, but they are avoidable pitfalls. . . .

U.S. Development Support

We urge a major increase in U.S. and other-country financial and economic assistance for Central America.

Reaching that goal will require a significant effort. External financing needs between now and 1990 have been estimated at as much as $24 billion for the seven countries (Belize, Costa Rica, El Salvador, Guatemala, Honduras, Nicaragua, and Panama) as a group. The World Bank, the International Monetary Fund, the Inter-American Development Bank, other official creditors, private investors, and commercial banks are likely to provide at least half of these funds—especially if each Central American country follows prudent economic policies, if there is steady social and political progress, and if outside aggression is eliminated.

The Kissinger Commission, *The Continuing Crisis,* 1987.

Even large amounts of financial aid will not help the region as much as the revival of international trade and the opening of markets in North America, Western Europe, and Japan. The Reagan administration's Caribbean Basin Initiative (CBI) has attempted to use trade openings to promote growth in the region, but, as Stuart Tucker points out, the trade concessions respond more to U.S. security concerns than to the region's development needs. What limited successes the CBI has had demonstrate the potential effectiveness of a broader liberalization of U.S. trade. Tucker adds that trade alone is not sufficient for regional economic recovery. The United States and other donor countries must support the reconstruction of Central America's infrastructure and the revitalization of regional trade and coordination through the Central American Bank for Economic Integration and the Central American Common Market. . . .

Certainly the Central American nations, backed by the international community, have taken some important steps toward achieving peace and laying the foundation for postwar Central America. If peace does come soon, the five Central American

239

countries will be in a position to tap into new forces in the region that will help promote balanced growth and the continuation of recent political openings. If the wars continue, the nations will almost certainly not be able to pull themselves out of their economic decline. . . .

The Study Task Force essays confirm the commission's premise that economic recovery and sustained, equitable development are critical requirements for any stable future for Central America. No matter what interpretation is given to the origins of the political instability and armed conflict in the region, the current economic stagnation and the precariousness of many segments of the Central American population present serious obstacles to regional peace and stability. It is fair to conclude that economic prosperity with equity for Central America is both beneficial in its own right *and* essential for peace. . . .

The commission's vision of a postwar Central America hinges on support from industrial countries—in the form of aid, more attractive lending, and improved trade—for both greater economic efficiency and greater equity. It also includes, through a series of reforms at key institutions, a more active role for women's groups, indigenous groups, labor unions, nongovernmental organizations, and peasants.

Understanding Words in Context

Readers occasionally come across words they do not recognize. And frequently, because they do not know a word or words, they will not fully understand the passage being read. Obviously, the reader can look up an unfamiliar word in a dictionary. By carefully examining the word in the context in which it is used, however, the word's meaning can often be determined. A careful reader may find clues to the meaning of the word in surrounding words, ideas, and attitudes.

Below are excerpts from the viewpoints in this chapter. In each excerpt, one of the words is printed in italics. Try to determine the meaning of each word by reading the excerpt. Under each excerpt you will find four definitions for the italicized word. Choose the one that is closest to your understanding of the word.

Finally, use a dictionary to see how well you have understood the words in context. It will be helpful to discuss with others the clues that helped you decide on each word's meaning.

1. Cuba would like to set up *DOCILE* satellites in Central America. Then it could get these Central Americans to do anything it wanted, including opposing U.S. goals in the region.

   DOCILE means:

   a) naughty   b) chaotic
   c) rich   d) obedient

2. The Spaniards had actively looked for valuable commodities in Central America. By the mid-1600s, they pronounced their search a failure and left Central America. Then the region lapsed into a period of *SOMNOLENCE*—little happened for two hundred years.

   SOMNOLENCE means:

   a) poverty   b) business
   c) sleepiness   d) wealth

3. Guatemala, El Salvador, and Nicaragua suffer from tremendous economic *INEQUITIES*. All three have been ruled traditionally by powerful people who rejected any economic reforms that would share wealth with the poor.

INEQUITIES means:

a) injustices   b) failures
c) pressures   d) stupidity

4. After the Sandinista revolution, Nicaragua *EMBARKED* on precisely the type of change needed to bring true stability. It began social programs that helped many people.

EMBARKED means:

a) refused   b) started
c) studied   d) fixed

5. The United States denounced the Central American peace treaty as inadequate. The U.S., instead, offered *VOLUMINOUS* new suggestions for revision, thus creating many new conditions for the Central American countries to follow.

VOLUMINOUS means:

a) vulgar   b) few
c) silly   d) many

6. The Reagan Doctrine made U.S. strategy in Central America more *ASSERTIVE*. Throughout his term in office, President Reagan challenged Soviet involvement in Central America.

ASSERTIVE means:

a) timid   b) bold
c) gentle   d) appealing

7. The U.S. should support Central American people who oppose *TOTALITARIAN* regimes. America must continue to reject Central American dictators like Manuel Noriega and Daniel Ortega.

TOTALITARIAN means:

a) authoritarian   b) immoral
c) kind   d) insane

8. The Reagan administration *SUBVERTED* an effort at a negotiated settlement for Central America, even while saying it supported negotiations and peace efforts.

SUBVERTED means:

a) found   b) permitted
c) helped   d) ruined

Periodical Bibliography

The following articles have been selected to supplement the diverse views presented in this chapter.

Laurie Abe	"New Soviet Thinking in Latin America," *The World & I*, May 1989.
Elliott Abrams	"The Deal in Central America," *Commentary*, May 1989.
Jorge G. Castaneda	"Latin America and the End of the Cold War," *World Policy Journal*, Summer 1990.
Noam Chomsky	"The Decline of the Democratic Ideal," *Z Magazine*, May 1990.
Georges A. Fauriol	"The Shadow of Latin American Affairs," *Foreign Affairs*, 1989/1990.
Michael Kramer	"Anger, Bluff—and Cooperation," *Time*, June 4, 1990.
Flora Lewis	"Central America Sweep," *The New York Times*, March 1, 1989.
John McLaughlin	"Central America at the Crossroads," *National Review*, May 27, 1988.
Ignacio Martin-Baros	"Reparations: Attention Must Be Paid," *Commonweal*, March 23, 1990.
Edwin Meese	"Making Distinctions in Central America," *Conservative Chronicle*, January 2, 1990. Available from the *Conservative Chronicle*, PO Box 11297, Des Moines, IA 50340-1297.
National Review	"Nicaragua: Losing the Peace," June 25, 1990.
Aryeh Neier	"Has Arias Made a Difference?" *The New York Review of Books*, March 17, 1988.
Christopher Orsinger	"A Trail of Missed Opportunities," *The Progressive*, February 1990.
Susan Kaufman Purcell	"Battle over Central America," *The World & I*, December 1988.
William Ratliff	"Reviving U.S. Policy in Central America," *The World & I*, February 1989.
Linda Robinson et al.	"Losing Ground in Latin America," *U.S. News & World Report*, January 22, 1990.
Rigoberto Padilla Rush	"Central America: Thorny Path to Peace and Liberation," *World Marxist Review*, April 1988.

Chronology of Events

1509	Spanish settlers arrive in Panama. By 1524, the Spanish have moved into the rest of Central America.
1812	Constitutional monarchy established in Spain; colonial rule liberalized. Election of town councils in Central America marks beginning of national political life.
1821	The confederation of Central American provinces proclaims its independence from Spain.
1822	Central American provinces annex themselves to independent Mexican Empire under General Augustín de Iturbide, later Emperor Augustín I.
1823-1824	Augustín I overthrown; Mexico becomes a republic. Costa Rica, Guatemala, Honduras, Nicaragua, and El Salvador form Central Federation, with capital in Guatemala City (later, briefly, San Salvador).
1825	United States and Central American Federation sign treaty of friendship, ratified following year.
1829-1838	Political conflict between federation members and the capital increases. In 1838, Central American Congress allows states to leave federation; Nicaragua, Honduras, and Costa Rica secede.
1847	Guatemala declares itself a "republic" rather than a "state," foreclosing possibility of reunion. Other Central American states follow suit.
1903	Panama proclaims its independence from Colombia. The U.S. negotiates the Panama Canal Treaty and establishes control over the canal zone.
1909	Dictator José Santos Zelaya overthrown in Nicaragua. Chaos and instability follow, leading to U.S. financial and military intervention (1911-1933).
1914	The Panama Canal is completed.
1927	Peace accord among fighting factions in Nicaragua provides basis for U.S. occupation and subsequent elections. General Augusto C. Sandino refuses to accept peace accord and leads guerrilla force against U.S. Marines.
1932	Marxist-inspired uprising by peasants and Indians in El Salvador quelled by General Maximiliano Hernández Martínez. Approximately 20,000 peasants massacred in revolt against landed elite. Martínez continues repressive rule for over a decade. Military regimes follow until 1979.
1933	General Anastasio Somoza García named director of new "non-partisan" National Guard in Nicaragua. U.S. Marines withdrawn.
1927-1934	General Augusto C. Sandino leads Nicaraguan guerrillas against U.S. occupation.
1934	Sandino murdered by members of Nicaraguan National Guard; Guard chief Anastasio Somoza domi-

	nates country until 1956.
1936	U.S.-Panama Canal Treaty abrogated; United States abandons protectorate powers over Panama and agrees to nonintervention.
1937	Somoza officially becomes president of Nicaragua.
1944	Dictator Jorge Ubico in Guatemala resigns under pressure of violence and protests.
1944-1950	"Spiritual socialist" Juan José Arévalo heads reformist administration in Guatemala.
1948	Government in Costa Rica overthrown by José Figueres and his Army of National Liberation; start of long period of democratic institutions and dominance of Figueres in Costa Rican politics.
	The Organization of American States (OAS) is established. Representatives of its thirty-two member nations meet annually to discuss issues that concern the Americas.
1949	Pope Pius XII forbids Catholics from supporting communism. This anti-communist position later causes dissension in the church when many Catholics begin to believe that a combination of Christian and Marxist ideas could ease Latin American poverty and oppression.
1950-1954	Jacobo Arbenz elected president of Guatemala. Revolutionary reforms intensify; Communist infiltration of government increases.
1952	Fulgencio Batista seizes power in Cuba and establishes repressive dictatorship.
1954	OAS "Declaration of Solidarity" against intervention of International Communism is directed against Arbenz government in Guatemala. After Eastern European arms arrive, Colonel Carlos Castillo Armas overthrows Arbenz with aid of Honduras, Nicaragua, and U.S.
1956	Anastasio Somoza is assassinated. His sons, Luis and Anastasio Jr., retain control of Nicaragua.
1957	Castillo Armas assassinated. Period of instability and violence begins in Guatemala.
1958	Conservative Miguel Ydigoras Fuentes elected president of Guatemala.
1959	Fidel Castro, a Cuban revolutionary leader, overthrows Batista.
1960	The U.S. Central Intelligence Agency (CIA) hires Panamanian cadet Manuel Noriega to provide information on leftist students.
1961	Sandinista National Liberation Front (FSLN) founded in Nicaragua.
	A U.S. attempt to invade Cuba at the Bay of Pigs fails. Castro proclaims Cuba a communist state and an ally of the Soviet Union.
	The Central American Common Market is formed. The Common Market establishes free trade among the

five nations and helps to strengthen the economies of four of the five nations. Honduras claims Common Market regulations harm the Honduran economy.

1962	U.S.-Soviet crisis over placement of strategic missiles in Cuba resolved by compromise: Soviet Union agrees to remove the weapons; U.S. promises not to invade the island.
1964	Riots in Panama Canal Zone lead to new canal treaty negotiations.
1965	U.S. intervention in Dominican Republic restores order after left-wing insurgency.
1967	Anastasio Somoza Debayle elected president in Nicaragua.
1968	Latin American Bishops' Conference held in Medellín, Colombia. The bishops announce their alliance with the poor, their belief that the class structure of Latin American society must be changed for oppression and poverty to end, and their conviction that the Catholic Church must help bring about this change. These beliefs are the basis of liberation theology.
	Panamanian president Arnulfo Arias Madrid is deposed by the nation's army, which establishes a military junta.
1969	Tensions between El Salvador and Honduras erupt into the six-day "Soccer War," which breaks out in July following a heated soccer match. The war causes the collapse of the Common Market.
1971	*A Theology of Liberation,* by Peruvian priest Gustavo Gutierrez, is published. It outlines the theory of liberation theology. Thousands of Catholic priests, nuns, and laypeople answer Gutierrez's call. The movement faces much opposition from government and military forces. In the 1970s and 1980s more than 950 Catholic priests, nuns, and bishops are arrested, tortured, or murdered in Latin America.
	Omar Torrijos Herrera, the commander of the Panamanian national guard, appoints Manuel Noriega as his U.S. liaison officer. Noriega had previously been Torrijos's chief intelligence officer.
1972	Christian Democrat José Napoleon Duarte wins the Salvadoran election, but the legislature installs army colonel Arturo Armando Molina as president. The military junta exiles Duarte.
	Panama reestablishes a constitutional government and installs Torrijos as president.
	Earthquake devastates Managua, Nicaragua; Somoza's mishandling of crisis and of international relief funds increases antipathy to regime.
1974	Election fraud ensures Somoza's reelection to six-year term in Nicaragua.
1977	U.S. agrees to new Panama Canal treaties giving Panama control over the canal on January 1, 1990 and

total ownership on December 31, 1999.

The CIA, suspecting Manuel Noriega of being a drug trafficker and a double agent, ceases to use him as an informant.

1978	U.S. and OAS fail in mediation attempts with Nicaragua; U.S. suspends military aid to Somoza.
1979	Somoza overthrown in Nicaragua; new governing coalition dominated by Marxist FSLN assumes power.

Salvadoran dictator Carlos Humberto Romero is overthrown in a military coup. A military-civilian government is established.

Latin American Bishops' Conference held in Puebla, Mexico. The bishops reaffirm their belief that the Catholic Church has a duty to help end poverty and oppression in Latin America through political, economic, and social change.

1980

March — Archbishop Oscar Arnulfo Romero, an outspoken critic of the Salvadoran government, is assassinated. Many Catholics and Salvadorans opposed to the government view Romero as a martyr. Opposition to the government increases, as does debate concerning U.S. support of the Salvadoran government.

April — Revolutionary Democratic Front (FDR), a rebel political arm, formed in El Salvador. Guerrilla umbrella organization, Farabundo Martí National Liberation Front (FMLN), created. Three strikes called by rebels in summer fail.

December — The Salvadoran national guard murders four U.S. Catholic churchwomen. In protest, the U.S. suspends economic aid for nine days and military aid for six weeks.

Duarte becomes president of a military-civilian government in El Salvador.

1981

February — The U.S. ends aid to Nicaragua after finding evidence that Nicaragua, Cuba, and the Soviet Union are supplying arms to Salvadorans rebels. President Carter lifts arms embargo begun four years earlier in El Salvador. U.S. Congress requires semi-annual certification of progress in human rights in El Salvador as condition for military aid.

July — Panamanian president Torrijos is killed in an airplane crash. Aristides Royo becomes president.

November — Roberto Suazo Cordova is elected president of Honduras.

1982

March — Guatemalan general Efrain Rios Montt takes power in a military coup.

July — Panamanian president Royo resigns and is replaced by Ricardo de la Espriella. The new president appoints a commission to amend the constitution.

	The new constitution calls for a general election in 1984.
December	The U.S. House of Representatives passes the Boland Amendment, which prohibits the U.S. from supplying the Nicaraguan contras (opposition forces) with arms for overthrowing the Sandinista government.
1983	
January	The foreign ministers of Panama, Mexico, Venezuela, and Colombia meet on the island of Contadora, Panama. They formulate the Contadora Plan, which calls for diplomacy and negotiation among the countries of Central America.
March	Pope John Paul II visits Central America.
July	U.S. president Ronald Reagan forms the Kissinger Commission to find ways to promote peace and prosperity in Central America. The Commission issues a report in January 1984, calling for an increase in economic and military aid to Central America and endorsing the policies of the Reagan administration.
August	After overthrowing Rios Montt in a military coup, General Mejía Victores becomes the leader of Guatemala
	Manuel Noriega gains control of the Panamanian national guard, renaming it the Panamanian Defense Forces. President de la Espriella remains president in name only—Noriega controls the country.
October	The U.S. invades the Caribbean island of Grenada after rebel Marxists seize control of the moderate Marxist government. American troops leave after a pro-U.S. government is installed.
1984	
February	The American CIA in a covert operation mines Nicaragua's harbors. Both America's enemies and allies condemn the action. Nicaragua sues the U.S. in the World Court, and in June 1986 the Court finds the U.S. guilty of violating international law.
May	Duarte is elected president of El Salvador, defeating opponent Roberto D'Aubuisson, the leader of the right-wing ARENA (National Republican Alliance) party.
June	Five guerrilla guardsmen convicted of the murders of four churchwomen in El Salvador.
July	Nicolas Ardito Barletta is elected president of Panama. Noriega, however, retains control over the nation.
November	Daniel Ortega, leader of the FSLN, is elected president of Nicaragua.
1985	
January	The U.S. suspends talks with Nicaragua.
February	U.S. president Ronald Reagan in a speech describes the Nicaraguan contras as "freedom fighters" and compares them to America's founding fathers.

May	Reagan initiates economic sanctions against Nicaragua.
June	The U.S. Congress approves humanitarian aid package for the Nicaraguan contras.
	The FMLN kills four U.S. Marines and nine others in San Salvador.
August	Guatemalans protest inflation and demand increased wages and a freeze on prices.
September	Eric Arture Delvalle is elected president of Panama. Noriega retains control.
November	Liberal party candidate Jose Azcona Hoyo is elected president of Honduras.
December	Christian Democrat Marco Vinicio Cerezo is elected president of Guatemala.

1986

February	Oscar Arias Sánchez of the National Liberation Party is elected president of Costa Rica.
June	FMLN attacks San Miguel military base, killing 250 members of the Salvadoran military.
	U.S. House of Representatives approves $100 million in aid to the contras, permits the CIA and the Pentagon to train the contras, and approves $300 million in economic aid to Guatemala, El Salvador, and Honduras.
	Nicaraguan government closes *La Prensa,* the opposition newspaper.
October	Plane carrying U.S. military supplies to the contras is shot down in Nicaragua. The Sandinistas capture American Eugene Hasenfus, the only survivor of the crash.
	Major earthquake kills 1,500 in San Salvador.
November	The U.S. government announces that, contrary to the Boland Amendment, the U.S. has been providing military aid to the Nicaraguan contras. The supplies were purchased with funds diverted from the sale of U.S. arms to Iran. The covert operation becomes known as the Iran-contra affair. National Security Advisor John Poindexter resigns, and Oliver North is removed from his position as an aide to the National Security Council. Reagan appoints the Tower Commission to investigate the scandal.
December	The U.S. House and Senate establish committees to investigate the Iran-contra affair, and Lawrence E. Walsh is named the special prosecutor for the case.

1987

| February | Costa Rican president Arias presents a peace proposal. In August the Central American governments sign the proposal, known as the Arias Peace Plan and Esquipulas II. The U.S. Senate later approves the proposal. Arias Sánchez wins the 1987 Nobel Peace Prize for his efforts. |
| | The Tower Commission reports that the National |

Security Council sold arms to Iran and used private and government funds to supply the Nicaraguan contras with arms.

April	American volunteer Ben Linder is killed in Nicaragua by the contras. His murder sparks debate over U.S. support of the contras.
June-July	House and Senate committees hear testimony concerning the Reagan administration's involvement in selling arms to Iran, in diverting funds from the sale to the Nicaraguan contras, in raising money for the contras, and in covering up these actions. Oliver North, John Poindexter, and several others are later convicted for their involvement in the scandal.
October	Nicaraguan leader Daniel Ortega begins a trip to the Soviet Union and Eastern Europe seeking military and economic aid.
	U.S. Congress approves $3.5 million in humanitarian aid to the Nicaraguan contras.
November	U.S. Congress approves $3.2 million in humanitarian aid to the Nicaraguan contras.
December	Peace talks between the Sandinistas and the contras break down. Ortega confirms rumors that the Soviets plan to supply Nicaragua with more military aid. Mediators begin new peace talks between the two sides, but these talks immediately collapse when the contras request direct negotiations with Sandinista representatives.

1988

January	Reagan requests $36.65 million in nonlethal aid and $3.6 million in military aid for the contras.
February	Reagan agrees to consult Congress before providing any military aid to the contras. The House, however, still rejects the president's proposed aid package.
	Federal grand juries in Miami and Tampa, Florida indict Noriega on charges of trafficking drugs and laundering drug money. Three weeks later, Panama's president Eric Arture Delvalle is overthrown after he attempts to fire Noriega as head of the Panamanian Defense Forces. Noriega appoints Manuel Solis Palma president. Panamanians respond to Delvalle's call for a general strike. Delvalle is forced into hiding to escape Noriega's Panamanian Defense Forces.
March	The U.S. freezes all Panamanian assets in the U.S. Mass anti-government demonstrations spread throughout Panama.
	The White House announces that 2,000 Sandinista troops have crossed into Honduras to attack a contra base. Reagan orders 3,200 U.S. troops to Honduras after Honduran president Azcona requests U.S. aid. Ortega denies that his troops crossed the border. Honduran jets bomb a Sandinista camp along the border. Two weeks later, U.S. troops withdraw.
	The Sandinistas and the contras agree to a cease-fire.

The House and Senate approve $47.9 million in humanitarian aid for the contras and for children injured in Nicaragua's civil war.

1989

March

Alfredo Cristiani of the ARENA party is elected president of El Salvador.

May

Panamanians elect opposition leader Guillermo Endara president. The Panamanian electoral tribunal nullifies the election, and Noriega retains power.

October

A U.S.-supported military coup fails to overthrow Noriega.

November

The FMLN stages an offensive in San Salvador, overtaking portions of the city.

The Salvadoran military murders six Jesuit priests, their housekeeper, and her daughter. Their murders incite debate about human rights and U.S. aid to El Salvador's government.

Rafael Leonardo Callejas is elected president of Honduras.

December

The U.S. invades Panama, ousts Noriega, and installs Endara as president.

1990

January

Noriega surrenders after seeking refuge in the Vatican embassy. He is taken into custody on charges of drug trafficking and sent to the U.S. to await trial.

Hector Oqueli Colindres, a leader of the Salvadoran National Revolutionary Movement, and Gilda Flores, a Guatemalan political activist, are killed by a Guatemalan government death squad. Human rights groups estimate that since 1954, 100,000 have been killed by left-wing and right-wing death squads in Guatemala. An additional 40,000 people have disappeared.

February

Rafael Angel Calderon of the right-wing Social Christian Unity Party is elected president of Costa Rica.

Violeta Barrios de Chamorro of the UNO (National Opposition Union) party defeats the FSLN's Daniel Ortega in the Nicaraguan presidential elections.

April

Nicaraguan Sandinistas and the U.S.-backed contras sign a permanent cease-fire.

June

Nicaraguan contra forces begin demobilization.

July

Nicaraguan government employees strike, shutting down banks and public transportation. Violence erupts, and at least four civilians are killed. President Chamorro agrees to the strikers' demands.

Portions of this chronology have been reprinted with permission from *Crisis and Opportunity: U.S. Policy in Central America and the Caribbean*, Mark Falcoff and Robert Royal, eds., published by the Ethics and Public Policy Center, 1030 15th St. NW, Washington, DC 20005.

Organizations to Contact

The editors have compiled the following list of organizations that are concerned with the issues debated in this book. All of them have publications or information available for interested readers. The descriptions are derived from materials provided by the organizations. This list was compiled upon the date of publication. Names and phone numbers of organizations are subject to change.

American Enterprise Institute for Public Policy Research
1150 17th St. NW
Washington, DC 20036
(202) 862-5800

The Institute is a conservative think tank that researches a number of issues, including foreign policy and defense. The AEI opposes the establishment of communism in Central America, and favors U.S. policies that hinder or prevent the growth of communism in the region. It publishes the monthly *Economist* and the bimonthly *Public Opinion,* as well as books and monographs.

American Friends Service Committee (AFSC)
1501 Cherry St.
Philadelphia, PA 19102
(215) 241-7000

The AFSC is a Quaker organization that believes in the dignity and worth of every person. The Committee opposes all U.S. military intervention in Central America. AFSC programs assist Central Americans by providing health care and education and by assisting in the development of the region. The AFSC publishes the monthly magazine *Friends Journal.*

Americanism Educational League
PO Box 5986
Buena Park, CA 90622
(714) 828-5040

The League, established in 1927, campaigns for private ownership, a strong national defense, strict crime control, and limited government. It publishes pamphlets and position papers, including *El Salvador: Target for Communist Violence!, Unmasking the Socialist International,* and *Cuba: A Bankrupt, Oppressive Soviet Proxy.*

Central American Solidarity Association (CASA)
1151 Massachusetts Ave.
Boston, MA 02138
(617) 492-8699

CASA protests U.S. involvement in Central America by sponsoring lectures by Central Americans, organizing demonstrations, and lobbying congressional representatives to change U.S. policy. CASA has an extensive library and functions as a clearinghouse for information on Central America. The organization publishes the monthly newsletter *The Central American Reporter.*

Central America Resource Center (CARC)
1407 Cleveland Ave. N.
St. Paul, MN 55108
(612) 644-8030

The Center supports the right of self-determination for the people of Central America and recognizes the need for fundamental economic, political, and social change in the region. CARC believes U.S. policy must be changed to one which respects the basic rights and needs of Central Americans. The Center publishes a directory of curricula, classroom resources, audio-visuals, the monthly publications *The Connection* and the *Executive News Summary*, and the quarterly publication *Religion Report*. The Center has an extensive library of books and publications available to the public.

Chicago Religious Task Force on Central America (CRTFCA)
59 E. Van Buren, Suite 1400
Chicago, IL 60605
(312) 663-4398

The Task Force opposes U.S. intervention in Central America by organizing missions to the region, by hosting speakers, and by publishing the quarterly magazine *Basta!* and a quarterly newsletter. The organization's goal is to inform U.S. citizens about the problems caused by U.S. involvement in Central America and to encourage people to protest U.S. policy.

Christian Anti-Communism Crusade (CACC)
PO Box 890
Long Beach, CA 90801-0890
(213) 437-0941

The Crusade, founded in 1953, sponsors anti-subversive seminars "to inform Americans of the philosophy, morality, organization, techniques, and strategy of communism and associated forces." The CACC supports U.S. intervention in Central America to contain the growth of communism. CACC publishes a free, semi-monthly newsletter called the *Christian Anti-Communism Crusade Newsletter* and the brochure, "Why I Am Against Communism." Its books include *You Can't Trust the Communists, Why Communism Kills,* and *What Is Communism?*

Committee in Solidarity with the People of El Salvador (CISPES)
PO Box 12056
Washington, DC 20005
(202) 265-0890

CISPES opposes U.S. intervention in El Salvador. The organization believes U.S. aid supports right-wing death squads and exacerbates the poverty and inequality in El Salvador. CISPES, which has 60 chapters and 450 affiliate groups throughout the U.S., sponsors around a hundred protests annually and provides humanitarian aid to El Salvador. It publishes the monthly newspaper *Alert! Focus on Central America* in addition to brochures and reports on the region.

Council for the Defense of Freedom
1275 K St. NW, Suite 1160
Washington, DC 20005
(202) 789-4294

The Council works against communist aggression and for U.S. national security. It opposes the establishment of Marxist-Leninist governments in Central America and supports U.S. opposition to such governments. The Council maintains a library and a speakers bureau and publishes the weekly *Washington Inquirer*, the monthly *Bulletin*, and monographs.

Eagle Forum
PO Box 618
Alton, IL 62002
(618) 462-5415

Eagle Forum promotes a strong defense and believes the U.S. must be involved in Central America to promote democracy and to conquer communism. It publishes a monthly newsletter, *The Phyllis Schlafly Report*.

Ethics and Public Policy Center
1030 15th St. NW
Washington, DC 20005
(202) 682-1200

The Center conducts a program of research, writing, publications, and conferences to encourage debate on domestic and foreign policy issues. It believes the U.S. has a right to protect its interests in Central America, and supports U.S. policies that hinder communism. The Center publishes the monthly newsletter *American Purpose*, as well as books such as *The Continuing Crisis: U.S. Policy in Central America and the Caribbean* by Mark Falcoff and Robert Royal, and pamphlets such as *Why Latin America Is Poor* by Michael Novak.

Freedom House
48 E. 21st St.
New York, NY 10010
(212) 473-9691

Freedom House is an independent organization that monitors human rights and political freedom in Central America and other regions throughout the world. It supports democratic elections in Central America, and monitors elections in the region. It publishes the bimonthly magazine *Freedom at Issue* and produces annual reports on elections and human rights in Central America.

The Heritage Foundation
214 Massachusetts Ave. NE
Washington, DC 20002
(202) 546-4400

The Foundation is dedicated to limited government, individual and economic freedom, and a strong national defense. It supports U.S. involvement in Central America to stop Marxist-Leninist influence in the region. Among its many publications are The Heritage Foundation *Backgrounder*, The Heritage *Lectures*, and *Policy Review*.

Institute on Religion and Public Life
156 Fifth Ave., Suite 400
New York, NY 10010
(212) 627-1985

The Institute is an ecumenical research and educational group whose purpose is to promote religious thought and philosophy in public debate. It supports U.S. government policies in Central America that promote democracy. The Institute sponsors seminars and conferences, produces the book series *Encounter*, and publishes the monthly magazine *First Things*.

The Inter-Hemispheric Education Resource Center
Box 4506
Albuquerque, NM 87196
(505) 842-8288

The goal of the Resource Center is to stop U.S. involvement in Central America by informing Americans about the region, its culture, and its economy. The Center publishes books, participates in seminars, organizes briefing sessions for Washington policymakers, and provides a clearinghouse of information for educators and organizers. The Center also publishes a quarterly newsletter, *The Resource Center Bulletin*.

Maryknoll
The Catholic Foreign Missionary Society of America, Inc.
Maryknoll, NY 10545
(914) 941-7590

Maryknoll was established in 1911 by Catholic bishops to recruit and support American missionaries in foreign nations, including the nations of Central America. Maryknoll believes peace will come to Central America only when the U.S. stops supplying military aid to the region. The society publishes the monthly magazine *Maryknoll* and many books on liberation theology.

North American Congress on Latin America
475 Riverside Dr., Suite 454
New York, NY 10115
(212) 870-3146

The Congress, which opposes U.S. involvement in Central America, is an independent research organization founded to document U.S. corporate, military, and political activities in Central and Latin America. It publishes an influential bimonthly newsletter that focuses on Central America, *Report on the Americas*, as well as pamphlets and books.

Organization of American States (OAS)
17th and Constitution Ave. NW
Washington, DC 20006
(202) 458-3000

The multinational OAS was founded to achieve an order of peace and justice among the American nations, to promote their solidarity, and to strengthen their collaboration. The Central American nations of Honduras, Costa Rica, Nicaragua, Guatemala, El Salvador, and Panama are OAS members, as is the U.S. The OAS publishes the bimonthly *Americas* in addition to reports on conferences and opinions on issues that affect the American nations.

Oxfam America
115 Broadway
Boston, MA 02116
(617) 482-1211

Oxfam America is an international agency that funds self-help development and disaster relief projects in many regions, including Central America. Oxfam's goal is to help Central Americans increase their food production and their economic self-reliance. Oxfam publishes *Oxfam America News* three times a year. It also publishes reports on the individual countries of Central America.

U.S. Department of State
Public Information Center
Bureau of Public Affairs
Room 5819
Washington, DC 20520
(202) 647-6575

The Department of State advises the president in the formulation and execution of foreign policy, including policy toward Central America. Write for a list of publications.

Washington Office on Latin America (WOLA)
110 Maryland Ave. NE
Washington, DC 20002
(202) 544-8045

With the goal of shaping a U.S. foreign policy that promotes human rights, democracy, and peace in Latin America, WOLA monitors human rights, political developments, and U.S. activities in the region. It publishes the bimonthly *Latin America Update* as well as editorials, articles, and investigative reports.

Bibliography of Books

Thomas P. Anderson	*Politics in Central America.* New York: Praeger Publishers, 1988.
Cynthia J. Arnson	*Crossroads: Congress, the Reagan Administration, and Central America.* New York: Pantheon Books, 1989.
Tom Barry and Deb Preusch	*The Central America Fact Book.* New York: Grove Press, 1986.
Tom Barry and Deb Preusch	*The Soft War: The Uses and Abuses of U.S. Economic Aid in Central America.* New York: Grove Press, 1988.
Humberto Belli	*Breaking Faith.* Westchester, IL: Crossways Books, 1985.
Phillip Berryman	*Inside Central America.* New York: Pantheon Books, 1985.
George Black	*The Good Neighbor: How the United States Wrote the History of Central America and the Caribbean.* New York: Pantheon Books, 1988.
Paul H. Boeker	*Lost Illusions: Latin America's Struggle for Democracy, as Recounted by Its Leaders.* New York: Marcus Wiener Publishing, 1990.
John A. Booth and Thomas W. Walker	*Understanding Central America.* Boulder, CO: Westview Press, 1989.
Daniel Cantor and Juliet Schorr	*Tunnel Vision: Labor, the World Economy, and Central America.* Boston: South End Press, 1987.
Noam Chomsky	*On Power and Ideology: The Managua Lectures.* Boston: South End Press, 1987.
Arturo Cruz Jr.	*Memoirs of a Counterrevolutionary.* New York: Doubleday, 1989.
Michael Dodson and Laura Nuzzi O'Shaughnessy	*Nicaragua's Other Revolution: Religious Faith and Political Struggle.* Chapel Hill, NC: The University of North Carolina Press, 1990.
Jose Napoleon Duarte with Diana Page	*Duarte: My Story.* New York: G.P. Putnam's Sons, 1986.
James Dunkerly	*Power in the Isthmus: A Political History of Modern Central America.* New York: Verso Press, 1988.
Patricia Taylor Edmisten	*Nicaragua Divided: La Prensa and the Chamorro Legacy.* Gainesville, FL: University Presses of Florida, 1989.
Marc H. Ellis and Otto Maduro, eds.	*The Future of Liberation Theology.* Maryknoll, NY: Orbis Books, 1989.
Richard R. Fagen	*Forging Peace: The Challenge of Central America.* New York: Basil Blackwell, 1987.
Marc Falcoff and Robert Royal, eds.	*The Continuing Crisis: U.S. Policy in Central America and the Caribbean.* Washington, DC: Ethics & Public Policy Center, 1987.

Georges A. Fauriol
The Third Century: U.S. Latin American Policy Choices for the 1990s. Washington, DC: The Center for Strategic and International Studies, 1988.

Georges A. Fauriol
and Eva Loser
Guatemala's Political Puzzle. New Brunswick, NJ: Transaction Books, 1988.

Pablo Galdamez
Faith of a People: The Story of a Christian Community in El Salvador, 1970-1980. Maryknoll, NY: Orbis Books, 1986.

Roy Gutman
Banana Diplomacy: The Making of American Policy in Nicaragua, 1981-1987. New York: Simon & Schuster, 1988.

Walter F. Hahn, ed.
Central America and the Reagan Doctrine. Washington, DC: United States Strategic Institute, 1987.

Nora Hamilton,
Jeffrey A. Frieden,
Linda Fuller, and
Manuel Pastor Jr., eds.
Crisis in Central America: Regional Dynamics and U.S. Policy in the 1980s. Boulder, CO: Westview Press, 1988.

Alfred T. Hennelly
Liberation Theology: A Documentary History. Maryknoll, NY: Orbis Books, 1990.

Joyce Hollyday
Turning Toward Home. New York: Harper & Row, 1989.

Susanne Jonas and
Nancy Stein
Democracy in Latin America. Granby, MA: Bergin & Garvey, 1990.

Michael J. Kryzanek
U.S.-Latin America Relations. New York: Praeger Publishers, 1990.

John Lamperti
What Are We Afraid Of? An Assessment of the "Communist Threat" in Central America. Boston: South End Press, 1988.

Robert S. Leiken
and Barry Rubin
The Central American Crisis Reader. New York: Summit Books, 1987.

Penny Lernoux
People of God: The Struggle for World Catholicism. New York: Viking Press, 1989.

Abraham F. Lowenthal
Partners in Conflict: The United States and Latin America. Baltimore: The Johns Hopkins University Press, 1987.

Frank McNeil
War and Peace in Central America. New York: Charles Scribner's Sons, 1988.

Max G. Manwaring and
Court Prisk
El Salvador at War: An Oral History. Washington, DC: National Defense University Press, 1988.

David Martin
Tongues of Fire: The Explosion of Protestantism in Latin America. New York: Basil Blackwell, 1990.

John Norton Moore
The Secret War in Central America: Sandinista Assault on World Order. Frederick, MD: University Publications of America, 1987.

Jack Nelson-Pallmeyer
War Against the Poor: Low-Intensity Conflict and Christian Faith. Maryknoll, NY: Orbis Books, 1989.

Michael Novak
Will It Liberate? Questions About Liberation Theology. Mahwah, NJ: Paulist Press, 1986.

258

Michael Novak, ed.

Liberation Theology and the Liberal Society. Washington, DC: American Enterprise Institute, 1987.

Robert A. Pastor

Condemned to Repetition: The United States and Nicaragua. Princeton, NJ: Princeton University Press, 1988.

Robert A. Pastor, ed.

Democracy in the Americas. New York: Holmes & Meier, 1989.

Douglas W. Payne

The Democratic Mask. New York: Freedom House, 1985.

Hector Perez-Brignoli

A Brief History of Central America. Berkeley: University of California Press, 1989.

Policy Alternatives for the Caribbean and Central America (PACCA)

Changing Course: Blueprint for Peace in Central America and the Caribbean. Washington, DC: Institute for Policy Studies, 1984.

Michael Radu and Vladimir Tismaneanu

Latin American Revolutionaries. Washington, DC: Pergamon-Brassey Publishers, 1990.

Ron Ridenour

Yankee Sandinistas: Interviews with North Americans Living and Working in the New Nicaragua. Willimantic, CT: Curbstone Press, 1986.

Richard L. Rubenstein and John K. Roth, eds.

The Politics of Latin American Liberation Theology. Washington, DC: The Washington Institute Press, 1988.

G.W. Sand

Soviet Aims in Central America. New York: Praeger Publishers, 1989.

Edward R.F. Sheehan

Agony in the Garden: A Stranger in Central America. Boston: Houghton Mifflin Company, 1989.

Jon Sobrino

Spirituality of Liberation. Maryknoll, NY: Orbis Books, 1988.

David Stoll

Is Latin America Turning Protestant? Berkeley: University of California Press, 1990.

Mark Tushnet

Central America and the Law. Boston: South End Press, 1988.

Ernest van den Haag and Tom J. Farer

U.S. Ends and Means in Central America: A Debate. New York: Plenum Press, 1988.

J.A. Emerson Vermaat

The World Council of Churches and Politics, 1975-1986. Lanham, MD: Freedom House, 1989.

Thomas W. Walker, ed.

Reagan Versus the Sandinistas. Boulder, CO: Westview Press, 1987.

Howard J. Wiarda and Mark Falcoff

The Communist Challenge in the Caribbean and Central America. Washington, DC: American Enterprise Institute, 1987.

Howard J. Wiarda, ed.

Rift and Revolution: The Central American Imbroglio. Washington, DC: American Enterprise Institute, 1984.

Ralph Lee Woodward Jr.

Central America: Historical Perspectives on the Contemporary Crises. Westport, CT: Greenwood Press, 1988.

Index

263